BOUND BY
HONOR

BOUND BY HONOR

A MAFIOSO'S STORY

BILL BONANNO

ST. MARTIN'S PRESS ✻ NEW YORK

Endpaper photo: Bill and Joe Bonanno in 1936.

Library of Congress Cataloging-in-Publication Data

Bonanno, Bill.
    Bound by honor : a mafioso's story / Bill Bonanno.—1st ed.
        p.   cm.
    ISBN 0-312-20388-8
    1. Bonanno, Bill.   2. Mafia—New York (State)—New York—
Biography.   3. Organized crime—New York (State)—New York.
I. Title.
HV6452.N7B65   1999
364.1'092—dc21   99-14049
[B]   CIP

First Edition: May 1999

1   3   5   7   9   10   8   6   4   2

To My Father, Joseph,
For the example of his life and who
throughout it all remained
scrupulous to his principles,
and
To My Wife, Rosalie,
Who married me for better or for worse,
and who for forty-three years
took both with confidence and strength

mafioso: to make oneself respected; to be strong enough to avenge yourself for any insult to your person, or any extension of it, and to offer any such insult to your enemies.

—Pino Arlacchi
Mafia Business

INTRODUCTION

People in my world usually don't write autobiographies. Or if they do, they are usually in the witness protection program. I'm not in anyone's program but my own. I've spent many years in prison, had federal, state, and local authorities down on me, had writs, judgments, verdicts, and offers of "leniency" directed at me. And, in my world, I've been the target of assassins and have been at the storm center of one of the most turbulent periods in modern gangland history—but here I am, like Ishmael, come back to tell you about it.

As I write this, I'm sixty-six years old. I'm in Tucson, Arizona, sitting at a picture window that frames a view of distant desert mountains. The mountains and the desert change color from hour to hour and sometimes, in the morning and the evening, from minute to minute. There is a Native American legend for almost every shadow and shape in the landscape. The high saddle-backed mountain that I can see from my window is a young warrior, the son of a great chief. When his father died, the warrior rode naked into the mountains. He pursued his father's spirit until his agonized heart was healed and his body was clothed in a great garment of many colors so that he could return to lead his people. These legends are like companions to me. You cannot live in this part of the country without feeling that kind of presence around you in the land.

Later in the day, my wife, Rosalie, and I will get in our car and drive to Phoenix to spend time with one of our three sons and several of our twelve grandchildren. Before we go, I'll drop by and look in on my father, Joseph Bonanno, who is ninety-four years old, still full of health and stories, a legendary survivor if ever there was one. It has been a matter of open speculation for years that he was the real-life model for Don Corleone in the book and the movie *The Godfather*. Yes, he was that—just as I was the model for his son Michael. But a fiction is only a set of colors, however beautiful, passing over the landscape for a time—the spirit, perhaps, but not the substance. Hence the reason for this memoir.

My story is an attempt to walk through a real and dangerous world— without police protection or anyone's prior approval—to say some things that need to be said, to dispel shadows and shapes that, over the years, have been turned into legends—and lies.

Anyone looking for confessions and self-incriminating chest pounding will not find them here. Yes, there is blood in these pages, blood in my father's history and in mine. Some of that blood ran in gutters and was washed away with a morning rain or with the passing of a city street sweeper. But much more of that blood is still in my veins and goes back centuries to traditions and values that can never be explained by the gaudy patter of movie mobsters and tabloid thugs.

I come from a long line of mafiosi. The Bonanno clan has been prominent in the area of Castellammare del Golfo in Sicily for centuries, and, most important, from the middle of the last century to the present. My paternal great-grandfather, Giuseppe Bonanno, was a supporter and combat ally of the great Garibaldi, who championed the movement for Italian unification. In Sicily, independence and honor have always gone hand in hand. That linkage ultimately was responsible for the formation of a secret society that later came to be misnamed the Mafia but, in reality, was only a gathering of men who were mafiosi.

Lest there be any confusion, there is a real distinction to be made between the terms *Mafia* and *mafiosi*. The former is a fictional term that conveniently has been used by law enforcement and the media as a catchall name for an organized central criminal conspiracy with worldwide, octopus-like tentacles. The latter term is rooted in reality, in the character and values of the men and women who were the everyday makers of Sicilian history. Some of those mafiosi became members of one secret society or another, emigrated to the United States, and formed themselves into Families.

Let me be as clear as possible. The word *Mafia* is both real and legendary in Sicilian history. For centuries, reality for Sicilians was living under the boot of foreign conquest. Sicily was the invasion route of conquerors. Whether they were Greeks before the time of Christ or the French in the time of the Bourbon monarchy, they tramped across Sicily with all the care and concern of barnyard animals. Sicilians, from time immemorial, had to adjust to these conquerors, to get along with them and, because they never had the strength to kick them out, to resist them by means of subterfuge, cooperation, and conciliation rather than by direct force. Traditionally, Sicilians buttered up their bosses during the day but broke the law at night. Great wealth in the form of landed estates was common on the island. These estates were established and belonged to absentee landlords who counted on the labor of natives and the force of conquering armies to safeguard them. Conquest, from the start, was a breeding ground for the peculiar formation of character in Sicily—one that led to the inevitable rise of the Mafia. It is impossible to understand anything about the Mafia, La Cosa Nostra, or whatever name law enforcement hangs on this group characteristic in this country, without first understanding this most essential aspect of its makeup: the character and personality of an individual mafioso.

First, it should be said that the term *mafioso* itself is ambiguous. It is used as both a noun and an adjective. A person can be a mafioso in the sense of being a member of an organized clan but at the same time may not possess those qualities that are defined as mafioso. On the other hand, someone who has no affiliation whatsoever can be mafioso just by being who he is. Gender has nothing to do with this, either. A beautiful, proud woman can be said to be mafioso. One does not even have to be a human being to exhibit mafioso. A horse with a certain bearing, a wolf, a lion can exhibit mafioso.

There is a story told in my family that illustrates this quality in a somewhat dramatic way. I had a grand-uncle, Giuseppe, who was a mafioso in the sense that he belonged to the Bonanno clan in Castellammare del Golfo. But he was also mafioso in his character. He had a young disciple at the turn of the century who wanted very much to become a "made" member of the clan. He followed my grand-uncle around and did everything that was asked of him. This quality of willingness to serve, though important in the clan, really was not the defining characteristic of a mafioso.

One day, my grand-uncle told his disciple to take off his shirt. The young man dutifully obeyed. My grand-uncle then took a bullwhip and literally beat the skin off his back. The young man said nothing all the while that this beating was administered. Surely, he had no understanding of what was happening. But he had correctly discovered in himself that it was not his place to ask, just to take on faith the relationship he had with my grand-uncle, that somehow the beating was necessary and good. When my grand-uncle finished, he then took off his own shirt and handed the bull-whip to his wounded disciple. He then ordered his disciple to beat him—with just as much force, for just as long. Again, the young man did what he was told—not understanding what was being asked of him but trust-ing the rightness of it because of the relationship that existed between the two men.

The quality exhibited by both the young man and my grand-uncle was mafioso. Call it pride, acceptance, a mystical form of sadomasochism, what-ever—if you try to define it too closely, you'll miss it. The quality is as mysterious as it is specific. It is in the soul, surely. It is unmistakable and indefinable. But it is in the way one person connects to another. Mafioso is, first and last, about the *nature* of relationships. Unless this most essential and traditional point is understood, nothing else about who we are and where we come from, what we have done and what has eventually become of us here in America is any way comprehensible.

The almost mythical origins of the Mafia are rooted in a very specific set of relationships. First, there was the one necessitated by outrage and misdeed. In 1282, the French occupied Sicily. They were, as conquerors go, unusually brutal. Power to them meant power to inflict harm, to take what was not theirs with the arrogant sense that it was. The relationship of ordinary people to the French was one of sullen and smoldering resent-ment. One evening in Palermo, all that changed. According to the story, a French soldier spotted a lovely young girl and her mother on their way to vespers at a local church. The soldier desired the girl, thought it was simply his right as an occupier to take her. He shoved the mother aside, seized the girl, dragged her into the shadows, and proceeded to rape her. This was the trigger for the uprising known as the Sicilian Vespers. The mother ran through the streets shrieking *"MA FIA! MA FIA!"* ("My daughter! My daughter!"). Crowds quickly gathered. Riots and insurrection broke out.

The relationship between occupiers and subjects had been exacerbated to a breaking point. For one of the only times in Sicilian history, outright general rebellion followed. The slogan of the rebellion—an acronym for Mafia—was *Morte Alla Francia, Itala Anela* ("Death to France, Italy Cries Out").

Such a rebellion, however, was not typical. More typical was the response of the young woman's suitor. Humiliated and shamed, outraged and inconsolable, he set out in his own private way to right the wrong that had been done. He learned the name of the soldier—a man named Droetto—who had raped his sweetheart and he quietly sought him out. When he found him, he did not make a scene, nor did he challenge him. He quietly came up behind him and plunged a stiletto into his heart.

A key component in all Mafia relationships is honor. Honor, in our world, is defined by respect. Respect has nothing to do with affection or even with a show of good manners. It is an acknowledgment of power and place, yours and someone else's. A Man of Honor—so called in our world—is someone willing to acknowledge the power of another, say a legislator, a judge, a wealthy and influential businessman, or another Mafia leader. But he is not willing to brook an insult to his own honor in that relationship. The rape of a woman, the abuse of the weak by a bully, is an act against honor and cannot be tolerated.

What is different in Sicilian tradition—perhaps because of all those centuries of occupation—is that no one steps up and demands justice—only revenge. And that act is personal, private, and passionate. Yet it is the heart and soul of an entire people. It is a key to understanding personal and social behavior. It's a knife in the back and a schoolyard fight. In the United States, if a kid has his lunch money stolen from him in the yard, he'll run to his teacher and ask for justice. In Sicily, the kid won't go to his teacher. He'll arm himself with a club, hide in an alleyway near the other kid's home, and then get him as he passes along the street. Justice? Who's to say? Revenge, it surely is, in the name of honor, of respect. That kid will not so quickly have his lunch money taken from him again, though he, in turn, may have to watch his back as he goes through the streets.

In the nineteenth century, after Garibaldi's great victories resulted in the unification of Italy, Sicily entered a new phase. A divided island till then, it officially—though very uneasily—became part of the new Italian kingdom. Though Sicilians enthusiastically supported Garibaldi and his call for independence and liberty, they soon found themselves under the boot of new conquerors. The social structure—which favored wealthy and powerful absentee landowners—remained the same. So did the general poverty of the island. The rule of law, extending from Rome, meant only that exploitation was given the usual sanction of authority. For Sicilians, disenchantment was inevitable—as was resistance. There was no great rising up this time, as there had been in 1282. Far more typical, Sicilians cooperated even as they revolted. They infiltrated the ranks of government and local administrative structures, using them to their own ends. When the Italian government got around to passing a universal military conscription law following the Italian unification in the 1870s, young men of draft age took to the hills, forming themselves into self-sustaining groups—"bandits," they were called. Their relationship to the authorities was a little different. They made no pretense of accepting laws they believed were illegitimate. They imposed their own way. They raided landed estates; they made sure that the running of those places benefited them as well as their owners.

In the main cities, where cooperation with government was the norm, resistance and rebellion were far more covert. Men who were government functionaries during the day, sworn to upholding Italian law, were law-breakers at night. Some of these men, out of their particular needs, banded together to create the modern Mafia.

A group of noblemen led by a man named Corleone della Forresta formed an early organization known as the Society of the Blessed Pauls. Around 1848, its members first met in a church basement in Palermo. The whole purpose was to redress the grievances of ordinary people secretly enough to avoid detection by the authorities. Thus strict codes of conduct were required. A blood oath of loyalty was mandatory. So, too, were honor, revenge, love of independence, and devotion to the weak (including women). The cause of the Blessed Pauls was the cause of the people, who were proud, suspicious, cagey, and deceptive, as only those who had been long conquered but never defeated could be. Word went out from Palermo to the surrounding areas. Clans or Families were formed—among them a clan led by the Bonannos. The network of Families that slowly extended across the island became the backbone of an ongoing and effective resistance to the authorities. By keeping to their own, by mutually helping one another while always seeming to get along with those outside who were in power, Sicilians used an essentially unequal set of relationships to their own advantage. Kinship, be it through marriage or blood, was the essential cohesive factor in the establishment of a clan. Even among Sicilians, there was a stratification; those who came from Palermo were essentially collective and different from those who came from Castellammare. Everyone within a Family or clan was an ally; everyone outside the Family was not to be trusted.

When Sicilians began emigrating to the United States in large numbers at the end of the nineteenth century, it was only natural that they carried their traditions and history with them. The Families or clans they had formed at home were brought with them—as were feuds and unsettled quarrels. The original Families established themselves in this country in the city of New Orleans in the 1870s. Up the Mississippi River in St. Louis was where the Families gathered next. After the turn of the century, there were three Families in the city of New York, these being the result of the massive immigration through Ellis Island in the latter part of the nineteenth century. By 1930, there were five Families in New York and they were all controlled by Joe Masseria.

The early Mafia in America did exactly what the Mafia in Sicily had done. It interposed itself between the authorities and the people—on behalf of the people. It acted, as it did at home, with subterfuge, wiliness, and, sometimes, where applicable, with force. And it did this all the while with the sense that building relationships, friendships, was absolutely indispensable to getting things done. There was no respect for law as such—because the legitimacy of laws that discriminated in favor of people in power against those who were not could never be seen as legitimate. But neither was there any direct challenge to such laws—only the attempt to manipulate them to the furthest possible extent.

How did manipulation work? By getting to know certain people, getting to know their needs, interests—and weaknesses—catering to them, and, yes, exploiting them. The cop on the beat, the union boss, the politician looking to get elected—all were amenable to working with our people. They were all willing to bend or break their own laws because they found it convenient to do so in the context of relationships that promised them gain.

What is little understood in this country is that the strength of the Mafia has never depended on force or violence. Though the media picture of the mob is saturated with images of colorful characters bent on mayhem, murder, and corruption, the reality is that the Mafia in this country has always depended for its survival on a strict code of discipline among its own in order to create a set of friendships or relationships with people on the outside—the same as in the old country. In other words, what the Mafia relies on is not firepower or money, but tradition.

Over the years, the Mafia, like every other group of immigrants in this country, became assimilated. The assimilation was slower, but the effect was just as dramatic: The Sicilians, like the Irish, the Germans, the Poles, and the Russians, eventually shed their old-world ways and joined the market economy, speaking fluent English, clipping their roots till they withered and died. The Mafia, like a successful American corporation, threw itself into the market economy, devoting itself exclusively to profit. And, like a number of corporations, it ultimately lost out to foreign competition, to firms that were leaner and hungrier, better able to keep order in their own ranks.

Everything I learned in my life in the Mafia grew out of tradition. I am an American, and a westerner to boot, but in my blood and in my mind, I have been in a time warp, back in the country of my forebears. I understand things as they did. Strength, to me, is about the way people are connected to one another. *Honor* and *respect* are meaningful words to me in the sense that they form the basis of all relationships, whether they are political or personal.

In the world I come from, it is impossible to understand events—whether they are marriages, political alliances, or killings—unless there is some understanding—literally—of just who was actually related to whom. The Lucchese and Gambino Families, political allies in our world back in the sixties, were actually connected by blood as well as by mutual interest. The same went for the Bonanno and Profaci Families. The killing of Gaspar Miliazzo, a leader in Detroit, in 1929 by the Joe Masseria element of New York touched off the major gang war of this century in the United States because Sicilian townsmen and relatives living in New York felt compelled to respond—to avenge themselves.

My experience came not from books but from being there, living side by side with men who have been romanticized, vilified, and distorted out of their human shapes. When I think of men like Vincent Mangano, Albert Anastasia, Joe Profaci, Thomas Lucchese, Carlo Gambino, and my father, I think of people whose lives were intimately bound up with mine. These were all men who had Families of their own, whose relatives all knew one another, socialized with one another, married one another, bore children to one another.

One summer in 1950, when I was eighteen—to give one example—a few of us had gathered at Joe Profaci's vacation farm at Hightstown, New Jersey. There were quite a few of us, children, grandchildren, along with top members of several of New York's Five Families. What kind of gathering was this? I was in an upstairs room when one of Joe Profaci's sons, Sal, came running in out of breath, laughing, telling me I had to go with him to see something I would not believe. He pulled me to a window overlooking a parking area below. There, my father, Profaci, Anastasia, Mangano—all in formal suits and ties (for that was the custom then, even in the country)—were on their hands and knees, having a peaceful argument about how to put together two giant kites so that the children standing nearby would be able to fly them.

As the men tried to attach a tail to one of the kites, Sal said to me, "What do you think people would say if they saw them now? These are supposed to be the most feared people in the country." I laughed but had no answer then. I do now. That little scene was crucial to understanding how Mafia power worked in this country. Those men were as bound to one another as they were to the task of building those kites. Once that unspoken bond between them vanished and the work of their Families became "just business," power—in any meaningful sense—was lost to the Mafia.

Ultimately, this is a book about the accumulation and dissemination of power. My story is not just about me but also about the way I fit into a history far older than myself. My tradition—the tradition of my fathers—allowed a small group of men, operating in secret, often against law and convention, not only to survive but also to thrive. The Mafia, for a time, was part of the power structure of the country itself. No history of the United States between 1930 and 1970 that does not take that into account will be a false history.

My story is my own but is also, I hope, a reflection of a true history.

BOUND BY
HONOR

PROLOGUE

I can see his head coming off. It slides backward like a clump of snow suddenly lifting off the hood of a car traveling at high speed and flying backward. Except that I see this in slow motion and it is not snow. There is an aureole of red where the spray of blood envelops the exploded parts of brain tissue and bone. I've seen this in my mind's eye thousands of times by now. It is almost thirty-five years since it happened, and though I was two thousand miles away eating a steak, it is as though I were actually there, soaking up the sunshine, standing on the pavement or at one of those windows along the parade route, thinking about something else when all of a sudden—

I can see the plane touching down at Love Field, taxiing to a stop away from the main terminal, in a secure area on the tarmac where the President and Mrs. Kennedy, wearing pink with a matching pink pillbox hat, step down the portable staircase, their smiles like light reflecting off glaciers, greeting local officials, nodding and glad-handing as they make their way to the open presidential limousine waiting for them. What are they talking about? The pleasant Texas weather? The great crowds that have been turning out, waving little American flags? The anti-Kennedy billboards and ads in the newspapers that have been suddenly springing up? Senator Yarborough's political problems? Liberals in Texas? Lady Bird's tulips? Who knows? I remember reading somewhere that Nell Connally, the governor's wife, leaned over and told the President as their limousine was moving slowly through the city streets, past the cheering crowds, "Ah, now you can't say Dallas doesn't love you, Mr. President!"

I can see the line of limousines and motorcycles making its way along Houston Street, through the very heart of downtown, approaching Elm Street, turning left, moving at about fifteen miles an hour so the people can all get a good glimpse of the famous suntans and professional smiles. The cars move out from a covering of trees, heading onto a stretch of roadway that straightens out. There's an underpass in the distance, people standing in an open grassy area to the left, facing the oncoming vehicles. Behind this knoll is an embankment that leads up to railroad tracks, a parking area, more trees. You know the rest, right? Or do you?

In your mind, do the shots come from the rear or the front? Are you one of those who long ago accepted, however uneasily or certainly, that there was a lone gunman lurking in an open sixth-floor window of the Texas School Book Depository, that he leveled an old bolt-action rifle called a Mannlicher-Carcano and in just 3.4 seconds, his hand flying from the trigger to the bolt between each shot, fired three bullets, the first striking the President in the neck, exiting from an area just above his polka-dotted silk tie—surprising him like a chicken bone suddenly getting caught in his throat—where it then, somehow, continued onward, striking Governor Connally, who was sitting in a jump seat, in his back, spiraling then through his body, gnawing out a long channel of bone and tissue till it exited again from the governor's wrist, where it would ultimately be retrieved whole and intact lying alongside him on a stretcher; then a second shot, one that missed completely, then a third, the one that took the President's head off, impacting the back of the skull as he was leaning forward clutching his throat, his body jerking backward violently—this improbable motion of the body due to the meltdown of neurological wiring as the bullet tore through the brain?

Or are you somewhat less credulous, perhaps believing that the shots had to come from the front, from the grassy knoll, and, therefore, involved more than a lone gunman? You would certainly have common sense—and a lot of conspiracy buffs—on your side if you leaned more toward the latter theory than the former. Bullets fired from the front certainly better account for the President first clutching his throat, for the debris of brain matter exploding upward and backward rather than upward and forward when his head was blown off. Also, believing the shots came from the front relieves the almost impossible difficulty of having to explain away three rapid-fire shots from the rear from an unwieldy Mannlicher-Carcano rifle. There are also plenty of eyewitness accounts of shots coming from the front, with virtually no testimony of them coming from the other direction. Any number of people claim they heard rifle cracks coming from the railroad trestle just above the grassy knoll. Others say they saw puffs of smoke—gunsmoke—coming from a clump of trees behind a fence at the top of that rise. Another eyewitness said he actually heard bullets whizzing by, inches from his head, as he watched the presidential motorcade from the front.

Why any of this still matters to me, decades later, is because in a most personal sense the truth of the Kennedy assassination went far beyond the killing of a single man. It was about the falling apart of my world, the world of the so-called Mafia.

There has been plenty written of late about how the Mafia killed Kennedy. I've read and reread the books and magazine articles, and like so much that's been recorded about my world, the mix of fact, fantasy, and speculation makes it almost impossible to get at what really happened. It's as though the public, craving the myth of Camelot, has needed to perpetuate a romantic truth rather than face a complicated set of measurable, if ugly, truths.

Because I happened, at the time, to be the acting leader of the Bonanno "crime Family," I eventually learned who shot the President—and why. What I know now—so many years later—is that the assassination, more than anything, was not a single event but, rather, was one link in a chain of events reaching back across many years, binding the lives of many people. The bullet that tore through President Kennedy's skull was the end of an era—but not the one people fantasized about.

1

Nineteen fifty-four. Spring. Mass has ended. A knot of people move out of a small adobe-style Catholic church in Tucson, along white walks framed by neat flower beds filled with desert plants: blooming cactus, epiphytes with pale green leaves and deep scarlet blossoms. There are two men in the center of this slowly moving group that surrounds them and shields them from the eyes of the curious: Joseph P. Kennedy and my father, Joseph Bonanno.

The men have known each other for almost thirty years. To all the world, these men are as different as night and day, as different as an ancestry that is Irish and privileged on one side, Sicilian and underworld on the other. But these two Joes, in my mind, are really opposite sides of the same coin. Their story is actually one, shrouded in the richness of disguise and irony: a Tale of Two Joes, an American Success set to the words of Emma Lazarus and the ideas of Niccolò Machiavelli.

Two men. Two seemingly separate destinies. Their lives are rooted in the neighborhoods of the American immigrant communities in which they grew up, among people new to this country, struggling to survive poverty, prejudice, and political powerlessness. Joe Kennedy is from a family that would not accept those limitations—the same as Joe Bonanno. Kennedy's father and then Joe Kennedy himself built out of the back rooms and saloons of their neighborhood a powerful answer to powerlessness. The building blocks were booze—and claps on the back: relationships. Out of the saloons of Boston's Back Bay, Joe Kennedy was raised to understand the importance of friendship. Like his father before him, he was there with money, contacts, advice, and support for those in need; in turn, he got back the kind of willing support and loyalty that allowed him to extend contacts and friendships: to the cop on the beat, the neighborhood shop-keeper, the local ward boss, the councilmen, representatives, mayors, and governors who supposedly ruled over them.

Joe Bonanno's father, Salvatore, my grandfather, at the turn of the century was also a man with a saloon and a thousand friendships, who understood that the nature of fellowship was decidedly political. But in the Sicilian wards of Brooklyn, political power worked a little differently. English was not spoken; relationships with the high and mighty were built more clandestinely. But the building blocks were the same. The men and women who did not have enough to eat or to pay their rent or to find good doctors for their children went to the Bonannos for help—which they received and for which they paid back in support and loyalty all that had ever been extended to them. Joe Bonanno and Joe Kennedy, from the time they were kids, understood this basic principle of friendship. That is what joined them at the hip (that and Prohibition). That was what made them men of power.

But as I was walking along behind them that morning, I was even more keenly aware of what it was that had pulled these men apart and set them on very different paths. It was not so complicated to understand.

One of the men was about six feet tall, with sandy reddish hair. He had a long, oval, freckled face—and he spoke English impeccably, so that it was easy to imagine him dining with diplomats or to see him as a diplomat himself, speaking for his country, skillfully, subtly, at official state dinners and at country clubs, in private negotiations with ambassadors, even with heads of state.

The other could never fit in that way. My father was shorter, stockier. His hair, though thinning, was still thick and dark. His face was broad rather than oval. His jaw was as solid-looking as a warehouse loading dock. Though he spoke six different languages and read philosophy and literature as eagerly as others pored over newspapers, his English was still heavily accented—enough so that when he met diplomats and heads of state, he would often, in spite of himself, feel out of place and embarrassed.

I knew why Kennedy was there that day. He was looking for money and support for his son John, recently elected to the U.S. Senate. Nineteen-

fifty-six was coming up, an election year, a chance for a little-known but well-placed senator from Massachusetts to grab a vice-presidential spot on the ticket, or at least to get his name up in lights so that he could position himself later on for better things.

What could Joe Bonanno possibly do for Joe Kennedy to enable a son of his to make a run for the sun? Begin with the Democratic party in New York State. No Democrat in New York got elected without the backing and approval of the Five Families. My father was the Father of one of those Families. As far back as 1932, when FDR was first elected to the White House, Joe Bonanno was involved. He was introduced to FDR at a Democratic party dinner after the election. FDR pulled him aside, had my father photographed with him, and gave him the picture as a keepsake and thank-you for all the help in the campaign and over the years. Don't expect anything as a presidential candidate without New York.

In Arizona and the West, where we had been established since the beginning of the forties (when, for health reasons, I was sent to school there), my father, though he kept a low profile, had a network of powerful business and social connections that included Judge Evo DeConcini (father of U.S. Senator Dennis DeConcini); Morris and Stewart Udall; Congressman Harold Patten; Governor Ernest McFarland; the state Democratic party chairman, Joe Walton; Larry D'Antonio, the state party treasurer; Gus Battaglia, the state party secretary; and Dick Jenkins, the Pima County Democratic boss. Joe Bonanno definitely was a man to see.

Joe Bonanno that day promised he would do what he could to help Joe Kennedy when and if the time came. This was a pledge made out of friendship—but also out of something else. My father knew Joe Kennedy, knew enough about his past to feel confident that any help offered would be returned. There was friendship—and a skeleton or two in the closet. Once upon a time, Joe Kennedy had been in the bootlegging business, and one of his partners at that time happened to be an associate of my father's, Frank Costello. My father regularly spent time in the twenties at Sag Harbor, New York, where Costello had a home. Kennedy used Sag Harbor as a drop-off point for contraband whiskey he smuggled into the country from Europe. My father clearly remembered a couple of occasions when Kennedy joked and bragged about having had to pitch an illegal immigrant or two overboard to divert possible interception by Coast Guard patrol

boats. The men joked about it over drinks in the library of Costello's rambling estate overlooking the harbor. Other people were present. My father remembered who they were. He had a memory like an elephant.

When Kennedy left Arizona that year, I thought a lot about my own future. Where was I going? What was I doing? Unlike Kennedy's son, I was not running for office; no one was out raising money for me. Though my father had shaped me as surely as the climate and soil of Sicily had shaped the olive tree, he was not campaigning for me to do anything. I wished he was. I was still uncertain, at the age of twenty-two, of what to do with the special legacy of my family's tradition, which I felt in my blood but not yet in my feet. What office was I going to fill?

I had recently been through college at the University of Arizona. I had been a good but fitful student, switching majors, never sure of what I wanted. For a time, I thought I wanted to be a lawyer or a diplomat. I didn't speak with an accent; my look was long and rangy—quite American. But I also knew that I was the son of Joe Bonanno, and the name Bonanno, if not the look, had already set a boundary for me I had to acknowledge. For a while, I had simply wanted to be a rancher. I had worked for years on our family farms, which grew livestock and special Pima County cotton, and then, for a year, I majored in agriculture at the University of Arizona. But ag school was the end of the line; it never suited me. Then I was a business major, largely because I was in love with a girl who was in love with numbers, too—but not mine. Because of the Korean War, I joined ROTC, which was mandatory.

I liked the military well enough to think seriously about it as a career for a time. I liked the discipline, the Bunker Hill to Iwo Jima sense of tradition and all that. Plus, I happened to be a very good marksman, skilled in the use of many types of firearms. I had an outlet for all that in the military. I went through special training one summer, and there was a chance my unit might actually be called, but it was at the end of the Korean War and the order never came. My unit was disbanded and the appeal of the military seemed to go with it. I was soon back in Arizona, back to figuring out what to do next.

I knew my father's history quite well by then. I knew he was a man of power and that his power was exerted behind the scenes rather than out front. I knew his activities reached into many areas, mostly legal, but

some—like gambling—illegal. A few years earlier, that alone would have attracted me. I considered myself something of a daredevil as a teenager. I fell in with a group of kids who were into running guns into Mexico. It was a lark for me, a way to make easy money on my own. Guns were legal in Arizona, so there was no problem purchasing them. There was also no problem taking them into Mexico and selling them at a huge profit, usually to big shots high up in the police or military who had their own little personal armies they needed to equip.

The guys I ran with weren't at all like me. They were guys "from the other side of the tracks," half-breeds and barroom hustlers. They talked tough, acted tough—and were tough, I guess—but I thought I was just as tough, just as daring. My running with them had an element of secret pleasure in it because I knew I wasn't at all like them but could keep up very well.

One day, five of us went into Mexico with a trunkful of guns, which we delivered to a "rancher" just outside of Agua Caliente, a town about ten miles from the border. It turned out our customer was an *"el capitano"* of some kind in the Federales. When we delivered our cargo, the *"el jefe"* tried to screw us out of the money we had coming. The guy was also a hothead—as were a couple of our guys. We got into a shouting match that quickly escalated into some serious pushing and shoving. Pretty soon, there were bodies flying in the dust all over the place. We got ourselves together, got back in our car, and took off, heading straight for the border. The big shot and his friends were in a couple of cars behind us, in hot pursuit.

As we neared the border and saw the pileup at the customs stations, we ditched our car, got out, and ran for it, with these guys a couple of hundred yards behind us. We never saw our car again, but that hardly mattered. I think the difference between our getting away and our spending years in some hellhole of a Mexican dungeon was, ultimately, the fact that we were in a little better shape than the *pistoleros* who were chasing us. We came steaming through the checkpoint, screaming, "We're Americans! We're Americans!" Even though the guys behind us were yelling to have us stopped, we were allowed to pass on the Mexican side. We were stopped by American authorities, questioned, and then, after it became clear what was involved, were charged with some kind of border violation and allowed to go free on our own recognizance, pending later court appearances.

When my father, who was in New York at the time, heard what had happened, he immediately dispatched my uncle Frank Labruzzo, my mother's brother, to Tucson to clear up the matter. I don't know what he did precisely, but Uncle Frank took care of things, and the charges were dropped. My friends got off, too. I then went back to New York and spent the summer with my family—and with Uncle Frank. He was a group captain in my father's Family. And, with my father's approval, if not his blessing, I remained at his side, watching and learning.

Because Uncle Frank was my favorite relative, because he was a generous and intelligent man, we talked a lot. We talked about books, about what I was doing—and not doing—in school, about what I wanted out of life. All the while, he kept me at his side as we went through different neighborhoods. I saw how he operated as a group captain, the respect people showed him—bookmakers, people in his "crew," cops who were friends—for a price—who could be counted on to turn the other way and who, in turn, looked to him to see that things remained quiet on their beat.

Uncle Frank was my teacher. I remember being with him in his office at the L&G Trimmings Company once when a man who had defaulted on a loan dropped by. The man was nervous, shifty-eyed, obviously fearful. When Frank asked him why he hadn't been making his payments, the guy went into what seemed to me to be an obvious song and dance.

"Oh, business is awful. I gotta fuckhead for a partner. I don't know if I can even stay in business. I got bills; my kids need clothes. . . ." And so on and so forth. Frank just stared the guy down and said very quietly, "I need the money."

The guy was shaking by now. "You'll get the money or I'll turn over my restaurant to you."

Frank got up from behind his desk and walked over to the guy. He put an arm around his shoulder and walked him to the door.

"I don't want your restaurant; you just do what you can to pay the loan back, okay?"

"Oh, I will, I will," the guy said, and slipped out the door as if he was late to catch a train. Frank walked back into the room, poured himself a cup of coffee, and then asked me what I thought. I told him. I told him I thought the guy was just playing the violin, that, in reality, he was one more person who was quick to borrow and slow to pay. Frank motioned for me to come over to his desk. He opened a drawer and asked me to take a look. There was a .38 revolver lying there.

"Pick it up," Frank said. "Is it loaded?"

"It is," I said.

"What else do you notice?"

"It looks like you haven't fired it in a while," I said.

"I haven't," Frank said, "because I haven't needed to. You know why that is? Because people know that I have the gun. That's all they have to know. The minute I use it, what they know about me changes. I'm their friend when I don't use it; I'm their enemy when I do. You understand? That violinist . . . we've known each other for years. . . . He's a good guy. He'll do the best he can. He'll pay me . . . and I can wait."

I think it was at that point—when I was not yet nineteen—when I sensed that this was the life that was waiting for me and that it was one that actually connected to traditions I believed in. When I returned to Arizona the following fall, after the military, I pursued my studies but also began to involve myself more directly in my father's world. I wanted to do this. It made sense, more sense than anything else. I carried messages and briefcases full of documents and, sometimes, cash to different places— California or Canada, where my father had business interests or crews. We had crews in Arizona, too. And, over time, my father allowed me to work with them. We had illegal activities that included gambling, slot machines, and bingo, which were all unsanctioned but allowed to flourish because of the wants and needs of the people in Phoenix. There were arrangements with other Families to stay out of the area, relationships with local officials, permits and payoffs to take care of.

It was on that trip of old man Kennedy's when it suddenly came to me that I knew exactly what I wanted. I sat in a pew behind and to the side of my father and Joe Kennedy at Mass that day. Out of the corner of my eye, I watched the two Joes with their heads bowed, kneeling side by side, brothers of shadow and sunlight. Joe Kennedy's son, I knew, had had his life picked out for him. He had no more choice in what he was going to do than he had had in selecting the college he went to or the color of his hair and eyes. Well, neither did I. In my father's world, though, he never had to say a word to me; tradition had already made me who I was. You could say that, sitting in that church, I had a revelation.

After Kennedy left, I sat with my father in the kitchen of our house. I remember the look and feel of the day very clearly. It was toward evening. Shadows had crept over the rear wall of the garden that closed our house off from the street. My father was sitting with his habitual glass of cognac, smoking a cigar. He must have known what was on my mind, because when I told him, he did not seem at all surprised. I asked him, in Sicilian, for his blessing.

"Ah, you are ready," he answered in Sicilian.

"I am," I said.

"Good," he said. That was all.

Within weeks, I went to New York for the summer—as I had every year for the past twelve years when school ended and the weather turned warm in the East. I visited all my relatives—aunts, uncles, cousins, in-laws; I hung out at the restaurants, street corners, and clubs I had always frequented; I traveled upstate for weekends at family farms. The only thing that set this trip apart from all the others was that on this one, I became a "made" member of the Mafia. I was formally and irrevocably initiated into the Family.

2

I remember that it was a chilly gray day in Brooklyn. It was in the spring
of 1954. I took my "oath of office" in a large warehouse in Brooklyn.
The heads of the four other New York Families—Joe Profaci, Tommy
Lucchese, Frank Costello, and Albert Anastasia—were there, along with
several other bosses from Buffalo, Milwaukee, Chicago, and Philadelphia.
Initiation ceremonies are usually attended by ten to fifteen people, and in
many cases, the Boss of the Family that the inductee is from is not even
there. After the initiation, we all gathered at an Italian restaurant, the
Enchanted Hour, which was across the street from the warehouse. At the
party, people came and went all night long, but it grew at times to be
seventy or eighty people.

The atmosphere was strange. The large, cheerless rooms that were usually
nothing more than storage facilities were literally packed with people, tables
of food, camp chairs surrounding barrels covered by planks with thick table-
cloths over them; there was a makeshift bar and liveried waiters, known to
and trusted by our people, who came and went. The whole setting resembled
a fabulous gallery opening except for the bare walls and dingy corners and
windows that were painted over or else caked with years of soot.

In those days, I watched as much as I participated. Part of my training,
informal but as rigorous as if I had had it drilled into me in military school,
was to observe body language. Body language first, words second.

What struck me immediately that day was the obvious difference between old-world people like my father and Joe Profaci and Americanized
leaders like Frank Costello and Tommy Lucchese. The older leaders carried

themselves with more circumspection, as though the energy in their bodies burned far below the surface, so that, outwardly, what was visible was a kind of compressed bearing. Joe Profaci, who in private could be gruff and almost pedestrian, seemed cool and courtly. The Americanized leaders, on the other hand, wore their disguises differently. Outwardly, they seemed more natural, more open—but they were not. Take Tommy Lucchese, who was the boss of the Gagliano Family, and Frank Costello, who ran the Genovese Family.

I always enjoyed being around Costello—without ever trusting him. Frank was a talker, not a doer. He was the ultimate politician, a person who could work a room better than anyone I ever met. He was a backslapper, a joke teller; he looked you directly in the eye, leaned forward when he shook your hand, and asked you questions in such a way that he conveyed the sense that he *cared* about you—even when he was planning to destroy you. He wore perfect suits; he was a guy who just looked as if his clothes cost thousands and his haircut hundreds. But I knew by then, because by now I had been around him enough, that he was an uncomfortable man. He was a little too tight in the shoulders, a little too mannered in the way he gestured. He seemed to me to have a more dependent than independent personality. Willie Moretti, a box-shouldered fireplug of a man, a guy who you knew was muscle from the second you saw him, was his right arm. Willie wore cheap suits, had a cheaper haircut, but you looked at Costello and somehow you just knew he couldn't get up in the morning without Willie around. Tommy Lucchese was, to me, a prototypical American short man. He was no more than five six and everything about him was quick. He spoke rapidly; his hands and feet were in constant motion. You had to jog to keep up with him. What made Tommy run? Who knew, except that his eyes were always darting this way and that, like a lizard or a snake looking for a meal. He dressed like a million dollars and his voice came out of some mysterious cavern in the middle of his little body, so that there was always something impressive as well as sneaky in his manner.

And then there was Albert Anastasia, boss of the former Mangano family. For Albert to be present that day was not just a testament to who I was but to who he was, as well. By all rights, Albert was lucky to be alive. Several years before, he was widely believed to have been behind the disappearance of his boss, Vincent Mangano, and the killing of Mangano's brother. Albert never denied that he was responsible, any more than he denied responsibility for other acts that gave him the reputation of being a hothead and a little crazy, although he was anything but that. Albert survived to become leader of the Mangano Family in 1951—with the grudging approval of other Family bosses, including my father, who, at the time, argued that in principle the internal affairs of other Families were private and therefore were not for others to judge. Alone among the Americanized leaders, Albert Anastasia had an appeal that went beyond his reputation for impetuosity and brutality. He was a fairly tall, athletically built man with rangy shoulders, a solid but not stocky build. He had been a physical education instructor in the army and was proud of that. This pride showed up when he entered a room; there was a purpose and a sense of confidence about him that was inescapable. But he also radiated a modesty that belied his fearsome reputation. Albert dressed in expensive suits, but no one would have guessed that. A two-thousand-dollar suit on him looked as if it had come off a rack at Robert Hall. In private, he was soft-spoken, almost gentle in his manner. He had a round face, large nose, and very soft eyes. He obviously doted on his wife, two daughters, and his son. And because he really was sure of himself, he was genuinely at ease in listening to other opinions, other ideas. He, alone among the Americanized leaders, had some sense of what our tradition was about.

Albert was especially kind to me. We had gotten to know each other over the years. Just two years before my initiation, he told my father and a couple of the other old-time leaders that he wouldn't mind having me join his Family.

The story, as it was later related to me, was this: The men were sitting around one day at my father's farm in upstate New York. They began talking about my recent gunrunning troubles in Mexico and Arizona. "Turn him over to me. Let him join my Family; we'll straighten him out," Albert said. Had I known about this at the time, Albert's words might have lifted all the confusion clouding my life. But my father then and always insisted that if I was ever to enter his world, it would only be because I came to that decision on my own, with no help from anyone else. He politely waved off Albert's offer with some words about my becoming a lawyer or a teacher.

I had learned all of that by then. I was as nervous as an actor on opening night, yet I felt as familiar with this world and its script as if I already had played my part for thousands of performances. This was my world as well as that of my father and all the other leaders. I was at home here; all of this felt right and comfortable.

There were speeches and toasts and endless plates of food as the waiters came and went through the entire day and into the night. The speeches were about the old country and about our traditions, who we were once and always would be. It is a sacred component of our tradition that, from time to time, on certain occasions, we all hear, once again, like parishioners in a church, the old stories, the biblical sagas about what made us who we are. This was one such occasion.

"Sicily, our country, was the invasion route of conquerors," said one speaker. "In the eighth century B.C., the Greeks landed in our country and pushed the native Siculi and Sicani inland, and then the Romans came and then the Byzantines. We were sacked by the Vandals and the Goths; then the Saracens invaded the island. Our people detested the Saracens, but we took their culture to heart, its beauty, its passion for secrecy and revenge. . . ."

And so it went, through the Sicilian Vespers up to the period when our people moved out and away, went to Europe and Australia and the United States. One of our group captains stood up and got the attention of everyone in the room. He turned and looked at me. Then he spoke, in Sicilian.

"Salvatore, I will remind you of your great-grandfather Giuseppe Bonanno, a friend and helper of Garibaldi himself. . . ."

I knew the story, set in 1870, when Garibaldi's ragtag army was on the verge of being wiped out by the occupying and far more powerful Bourbon armies. Our Family, which by then had become prominent in the area around Castellammare del Golfo on the western tip of the island, came to Garibaldi's rescue. The story was a reminder of who the Bonannos were, of the blood that connected me in 1954 to my forebears, going back for centuries.

"Remember the Battle of Segesta [actually fought in Calatifima]? Who was there to help Garibaldi? Who did he turn to for help when the Bourbon armies were ready to annihilate him? . . ." The words came tumbling out, but it was more in the manner of a church service than a narrative.

"They turned to the *piciotti,* 'the boys.' And so, Salvatore, your great-grandfather rounded up a herd of sheep and cattle and drove them toward the Bourbon army so that they raised a cloud of dust as they went. . . ."

There was excitement in the speaker's face, his skin was flushed, and his hands moved before him, almost as if he was leading an overture to an opera. "A great cloud of dust was raised, the Bourbon soldiers could not see, and so Garibaldi's men, few though they were, moved in and around them, destroyed them, once and for all. . . . The great and historic Segesta . . . it is with us today. But it was not liberation, only the illusion of liberation, for Sicily has never been free. . . ."

Another person got to his feet, rapped a glass with a spoon, calling for attention. I was reminded about my father's success in this life and how it should always be my guide, my model. Someone else told a story about the Beati Paoli, the Blessed Pauls, and Corleone della Forresta, who worked for the government during the day but who wore a hood over his face at night like a modern Robin Hood; there were stories about his contemporaries, the practical organizers Count Blasco and old Don Raimondo . . . on and on into the night.

The speeches finally ended. The ceremony itself, simple, stark, and chilling began. I was asked to write a number down on a little piece of paper, a number larger than the number of people in the room. I wrote down 115 (my birthday is November 5: 11/5). Then everyone in the room held up one, two, or three fingers of one hand. When the number I had selected was reached, the designated person drew blood from my finger with a pinprick. The drops of blood were spattered onto a picture of Saint Sebastian; the picture was then burned while I held it so that I could feel its heat, feel what would happen to me if ever I broke the vow I now was taking.

I did not feel like a different person when I left that day, but I knew I was, just as Joe Kennedy's son had to have known he was different the day he committed himself to his father's world. Hours before my initiation, I was a young man with a specific, individual history. I left that warehouse knowing that everything I had been, everything I had done, for good or ill, all my sins, my accomplishments, had literally been wiped clean. This was not only a matter of symbolism but also of actuality. The ritual wiping of the slate eliminated any allowance of old grudges and unfinished business. There were no sins, no "problems" left—only a pure commitment to a future defined by something larger than myself. The ceremony I went through was a baptism and a purification both—as well as a kind of marriage vow that, as in the Catholic Church, could be undone only with my death.

It is odd. My actual marriage took place during this period. Just as if I were a political figure about to set out on a career where the possession of a suitable wife would be considered a necessary asset, it was apparent to me—by all that I sensed in our tradition—that the time had come to find the right mate to go along with the life commitment I had already made. No one ever came to me and said I had to get married, that among the women I was seeing this one or that would be acceptable or not. It was not necessary for anyone to do that. Nor would it have worked. I still thought of myself then as a free man, as an independent, very American type, able to choose for myself. But my life was already being driven by forces deeper than choice, or at least by the choosing power of people other than myself—which I was duty-bound to respect and absorb. So subtle was this part of my tradition that I never quite saw it then—and still do not quite fully comprehend it now.

In my world, as in politics and royalty, marriage always involved the interests of people other than the happy couple. As immune as I felt from all of that, it was clear to me that Rosalie Profaci, the niece of Joe Profaci, leader one of the Five Families and an ally of my father's, was seen by my father—and his allies—as a desired mate. That same summer that I took my vows to my Family, I happened to decide—for myself—that Rosalie was a woman I wanted to spend more time with.

I had known her for years without ever thinking of her romantically. She was four years younger than I; she was always a kid hanging around the different family farms and houses during the summer months when I went east. In addition, she was a very shy and withdrawn person, someone who rarely raised her voice or spoke out about much of anything. Because her father and uncle were both powerful men in our world, she was also kept at arm's length from the everyday dangers of life in the Mafia. She was, at an early age, shipped off to convent school, as were the other daughters of the men who belonged to our world. The school she attended, Mount St. Mary's, in Newburgh, New York, was also attended by my younger sister Catherine, a girl whose mind and temperament were as outgoing as Rosalie's were introverted. Over the years, Catherine befriended Rosalie, so that when the time came, she, alone among people in our families, expressed the opinion that Ro and I would not really be suitable for each other. Catherine's objections actually deepened my interest in Rosalie. Like a thirteenth-century Sicilian, I wanted to protect her from the French of the world. Rosalie's obvious vulnerability fanned all kinds of traditional stirrings in me.

My father never came to me, as Joe Kennedy did to his son, and told me, "This is the woman I want you to marry for the sake of your career." But I also knew from the moment I began looking at Rosalie as a woman rather than as a kid that he was pleased. And that mattered to me. For years, I had gone my own way with women. I had lots of girlfriends, a couple of them more serious than others. I thought of marriage once, briefly, with a girl whose family was scandalized by the idea of having a rather prominent Sicilian for a son-in-law. My father, while not outwardly scandalized, was not especially approving, either. I took note of that. I felt disappointed, aware that in the choice I had wanted for myself, I had somehow let him down. With Rosalie, I knew I was on solid ground. Yet, all the while, I never felt pressured. I always felt I was choosing, and that my choice was based on attraction, an attraction that evolved slowly over time.

During the summer of 1953, when I was taken back east after the Mexican escapade, I wound up spending a little time with Rosalie at our farm in Middletown, New York. For the first time, I noticed that she was no longer a little kid. She had turned seventeen and she had a kind of dark-eyed beauty that appealed to me. Still, I had only the stirrings of romantic feeling for her. While she was a teenager, Rosalie was not permitted to date boys. So when we began spending some time together that summer, it was no big deal. In fact, I felt a little on guard because I thought her perceptions of me were a little dreamy. She said later on that she saw me as an Arizona cowboy, not the son of a Sicilian Mafia leader. I told her before I went back west that it had been nice seeing her and that I hoped we'd see each other again soon—maybe over the winter—but that was it. I wasn't making plans and I didn't think she was, either.

That winter, Rosalie and her brother came to Arizona for a visit. I was surprised, and because I was so busy with school and my outside business commitments, I had little time for her. Ro and her brother stayed for a week and then went home, but I was actually pleased to see her and I found myself wondering for the first time whether we could be a pair. However, I was not thinking of that when I went east in the spring of 1954 to take my "vows." Yet when I began seeing Ro again, my father let me know how pleasing that was to him.

Weeks after my initiation, many people from our world attended Rosalie's high school graduation in Cornwall, New York. There was a lavishly attended dinner dance held in her honor at a local hotel which was sumptuously decorated and serviced. Bands played till the small hours; the young women, all in flowing gowns, had dance cards; the men, some in cutaways, some in white dinner jackets with dark carnations pinned to their lapels, all looked like figures who belonged on wedding cakes. I danced with Ro often that night and I remember feeling jealous when I saw her dancing with anyone else—yet nothing had happened between us; there was still nothing like a commitment. Later that summer, I returned to Arizona. I did not think about much Ro until one day in late August.

During the hay fever season, Ro's father, Sal, a group captain in the Profaci Family, went down, as he always did at that time of year, to Point Pleasant, New Jersey, where he had a boat moored in a marina. It was his habit to take the boat out from shore for days at a time when the ragweed pollen was at its worst. He was working on his boat one morning when the engine exploded, hurling him into the water and causing third-degree burns over three-quarters of his body. News of the "accident" (there was suspicion, never proven, of a hit) quickly circulated through our world. Ro's father lingered in the hospital for almost three weeks before he died, in agony, in an oxygen tent, his body covered with a rubber sheet smothered with ice.

Sal Profaci's wake and funeral in Brooklyn were extraordinary. Thousands of people passed through the funeral home where he lay in state. More and more rooms had to be opened to accommodate guests. Massive banks of flowers and crucifixes were placed everywhere. And the cortege and burial service befitted that of a major political leader, which Ro's father was not. He was the brother of a major leader and very possibly the target of someone or some group intent on injuring that Family and, by proxy, ours, as well.

I did not think of this in political terms but, rather, in terms of what effect Sal Profaci's death had had on Rosalie, a young woman who knew almost nothing about the world, who was now unprotected and terribly wounded herself. I corresponded with her over that winter, and while my goal was to offer her only solace and understanding, I was also acutely aware that with the death of her father, her station in life had been dramatically changed. I was not yet ready to propose to her—we hadn't yet even dated—but I did feel enormously protective toward her. And that feeling, for me, was larger than simple attraction.

I saw Ro when I went east the following summer, 1955. I spent time with her at her family's farmhouse near Cornwall. We took walks together, we held hands, and we kissed for the first time. Mostly, we talked. We talked about tradition, history, the Catholic religion. We also laughed and joked a lot—and for the first time talked about marriage: not about the two of us marrying in particular, but about marriage in general, about its absolute value in the society we came from, its importance in the maintenance of family and tradition. We talked about our parents—and their parents. And only then did we begin to date.

Following her father's death, Ro had become the ward of her uncle, the leader of the Profaci clan. Joe Profaci, my father's friend and ally, was flamboyant, strict, and dictatorial. Whom Rosalie went out with, where she went, who went along for the ride became matters of state. It was oppressive. Ro and I couldn't go to a movie together unless I bought tickets for a whole row of cousins and other relatives. It was crazy. I finally made a point of asking her uncle to let us have some time alone, and he relented—somewhat.

But now, having to fight for time alone and because dating had been elevated to a matter of state, the feelings we had for each other almost inevitably were heightened, though, to this day, I cannot say that it was simply my heart speaking when I proposed. I felt stronger in my desire to protect Rosalie from the dangers of a hostile and unpredictable world. I knew this was the right move for me, for Rosalie, and for the two Families involved. Not a word, not a gesture of coercion had been used, and yet the effect—I can see now—was one of silent persuasion. Our families all along wanted this for us and, mostly, for themselves. The effect on Rosalie and me of this invisible undercurrent was profound. We knew we were meant for each other in only the way the sons and daughters of people from our world know those things. No matter what is said or felt outwardly, there is this other inescapable sense of cementing bonds as deep as blood, as tangled as politics. Ro, though innocent in any of the details of the world she came from, knew this in her bones in the same way I did. My father and Joe Profaci, allies to begin with, obviously saw a marriage between the Families as a way of strengthening an already-solid friendship at a time of uncertainty and trouble. Neither Rosalie nor I ever had to be told that our marriage would be especially pleasing to the heads of our Families.

I wrote her from Arizona in the fall of 1955, telling her that I wanted to marry her and that, if she was so inclined, she should not tell anyone until I returned to the East and made a formal request of her family, as our tradition demanded. When she accepted my offer, I then traveled to New York for the holidays. I had a giant engagement ring in my pocket and another set of lifetime vows ready to offer.

3

The year I got married, 1956, was also the year President Eisenhower was reelected. Eisenhower won in a landslide over Adlai Stevenson, whose running mate, Senator Estes Kefauver, was a familiar name in our world. Kefauver had muscled his way into the national spotlight by holding a series of Senate committee hearings on organized crime in 1950 and 1951. The hearings made headlines at the time and created quite a stir in our world, because until then there had been little publicity about the Mafia, its leaders, or its activities. In fact, prior to that, the word *Mafia* itself was little used by the general public. But Kefauver, though he knew little and though his hearings turned up less, got a name for himself and so eventually found his way onto the Democratic ticket with Stevenson.

Kefauver's rival that year for the vice-presidential slot was John F. Kennedy. And just as he had in 1954, Joe Kennedy came through Arizona in late 1955 looking to drum up support for his son. He and my father spent a couple of days together huddling, talking about the possibilities of fundraising and political backing.

It might seem odd, even a little preposterous, for a man with Joe Kennedy's savvy and background to have persistently courted a known Mafia leader like Joseph Bonanno. But at that point, despite the Kefauver hearings, which were quickly forgotten, our world was at the zenith of its power, as much a part of the system as the electoral process itself. Anyone who knew anything about the way politics worked in the United States then understood that candidates and special-interest causes were largely beholden to big-city machines, which were, in almost all cases, heavily influenced, if not controlled, by the Mafia.

Kennedy and my father huddled at the ranch of Gus Battaglia, the Arizona state Democratic party vice-chairman. Kennedy told my father that he wanted to get his son on the national ticket—if only to prepare the way for a real run at the presidency in 1960. Kennedy correctly judged that President Eisenhower would be unbeatable that year but that by being well positioned, a losing vice-presidential candidate would likely go to the head of the pack after the party's presidential candidate went down. My father— and his allies in New York and in the Arizona Democratic establishment— agreed. They told Kennedy they could support a move to get his son on the ticket as a vice-presidential candidate. Though they knew little about the son, it was clear to them that the father was very much in control of his unfolding career. That was enough. They would spend time and a modest amount of money politicking other delegations, notably California, which had a large block of delegates, many handpicked by bosses who were controlled by friendly Families such as the Desimones in Los Angeles and San Diego and the Lanzas in San Francisco. Joe Kennedy was more than satisfied.

Because I spent much of my time in Arizona and because my heart was comfortable in the mountains and my feet in well-worn cowboy boots, I did not pay too much attention then to the look and feel of national power. But it was unavoidable, nevertheless. It was obvious in Arizona when Joe Kennedy came visiting; it was all around me in the East in the weeks, months, and days leading up to the election—and in my marriage to Rosalie.

Back east, I spent time with my father and his associates, enjoying the prospect of a big change in my life. I often went with my father and some of his associates to some of New York City's big nightclubs like the Latin Quarter and, especially, the Stork Club. The Stork Club in those days was where anyone who was anybody sooner or later turned up. The place was run by Sherman Billingsley, an old bootlegger, who had done time in Leavenworth federal prison and who thereafter had been set up in business by people in our world to create just the sort of central gathering place that the Stork Club became. Famous personalities who might otherwise never have come into contact with people like my father and other Family leaders rubbed elbows with them night after night. On any given night of the week, you could find luminaries from the entertainment, sports, and political worlds: Milton Berle, Dorothy Lamour, Clark Gable, Tony Bennett, Marilyn Monroe, Mickey Mantle—everyone sooner or later turned up at the Stork Club. Some celebrities had regular tables—people like Walter Winchell or, whenever he was in town, FBI director J. Edgar Hoover. In those days, we were one big happy family.

One night, Walter Winchell, who fed us as many "hot tips" as he did to the authorities and the general public, came over to our table and sat down for a few minutes. I reached over to shake his hand when we were introduced and Winchell said, "I've heard about you. Your father says you can rope a calf and recite Virgil in Latin?"

"I can do whatever my father says I can do," I answered. Winchell laughed.

"Good. You've raised a diplomat," he said to my father.

"No, an obedient son," my father said.

"I've heard something else," Winchell went on. "Any truth to the story that there's going to be a marriage between the Bonannos and the Profacis?"

"Whose been talking to you?" my father said, looking left to right around the table with an expression of feigned surprise.

With the same sort of theatrical flourish, Joe Profaci looked right to left. "Marriage between us?"

"If there is, you'll be the first to get an invitation—if you give us a good review," my father said. There was a rumble of laughter, joined in by Winchell, who soon got up, shook hands, and then moved on to Hoover's table.

I have no idea how Winchell knew anything about my plans, who had spoken to him, what was said. It did not matter. In that setting, it was clear to me that the world I belonged to included gossip columnists, presidential candidates, movie stars, even the head of the FBI—who was a special friend of Winchell, just as Winchell was a special friend to us. My upcoming engagement to Ro was intertwined with all of it. The sense of everything growing, expanding, merging—of national power—was as palpable to me as the heavy blue layer of cigar and cigarette smoke that hung over the brightly lit room in which we were all sitting. My marriage to Rosalie would ordinarily have been a family affair. But in our world, at this particular moment, it was much, much more.

My first order of business through the coming Christmas season was to make the private decision Rosalie and I had made into an acceptable public one. That was not quite so automatic. In my world, there was form and tradition to follow. Though it was the end of 1955 in Brooklyn, New York, it might just as well have been 1855 in a mountain village in Sicily.

Because the titular head of Rosalie's family was now her oldest brother, Sal, I was obliged to ask him formally for permission to marry his sister. I was not particularly thrilled to do this because I was aware that Rosalie's mother and siblings were not fond of me. I am sure that if it were left to them personally, Rosalie would have been packed off to a convent in Europe rather than be turned over to the likes of me—but that was quite beside the point. Wearing a suit and tie, my hair neatly combed in place, I did my best to appeal to Ro's brother. I did everything I could to make him feel as important as a nineteenth-century grandee, though he was, in reality, a short, stout, sallow-looking kid with dark circles under his eyes.

"You wanna get married? Sure, that's a good idea," he said as he glanced at his watch. He cared for his sister, but he had a lot of things going through his mind at the time.

His personal feelings, whatever they were, were no more important than mine. He, like me, was also bound by form and tradition. He was obliged to take my request to the next stage: to seek formal approval to ask for Rosalie's hand from his uncle Joe Profaci, the actual head and protector of the family.

The occasion was as formal and traditional as it could get. Though Uncle Joe had already indicated his satisfaction, strict protocol was followed every step of the way. The Profacis, all of them—Uncle Joe, Rosalie's mother, her two brothers and two sisters, a roomful of cousins—were gathered for the occasion in Uncle Joe's living room. In the middle of the room in a high-backed chair that looked like a gilded throne, sitting stiff as a figure in a daguerreotype, Uncle Joe stared at me with blazing and unsmiling eyes as I presented myself. We exchanged pleasantries—about the weather, my parents, Uncle Joe's children. Then I informed him—in Sicilian—that I hoped to marry his niece if she would have me, and if her family would approve. Uncle Joe nodded gravely and thanked me for informing him and told me that he was honored and would take my words under advisement.

Then, rigidly and exactly, he turned to each person in the room and asked them if they approved of my marrying Rosalie. The brothers, asked first, mumbled their weak-as-tea assent. Rosalie's mother, who thought I was someone from the fast lane, too worldly for her daughter, simply turned down her lips. That was a yes, even though she looked as if she was gargling castor oil. But Rosalie's fourteen-year-old sister, Annie, a very American kid, mindless of Sicilian tradition, made a face, turned up a shoulder, and said, as though she was being asked a question about nail polish, "If she loves him, she should marry him, but if she doesn't, then she shouldn't marry him." A remark like that, innocent as it was, was like a boulder landing right in the middle of the family's priceless crystal collection—but not to Uncle Joe, whose political objectives remained, shall we say, crystal clear.

"In a few more years, we'll find somebody for you," he said, laughing like an indulgent parent, which infuriated Annie but which also shut her up.

Then we were on our feet, listlessly embracing. Within a week or two, Joe Profaci threw a huge party for the two families at a fancy restaurant, Ferdinand's, in Queens. Hundreds of relatives, *compares* on both sides of the family, were there. Children were running to and fro; there was singing and dancing into the small hours of the night.

And all of this was just another stage in the preliminaries, as formal as it was outwardly spontaneous.

Once Rosalie and I had announced our engagement to the public (Winchell got news of it that same day, January 1—which, coincidentally, was J. Edgar Hoover's birthday), there was a wedding and reception to put together. This became as complicated and as delicate as a massive military operation. The devil was in the details and there were devils lurking in every corner. There were hundreds of invitations to send out, arrangements to be made for hotels, transportation, entertainment, flowers, security, name it. Personally, Rosalie and I both would have been happy with a small private ceremony and a quick getaway to our honeymoon. But what say did we have? Rosalie insisted that the wedding ceremony be held in the parish church in Brooklyn where she grew up—and that was allowed. The rest was logistics and strategy on a grand scale.

Because we were preparing to accommodate multitudes at the reception, we had to make sure we selected a suitable hall. The only choice we had was in another borough. Did we want the reception in Brooklyn—which meant the elephantine and slightly seedy St. George Hotel—or in Manhattan? Even though both families were Brooklyn-based, we still decided on Manhattan. But once that was decided, we had to pick something suitable, something between a roof garden and Madison Square Garden.

Rosalie and I traipsed around for days looking for a place that had a ballroom with a main floor and overhanging balconies, some place large enough to accommodate all the guests and that would allow them room both to dine and dance till the small hours. There had to be a stage and room for a good-sized band. There obviously had to be room for a dais.

We walked our feet off, burned our eyeballs out taking in different hotels until we eventually found what we were looking for at the Sheraton Astor. Of all the hotels we had seen—the Waldorf, the Plaza, the Commodore— only the Sheraton Astor had a large-enough ballroom. Then, once we booked the hall, we had to arrange everything else. We had to hire food preparers, florists, cake makers, photographers, filmmakers. Arrangements had to be completed to fly in 100,000 daisies from California so they could be displayed in individual flower baskets on each table. We had to provide one hundred limousines and reliable escorts to and from local airports for different celebrities and associates. We had a liquor problem—a big liquor problem—and then last, but not least, the entertainment had to be perfect.

Fortunately, because there were friends we could call on, we had help. Peerless Importers donated all the liquor for the occasion. Many foot soldiers in our ranks became escorts for people flowing into the city. The entertainment featured a protégé of an old friend of my father's, Tony Bennett, along with the Four Lads. We got Chic Cambria's Orchestra, the best dance band in the business in the fifties, signed up and they were willing to play all night and into the next day if need be.

The security arrangements were as complicated and demanding as moving an army from one country to another. Secrecy, mobility, timing were crucial. Because an occasion like this was a perfect opportunity for law enforcement to snoop and gather names, we had to convert our guest lists—involving thousands of names—into code. Drawing up a seating chart was just as tricky. All twenty-four of the nation's Families were going to be in attendance. There were some who carried grudges, animosities, unresolved conflicts with other members that went back to the last century in Sicily. There were big shots—senators, congressmen, judges—all who needed to be seated in a manner that accorded with their prestige and that yet would not embarrass them by making their presence too visible. The proximity of all the tables to the dais had to be calculated. Closer meant more important; farther back meant more obscure. It took a diplomat's skill, a politician's guile, and a mathematician's genius to bring it all off.

And then there was the wedding itself. The ceremony was going to be in Brooklyn, at St. Bernadette's, a parish church where the Profacis had worshiped all their lives. Though there would be room for only a few hundred guests—members of the immediate family, relatives, and the closest friends—the event required, in its way, as much planning and care. Because this was not going to be just another neighborhood wedding, security and appearances had to be followed to the letter. Everyone coming and going within a block of the church had to be carefully but discreetly screened. Photographers and reporters from the media were barred from the service, but we had our own crews to record every step, every gesture of the event. From the moment the first guests began arriving to the moment when we spoke our vows, motion picture cameras were rolling. The look of the church, therefore, had to be up to the event. That week, the church was celebrating the Feast of the Assumption. A neon sign had been erected advertising the feast day. Much to the chagrin of Rosalie's mother, I asked that the sign be dismantled—because it simply did not fit with the appearance we wanted. Whether we liked it or not, our union was like a coming together of royal families. The look was every bit as important as the reality of the event. Rosalie's mother did not want us presuming on the church—and the sign stayed.

Just days before the wedding, after all the plans and arrangements had been taken care of, Rosalie and I took a ride out to a park overlooking New York Harbor. It was a warm, clear summer night. We sat close to each other on a bench where we could watch the black water and the lights of distant ships. We talked: about our upcoming honeymoon in Sicily and Europe, our plans of returning to the States and living in Arizona. I had what you could call the cold feet of a bridegroom, I suppose, but it was something more, too. I was feeling uneasy because I knew just how dreamy and unaware Rosalie really was. I wanted to tell her something about the real day-to-day world I lived in. Till then, I had been unable to. And sitting there with her, I found that it was still hard, nearly impossible to say much of anything. She leaned her head against my shoulder and told me that one night years before she had seen Jesus floating above a streetlamp but that all she wanted now was to live in the world as my wife.

Then she began talking about her father that night and how she wished he could be there for the wedding. She was afraid for him, she said, because he had not prayed enough in life and so she feared he might be trapped in purgatory.

"I don't believe in all that," I said matter-of-factly.

She looked at me as though I were a stranger. I explained that my belief system did not include room for eternal damnation. She wanted to know if I believed in sin. She asked this as innocently as if she was inquiring about my belief in virginity.

"No," I said, "I don't, not in any sense that you mean."

"What do you mean?" she asked, a tremor in her voice.

"One person's sin is another person's virtue," I said. "Good or bad, right or wrong. There are times when what appears right to one person appears wrong to another, especially if that person doesn't live by the same philosophy and set of values as the other person."

My own words sounded hollow to me, almost as though, in disguising what I really wanted to say for fear of confusing or injuring Rosalie, I wound up talking to her in abstractions, as though I was her professor and she was my student. All I really wanted, though, was to let her know in some way what she was letting herself in for marrying me.

"Ro, I need to tell you something," I said finally.

"What?" She said.

I measured my words as carefully as I could.

"I already am married."

"What?"

"No, no, it's not what you think. I am married to a philosophy, to a way of life. And that will always come first."

"I don't understand," she said. "I don't understand." Her voice was thin and strained. I took her in my arms as gently as I could. For a long while, I just held her.

"You'll understand," I said. "In time, you'll understand."

And so we were married, as hopeful and as in the dark as any other young couple setting out—except for this secret double life of mine, this burden our forefathers had brought with them from the Old World and which I carried with me as surely as Aeneas carried his father on his back.

The day of our wedding was scorching. The temperature was in the nineties by midmorning. The men in their formal tuxedos, the women in their gowns, with their layers of makeup and careful hairstyles, were like ice-cream figures melting in the sun. There were over three thousand guests at the reception at the Astor. Filet mignon and champagne were served, Rosalie and I and my father and Joe Profaci stood in a reception line for hours, till our hands turned thick and red as lobsters, till our cheeks were worn away from all the kissing and hugging. My uncle Frank stood nearby with a big satin pouch into which each wedding guest dropped an envelope—luck to the tune of more than $100,000. And then the dancing swirled on into the night; the big air-conditioned room was simply overwhelmed with the heat of so many bodies caught in so much energy.

Later, much later that night, Rosalie and I faced each other for the first time as husband and wife—as lovers. Rosalie, so shy and demure, dressed herself in a filmy white negligee, let down her hair, and curled herself into my arms. I felt her lying against me with all the trust and longing of an innocent heart. I was aroused by her, but I knew, too, that she did not know what to expect. She was unaware that this moment, this actual moment of marriage, was going to hurt. I told her this. She did not believe me. I tried to be as gentle as I could, but I heard her cry out, not in joy but in pain. And then afterward, when there was blood on the sheets, she turned away. I had no idea what to say, how to comfort her.

"Didn't your mother tell you?" I said.

"I didn't know," she said. There was a catch in her throat, as though she was trying to stop herself from crying.

"Didn't your mother tell you?" I said again, because I could think of nothing else to say—and no one else to blame. Ro's mother should have said something. That was a mother's obligation to her daughter as surely as it had been to feed her as an infant. In our culture, mothers always counseled their daughters, always whispered to them, laughed with them so that they would have some prior knowledge, some familiarity that would allow them to anticipate and even savor that shock and surprise of pain— and blood.

The day following, Rosalie and I set out on our honeymoon—to Sicily. My secret hope was that in the land and tradition we both came from, she would begin to feel more at ease with all that she had discovered and pledged herself to when she married me.

4

Summer in Sicily is like summer in Arizona. In the flat areas of the east, it is dry and blazing; along the coast in the west and in the ruined old fishing villages nestled in the hills, the colors turn from soft copper in the morning to hueless white at midday, then to something like glowing-coal red at dusk. The air is an invisible fire that sears your flesh; when you step into sunlight from shadow, there is weight and force in the heat waves that slam into you. Yet the country's beauty lies hidden in this inferno, lurking in vineyards and old courtyards, in rugged, crumpled mountains, in countless cobblestone alleys and old stone farmhouses, in churches centuries old, whose day-to-day life is still as vibrant as the entire country is poor, primitive, and traditional.

My father took me aside before Ro and I left on our honeymoon. There were people he wanted to make sure I saw, relatives in and around Castellammare del Golfo, clan leaders he was still friendly with in the Palermo area who would make sure our trip was a happy one. I was asked to convey our family's greetings to these men and to assure them that any problems they had could be shared with us back in the States. And then my father had a special warning for me.

"If your wife wants to visit Villabate, do not let her convince you to stay. Stay away from Villabate; there is trouble there. You understand?" he said.

"I understand." I asked no questions. I did not need to know more.

Before we arrived in Sicily, Rosalie and I made an itinerary for ourselves. We would spend a day in Palermo, visiting friends and touring the historic parts of the city; then we would take a leisurely trip up the coast into the hills past Mondello till we eventually got to Castellammare, where we would spend several more days. Rosalie was excited and eager to see the land where both our families had come from. Then, predictably enough, she said she wanted to visit her family's hometown, Villabate, and I had to tell her that was out. She looked at me as though I was kidding.

"But I want to see my family's hometown, Bill," she said, "come on!"

"We can't go there."

"Can't go there, why not?" She was disbelieving—but very innocent.

"Because there's fighting in the area involving your family. We would not be safe."

"Fighting? I don't understand."

"What's to understand? Our safety can't be guaranteed, that's all."

This was a brief passing shadow, but for just an instant I could see the light go out of Rosalie as she digested what I had told her. I saw again how unprepared she was for the life she was about to take up, but I, like her, was thinking then only about the pleasurable prospect of our upcoming days in Sicily.

After stopovers in Paris and Rome, our plane touched down in Palermo early one afternoon. We were told that a driver would be there to meet us, to escort us around Palermo and then on to Castellammare. The first big surprise of our trip occurred, literally, looking out the window of the plane as it taxied toward the terminal in Palermo. There was a crowd of people jammed behind a high chain-link fence and atop an observation deck on the terminal building. From a distance, they looked like protesters of some kind. They were carrying signs that I could not make out initially. As the plane taxied closer, I could make out a word on a banner: BONANNO. I froze. My first thought was that we were going to be arrested and deported. SON AND DAUGHTER-IN-LAW OF FAMOUS MAFIA CHIEFTAIN SEIZED IN SICILY. It would make a good headline back home. I was debating with myself whether and what to tell Rosalie, who had an aisle seat and could not see. Then as the plane grew closer to the crowd, I was able to make out the signs and banners more clearly. The headlines would have been very different. WELCOME HOME SALVATORE AND ROSALIA! CONGRATULATIONS TO THE NEWLYWEDS! LONG LIFE TO THE BONANNOS! WELCOME SON OF JOSEPH BONANNO!

It was beyond comprehension. There had to have been two or three hundred people waiting to welcome us. When I had Rosalie lean past me to get a look out the window, she laughed nervously and then said, almost under her breath, "Oh my God!"

An official delegation from Castellammare greeted us at the gate with flowers and baskets of fruit. A little girl handed Rosalie a huge bouquet of roses. Someone even read a brief welcoming speech and then we were literally swept away. People I did not know took our luggage, cleared a path for us through the terminal to the front of the building, where an official car was waiting for us. Our luggage was loaded; we were given hugs and kisses on both cheeks from dozens of people before we were able to settle into the backseat of our vehicle and move out of the airport area.

Palermo in the mid-fifties was like no city I had ever seen. It was ancient, modern, ruined, rising, all at once. Its old streets and neighborhoods were lined with odd-shaped creamy- and pastel-colored buildings, stucco walls that looked like they had been bleached by several centuries of sun and which were spotted with handbills, some of which had been peeled away, while others seemed newly plastered over the shreds of the old. There were little sidewalk cafés and mysterious alleys that seemed to twist in and out of sight everywhere and from which people—young lovers, old men with bicycles, women lugging armfuls of laundry—appeared and disappeared. Then, seemingly contiguous with the old neighborhoods were towering new apartment and office buildings rising into the azure sky. These were functional and powerful structures rather than beautiful ones, as if they belonged to movie sets of the cinema verité of the day. The look and feel of the city was chaotic, frantic with energy, noise, and activity. Every block of the way, car horns sounded in jammed traffic; the sound of people cursing each other good-naturedly filled our ears. Rosalie pushed herself back into the cushions of the car seat. I could sense how assaulted she felt by the explosion of noise and color. I felt stirred by the excitement, though I could not imagine myself ever living in this.

Our driver took us to an address I had given him in the middle of the old part of the city. We were greeted at the door of a walled private home by a large, full-mustached man, Benedetto Russo, the boss of a major Palermitan Family. He was flanked on either side by aides. The women of his family—it looked like three generations—stood discreetly in the background.

We were served a sumptuous lunch in a beautiful outdoor garden. The surprise for both Rosalie and me was the almost intimate awareness our hosts seemed to have about our wedding, as though they had attended it. The women talked about Rosalie's beautiful bridal veil, which they knew she had designed herself. The men asked about Tony Bennett and the fabulous eight-story cake they had heard about. At the end of the meal, we toasted one another with expensive cognac. Russo said, "Your father's favorite, Louis the Thirteenth!"

I formally offered greetings on behalf of my father and told them that I had been instructed to carry back with me anything they wanted to tell him. Russo wanted to know about my father's health. He had had a heart attack a few years before—nothing serious—but it was a point of concern among friends. I assured them he was fine. Russo wanted to know if he was talking any more about retirement.

"The last time I saw your father," he said, "all he could talk about was how beautiful the spring and the mountains in Tucson were."

Before we left, Russo took me aside and said, "Please tell Don Pepino that we miss him and would like to see him soon. His wisdom and counsel are invaluable to us."

This exchange, seemingly innocuous, was very typical of the way men in our world conveyed important information. Code words, analogy, ellipses rather than direct speech were inevitable in any secret society, more so in the Mafia, where Sicilian tradition over the centuries had distilled to an essence realities of secrecy, betrayal, and revenge. During the course of this innocuous lunch, Russo told me—in code—that he and his Family wanted my father to visit them to help straighten out serious though unspecified problems they were having. I assured Russo, using his exact words, that I would convey the message.

Then we were off. The driver assigned to us took us through some of the more venerable neighborhoods in the city and its suburbs. We stopped at a particularly old and beautiful Norman cathedral with great bronze doors that had been designed by an artisan and distant relative named Pisano Bonanno and then we were on our way again, heading up into the mountains, bare and sun-blistered in places, strangely abundant with olive trees and vineyards on others. The road we followed wound along above the sea, which came in and out of view as we proceeded toward the ancient fortress town of Castellammare del Golfo, protected like a large pearl in an oyster, set as it was deep in an inlet facing a broad bay and the open sea. We arrived before nightfall to another large, welcoming crowd in the town center near the church in the main square. Bells were rung, the mayor read a short proclamation, a priest blessed us, and there were more flowers and kisses and a parade through the streets. And then we moved on to the inn where would be staying for the next few days.

The inn was the converted home of a nobleman. Its large rooms had been made over into a comfortable hotel that could accommodate thirty or so guests in a setting that was both intimate and elegant. There were no other guests when we visited. Just the host and his wife and family, who served us dinner and waited on us as though we were aristocracy—a fact that was initially discomforting. But the feeling vanished over the course of a long meal washed down with lots of wine. My Sicilian was good enough to converse easily; my interest in the town and its people was genuine and put our hosts at ease. I never thought of myself as a big shot and neither did Rosalie. There were so many relatives and friends in the area, there was so much here, in the dust and dirt of the soil itself, that accounted for who I was, I could not have been a lord of the manor even if I had wanted to be. What I wanted was to cry for joy in this place, a place I knew was home, though I had never before set eyes on it in my lifetime.

Sometime before we retired for the evening, an old man stopped by the inn to say hello. He was bent and gnarled as a gnome. His hair was wild and disheveled, and he was in the rough, ragged dress of a well-to-do landowner. His hand was trembling as he extended it to shake mine. He looked as though the effort of breath itself was a threat to his well-being. Then he told me his name—Giuseppe Maggadino.

Maggadino was a name that went back for generations in our family. It would take the better part of an afternoon to draw a tree connecting the Bonannos, the Maggadinos, the Bonventres, Brunos, Labruzzos, all those family branches that connected with ours somewhere between root and leaf. But the name Maggadino leapt out at me with a force that was almost palpable.

There was a Stefano Maggadino in the United States, the boss of a Mafia Family in Buffalo. He was a cousin of my father's and had at first been his patron when he arrived there as an illegal immigrant in the 1920s. My father's arrival in the United States was inextricably bound up with the Maggadino family. Originally, my grandfather Salvatore had settled in the United States when my father was an infant. He had returned to Sicily—with my father—when he learned that it was safe to do so (he had for years mistakenly believed he was being sought for murder in his homeland). My grandfather died from wounds suffered in World War I, my grandmother died shortly after that, and the care of my father, a teenager then, was placed in the hands of one of the Sicilian Maggadinos—also named Stefano—a relative of both my father and Stefano Maggadino in Buffalo. The man standing before me now, Giuseppe Maggadino, was the Sicilian Stefano's brother and the father of my father's closest friend, Peter Maggadino, who was ultimately involved in the long adventure that brought both young men to America.

The story was that my father had gone off to the Naval College in Palermo during the early days of Mussolini. There had been an edict requiring all young men at the school to wear black shirts in honor of the dictator. My father, passionately opposed to Mussolini and fascism—as many Sicilians were—was one of a handful who wore white shirts. One particular day on the parade ground, he and his group wore their white shirts. He was expelled from school, and shortly thereafter, to escape the fascists, he and his cousin and friend Peter Maggadino—with Giuseppe's blessing—set out for Tunisia and then France, hoping to make their way to America, where there was a large immigrant community of Castellammarese. The two men eventually took a steamer to Cuba and then a midnight fishing boat to Florida, where they were later arrested by immigration authorities, only to be bailed out by Willie Moretti (the eventual right arm of Frank Costello), who had been dispatched to Jacksonville by the Buffalo boss, Stefano Maggadino.

The old man asked me if I wanted to take a walk with him the following morning. I was somewhat apprehensive about having him exert himself in any way on my behalf, but I could never have insulted him by declining his offer.

"Of course," I said. "I'd be honored to accompany you."

"Good," he said. "Be ready at four o'clock in the morning."

Rosalie and I had a good laugh at the predicament I had landed in. I surely did not look forward to getting out of bed in the middle of the night—but there I was the next morning, waiting for old Giuseppe downstairs. The owners of the inn had gotten up, too, just to make sure I had coffee and biscotti to take along for later.

The old man arrived exactly on time, dressed in the same rough getup as the night before. He had a cup of coffee, too, and then, while it was still pitch-dark out, we started our walk. I was surprised by the relative briskness of the old man's pace. He seemed almost to be in a hurry. I wanted, for his sake, to slow him down, but I said nothing—again, for fear of insulting him. We walked through the neighborhood we were in and proceeded up the Madonna Scala. Suddenly, the old man stepped off the road and into a field. I stayed at his side as his pace seemed, if anything, to quicken as we marched through tall grass, then onto a narrow boulder-strewn path that caused me—but not him—to stumble, bruising my toes and shins. All the while we walked, he said nothing. I found myself a little out of breath after awhile. I had no idea where old Giuseppe was leading me and, even less, where he got the reserves of stamina that allowed him to forge ahead as tirelessly as a mountain goat.

We were headed toward the mountains. After awhile, as the first light of day appeared, I could make out the town behind us and how far we had already climbed into the hills. The old man kept going, straight up the side of the mountain. I was stumbling and scrambling to keep up with him. I had a hard time breathing. And now my reticence in saying anything had to do with me, not him. I did not want him to see that I was unable to keep up. I was young—and a Bonanno. And I was desperately out of breath.

Eventually, we reached the place he wanted to show me, an old abandoned farmhouse—which was little more than a pile of foundation stones now—at least six or seven miles from where we had set out. My lungs were burning and my eyes swimming with sweat as I let myself collapse, sprawling out under the shade of an olive tree next to the old man, who sat bolt upright and unwrapped a bandanna containing bread, cheese, and a nice huge *cibolla*. He pointed to a well, which he said had good wine in it, and I went and drew up a bottle chilled in cold water. The wine and food were perfect, but I had to take them slowly to keep from throwing up.

For a long while, the old man said nothing. We sat watching the gulf and ocean in the distance, the dusty, rocky mountains surrounding us, feeling the hot wind on our faces. Finally, old Giuseppe said to me in Sicilian, "You know the name Bucellato?"

The name was familiar to me. I remembered something about an old feud between the Bonannos and members of a family named Bucellato.

"The Bucellatos and Bonannos were once in a shooting war. Members of our family were shot and killed tending their lands, minding their own business; so were men of the Bucellatos—shot and killed. This went on for years. Your grandfather, the head of our clan," Giuseppe said, "wanted to make peace with the head of the Bucellato clan and did not know how to do it because the killing had gone on for so long. Then your father was born. It was 1905. You know the story?"

I remembered now. But I said nothing because I wanted to hear the story as old Giuseppe, one of the actual participants, told it.

"Your grandfather, after your father was born, came to us and asked what we could do to end the war we were in so his son might have a chance to live. 'Cut off the head of the snake,' I said—kill Felice Bucellato himself. You know, every day Bucellato went to a café in the town square with his bodyguards and sat there like he was a king or a potentate. He thought he was invulnerable—but he was not. I knew how to get to him because I knew the owner of this café, and I told your grandfather this. And he said, 'As usual, you are right, Giuseppe. But I was taught that a good Father brings peace to his family, not blood.' What was he saying to me! You know what he was saying?"

The old man took my arm and looked me in the eye. His eyes were coal black and on fire. I knew this look well; it was my father's face, the eyes, the darkness and light present at the same time. The old man continued: " 'What the hell are you talking about?' I said to your grandfather. 'This is no time for philosophy.' 'No,' he said. 'This is not philosophy. You stay here.' And then he walked—by himself, no bodyguards—through the center of town to that café where Felice Bucellato was sitting. He walked up to his rival, whose bodyguards immediately stepped in the way. 'I am unarmed,' your grandfather said, raising his arms, allowing himself to be searched. Then he stood face-to-face with Felice Bucellato. He bid him good morning and he said that he came in the name of peace and had a request to make of him. 'What is that?' Felice asked. 'Will you be the godfather to my son?' your grandfather asked him. Felice was completely unprepared for this, so much so that he could only answer in the positive.

'I would be proud and honored to be the godfather of your son.' And then the two men, to the complete consternation of everyone nearby, embraced each other and drank to each other's long life and health. Two days later, your father was carried to this farm where we are sitting now. There was a celebration and then a procession to the church, where your father was baptized, with Don Felice holding him in his arms. Your father was born an Angel of Peace!"

Though I had heard this story, told somewhat differently by my parents and relatives—it was part of our family mythology as much as the Battle of Segesta—I had never heard it from an eyewitness, a participant. It was as though I could feel for myself, for the first time, my grandfather's heartbeat and the force of his thinking. I was stirred not only by the story but by the storyteller, as well. The man sitting next to me was no ordinary person. He might have looked like an ancient stick figure from a misty pastoral romance, but he was a living connection to my own history, to the life force of the tradition that was already in my blood. My father had once said about Uncle Stefano that he was the one who had endowed him with a love for our tradition. Tradition, my father said so many times, was our bulwark against chaos. And here, sitting with this man, I understood something that went far beyond the use of violence or the accumulation of wealth, fame, power. In this not-so-frail old body was a different kind of power, the power of a specific tradition, one that had enabled a small group of island people to survive more than twenty centuries of conquest, then one day to mix with and become part of the ruling establishment of the strongest country on the face of the earth.

We lingered here through the hottest part of the day and then made our way back down the mountain. I heard many more stories—some that I knew, some that I did not—and they all reinforced in me the awareness I had been given, almost from birth, that the way of life I had entered upon was a sacred trust, whatever anyone else said about it. I was, in ways I never could have explained to my new wife, married to it as I could never be to her or any other living soul. Was that my blessing or my curse? To this day, I do not know. I know only that my life, like my father's, was determined for me at the moment of my birth—though, like him, I have always cherished my independence and my sense of freedom. A paradox? Of course. This way of life has always been a paradox. It is a life defined by sins of honor, punishable by law but cherished by its adherents.

5

There is so much blood, rebellion, and loss in my father's history, the designation "Angel of Peace" seems to me, today, to be profoundly ironic. When my father arrived in Brooklyn as an illegal immigrant during the 1920s, he soon became involved with a community of fellow Castellammarese, many of whom were, like himself, "connected." He became associated with a man named Salvatore Maranzano, a Man of Honor and a dynamic leader who soon turned into a wartime leader when a long and complicated struggle broke out between the Castellammarese and New York's most powerful Family, headed by Joseph Masseria. The war raged for almost two years and was one of the mythical sagas in American gangland history. There were bodies all over the streets of several major cities. Al Capone of Chicago, for example, rose out of the flames of this war like a gaudy phoenix, only to be plucked naked for his arrogance and stupidity. My father, as Maranzano's chief aide, also rose to the top out of this war, but he did not dress himself in feathers or airs. When Maranzano, the leader of the Castellammarese, was struck down by Charles "Lucky" Luciano, the surviving leader of the Masseria faction, my father made peace—not war—with him.

Young as he was, my father had the loyal backing of all the Castellammarese because they knew he was a man of integrity who would honorably represent their interests. My father's interests, for himself and his Family, were for peace. He met with Luciano at a heavily fortified location in the Bronx and told him, "I have no quarrel with you." He declined Luciano's offer to carve up New York between them into spheres of influence and, instead, at my father's insistence, worked out a real peace between them, one that recognized the five different New York Families and a system of consensus and negotiation to mediate any future disputes. The idea was to form a Commizione del Pace, as it was called in Sicilian, a Committee of Peace. Commission was the Americanized name, insisted on by Luciano, who was ignorant of Sicily, its language, and its traditions.

"I don't even know how the fuck to pronounce it; just call it the Commission," Luciano said at the time.

By whatever name, the Commission, made up of the fathers of New York City's Five Families and Buffalo—later the heads of the other Families around the country were added—worked. The peace held for more than thirty years. The Angel of Peace, invisible to the rest of the world, was visible to all mafiosi because what he stood for was steeped not only in tradition but in practice. The peace worked. Business prospered.

How did this peace work? The heart of it was live and let live. Let each Family run its own business in its own way, don't interfere, and if any disputes arise, mediate them through the Commission. When a matter came up in one Family that might have a spillover effect for all, *mediation*, not *warfare*, was the ruling word. In 1938, for example, Albert Anastasia, the underboss of the Mangano Family, at the instigation of Dutch Schultz, wanted to assassinate the New York district attorney, Thomas E. Dewey, who had been responsible for prosecuting and jailing Luciano a couple of years earlier. When Anastasia appeared before the Commission, the plan had been tentatively set. All that was needed was the signal to go. My father talked Albert out of the plan, made him see the danger in it to all the Families.

When I was talking with him about it awhile ago, my father said, "How long would we have lasted if we went around killing cops and politicians. Kill Dewey? No, our way was to find an accommodation with him. If we had not found that way, the fault was ours, not his."

The way of accommodation was found. A secret $250,000 fund, large for those days, supporting Dewey's bid for the governorship of New York was established in 1939 by Frank Costello and Meyer Lansky, who had strong gambling interests in Saratoga, New York. Dewey lost that year, but his campaign accepted—and used—the money. He was never again a threat. He became a "friend," thereafter, a politician who could be worked with—as in the old country, according to a tradition where, always, co-operation with rulers and potential enemies was the order of the day.

The long peace built up by the Commission earned my father a reputation as "a Godfather," a man of extraordinary wisdom, a carrier of the old tradition into the New World. The New World was a challenge, but for a time the idea of cooperation seemed just as fruitful here as it had been in past centuries in Sicily.

During World War II, for example, the government and the Mafia actually went into a partnership of sorts. When German saboteurs sank the French liner *Normandie* in New York Harbor in 1941, New York District Attorney Frank Hogan, acting on behalf of Naval Intelligence, tried to work out a deal with Lucky Luciano. Hogan contacted an aide of Luciano's, "Socks" Lanza, and asked him for help. Luciano said he would help if the government moved him from Dannemora, a federal facility far from New York, to Greenhaven, a facility closer to the city—and to his business interests. Luciano was transferred to Greenhaven. Luciano then told Lanza to get hold of the leaders of other Families because they, not he, would be in a position to help. Lanza approached my father and others and appealed to them for support. Support was given. There was not a single further act of sabotage on eastern docks till the end of the war.

Then there was the Allied invasion of Sicily. Naval intelligence again approached Luciano. A lieutenant commander named Charles Haffenden met with Luciano in prison, asked for his help, and offered in exchange to see what he could do about shortening his sentence. This proposition, as well as being a cynical one, demonstrated the ignorance of Naval Intelligence. Luciano had only the most limited contacts in Sicily. Though he had been born there, he came here as an infant and was a thoroughly Americanized product. He never had the kind of connections and power in the old country that would have enabled him to set up anything.

But he did tell Haffenden that he would help. What he did then was to contact Socks Lanza and told him to go to the old Sicilian leaders in this country who did have those connections—Vincent Mangano, Joe Profaci, and Joe Bonanno. These men not only knew the old country but also had active and ongoing contacts there. Friends, relatives, associates—whole towns still regarded these American Family leaders as native sons.

Mangano, Profaci, and my father agreed to cooperate. These men all hated Mussolini and the fascists—and they could not pass up a golden opportunity to cement their relationship with the government.

They knew Sicily like the backs of their hands, were able to locate people, have messages sent to them, provide the government with exactly the sort of fifth-column help it so sorely was looking for. The guerrilla force put together by my father and his friends had a real impact—in Sicily and back home, where results produced benefits. Luciano, predictably, was not given his freedom. He was deported, but the Families, the Commission, flourished and prospered along with the rest of the country. At the local, state, and federal levels of government, communication and cooperation were routine because by then the mob was embedded in unions, businesses, and legislatures all across the country. Things got done.

For the Angel of Peace, postwar prosperity represented a new and far more difficult challenge. How to keep a traditional way of life intact in a country that scorned tradition or, at least, operated according to very different traditions. This was not a question of philosophy, but of practicality. How to keep the peace, how to preserve unity among a relatively tiny group of people—about five thousand nationwide—who had accumulated extraordinary power and prosperity.

In the beginning of 1947, there were a couple of fateful meetings to decide the future. Lucky Luciano, deported to Italy, got a visa from the Italian government that allowed him to travel to Cuba. Once there, leaders from many of the Families, including my father, wined and dined him and talked generally about the future. This Cuban get-together has been the subject of countless Mafia exposés because it supposedly was there that an agreement on shipping drugs into the States was worked out. That, in fact, did not happen. Nor, for that matter, were any agreements of substance worked out in Cuba.

A month later, however, in a yacht off the coast of the Florida, there was a full Commission meeting—so far as I know, never reported about—at which time very fundamental policy decisions regarding the future were made.

One decision was that Frank Costello would be formally named head of the Luciano Family, later to become the Costello Family—because Luciano, as a leader, was in permanent exile. Another decision taken was to eliminate Bugsy Siegel, the West Coast mobster who had gone too far in trying to colonize gambling interests for himself in Las Vegas. The decision actually was that Siegel was "a Jewish problem," and therefore the responsibility of Meyer Lansky, who, it was clearly understood, would do what he had to—namely, kill Siegel.

The subject of drugs did come up at that meeting. Once again, the liberal bloc of Americanized leaders wanted to get involved in the heroin trade, but a specific decision by the conservatives, headed by my father, was made not to. There were practical reasons for this. Narcotics trafficking was a dangerous and not-yet-profitable business. Plus, it raised the possibility, like counterfeiting (which the mob generally never got involved with), of federal intervention. My father opposed drugs—and prostitution—on principle. He passionately believed that narcotics and prostitution undermined family life, the backbone, in his mind, of traditional life. He urged—and the Commission passed—a specific resolution forever forbidding narcotics trafficking. This decision, it turned out, was the beginning of the end. The ultimate prospect of big profits far outweighed the lingering attraction of old traditions—at least in the mind of newer leaders who were coming up through the Families. The conservatives had their reservations about narcotics and prostitution, but that's not to say they didn't know they existed *or* that they didn't profit from such activities. Lucky Luciano, for example, was a dapper man-about-town in New York in his time. He lived lavishly in the Waldorf-Astoria and dined regularly at the Stork Club with a host of beauties on his arm. The public naturally interpreted from these activities that he was dealing with prostitution. He may very well have controlled districts where prostitution existed and received money from the proceeds, but he himself did not take part in the actual process, condone, or even advocate the practice. It was the lower eschelons, the foot soldiers, that controlled the illegal activities. And they paid up to allow themselves these privileges.

I did not know it at the time, but during my honeymoon trip to Sicily, when Roaslie and I had lunch that day in Palermo with Benedetto Russo, the Palermitano boss, the coded message I carried to my father was all about drugs—drugs in Sicily and in the United States. The same split between the conservative factions and the liberals was happening in Sicily, as well. The liberals there were mostly younger men who after the war had healthy appetites for wealth and all it stood for.

Without knowing it then, the seemingly innocuous message I passed on to my father when Rosalie and I returned from our honeymoon was about the end of the era of peace and cooperation that had been so carefully worked out and which had resulted in such great power and profit for all.

During the early part of 1957, still flush with happiness, Rosalie and I accompanied my father, along with several of his friends and their wives, including Albert Anastasia, Joe Profaci, Frank Costello and Meyer Lansky, to Cuba. The occasion was to celebrate Costello's early release from prison on an overturned wiretap conviction. We stayed at the Hotel Nacional, as guests of Lansky. We were there for pleasure, not business, but business came up.

We were lavishly entertained by Fulgencio Batista, the Cuban dictator, a bantam cock of a man, full of swagger and bravado but shrewd, as well. One evening, he provided unlimited chips for the wives to use in the sumptuous casino of the hotel and he sat with us and openly appealed for our support. He wanted us to use what influence we had to get the Eisenhower administration to commit to blocking Fidel Castro's insurgency.

"You can tell your friends I will not oppose an American invasion of my country," he said. Batista counted on our support because he knew that Anastasia, Costello, and Lucchese—as well as Lansky—had big money in the casinos and, more than likely, in a flourishing drug trade in which Cuba had become a transshipping point.

My father said to Batista—and I can still hear the even tone of his voice and see the cold blue glitter of his eyes—"Perhaps you think we have more influence than we do." Batista pushed his case, but we left that evening with no offers proffered, no commitments made. When we later took a drive through the streets of Havana, you could hear the thump of artillery in the hills. In the back of our sedan, Anastasia said to my father, "I think we should try and support him. You know, do the Communist thing on Castro; that'll get some attention." My father, unimpressed, mumbled something about Sicily and the fascists in the twenties and not trying to thwart the will of the people. "We have interests here, Joe; you don't," Anastasia said. My father shot back, "And Batista gets fifty percent; when Castro wins, maybe you'll be able to cut a better deal with him."

Later that night, in our hotel suite in the Nacional, Rosalie laughed over the winnings she had brought back from the casino.

"We couldn't lose," she said, combing out her hair near the balcony, which overlooked the city. "I don't think it's fair for us to win like that."

"Are you complaining?"

"No. It was just a little obvious, that's all."

True. But my mind was elsewhere.

When we boarded our Eastern Airlines Electra for a flight back to Miami, I sensed tension in our group; there was something in the air that seemed all of a piece with the distant and unsettling thump of artillery in the hills surrounding the city. But what was it?

Less than two months later, in May 1957, Frank Costello was returning home to his apartment on Central Park. He was striding through the lobby when a gunman stepped out of the shadows and called out to him. "Hey, Frank, this is for you!" Costello turned his head in the direction of the voice—which probably saved his life—as a shot was fired, creasing his skull. He fell in a pool of blood. The gunman later was identified by the doorman from police photos as Vinnie "the Chin" Gigante, a street hood who was loyal to a rival within Costello's Family, Vito Genovese.

I did not know then—though it is clear now—that Vito Genovese's interests in eliminating Frank Costello involved something more than personal rivalry. Vito, underboss in Costello's Family—the old Luciano Family—was into drugs. Costello, following the 1947 Commission edict, was not—or at least had severely limited the opportunities for trafficking in his Family. It is ironic, too, that "Chin" Gigante should have had any kind of career after that botched assassination job. In our business, you did not call out to a victim; you never gave him an opportunity to take any kind of evasive or defensive action. When it was your job to kill someone, you moved up as close to him as possible, preferably from behind, unseen, where you could get off a point black shot to the back of the head, then turn and walk away. Just that. Gigante was an ex-prizefighter and in our world was said to have taken one too many punches—something he later tried to exploit as a Family boss when the government prosecuted him in the mid 1990s for conspiracy to commit murder.

My father at that point was making plans to answer the invitation to visit Sicily—a trip that would combine pleasure with serious business. Just after the attempt on Costello and just before my father left for Sicily, Albert Anastasia, in a rage, paid him and Joe Profaci a visit. Anastasia knew that

Vinnie Gigante was Genovese's man and therefore wanted to go after Genovese. He went to the old-timers—as a courtesy—and told them he wanted to take out Genovese.

"All I want is for your Families to remain neutral in this," he told my father and Profaci. My father, feeling that his trip to Sicily was now urgent, argued for time.

"I understand your feelings, Albert, but I would like you to do nothing. If this escalates, there will be a war and everyone will be drawn in. That must not happen," said the Angel of Peace. And Anastasia, at that point, committed himself to waiting.

"My life is in your hands," he said. A fateful moment indeed.

My father left for Sicily at the end of that summer. In Sicily, Benedetto Russo and other Family bosses told him that there was a developing split in Sicilian Families, a split between older members, who were loyal to tradition, and younger ones, who were not, who put money first. One of the old-timers told my father then that Turkish opium was at the heart of the problem and that Families in the United States were deeply involved.

"Impossible," my father said then. "There is an absolute ban against trafficking with us and there is a death sentence in our Family for anyone who disobeys."

Don Vincent Vercelli, another Palermitano, told my father, directly, "Maybe there's no trafficking in your Family, Don Pepino, but there are other New York Families who are up to their asses in it. They will lie to you, tell you anything, but they are nothing more than *cocciu di taca;* they are lice devoted exclusively to money. They couldn't care less about our glorious tradition."

My father became ill on this trip abroad and decided to cut his visit to Sicily short and head back to the United States. But by the time he boarded a plane in Rome and headed for New York, all hell had broken loose.

6

On October 25, 1957, Albert Anastasia was reclining in a barber's chair at the Park-Sheraton Hotel in Manhattan, in the process of getting a luxuriously fashioned shave and haircut. Hot towels covered his face. Music was playing on a nearby radio. The salon was quiet when two men, unnoticed by others, walked into the room and up to Anastasia's chair and pumped him full of bullets. The gunmen turned and fled even before the terrified barbers and other patrons could sound an alarm. Anastasia's blood-soaked remains hung from the chair where only seconds before he had been floating in dreamland.

In our world, the open murder of a Family leader, a Father, was the equivalent of killing a head of state. It was a political act of monumental importance because it was a blow against the existing order.

In 1951, when Vincent Mangano, the head of the former Mineo Family, had disappeared, it was not immediately clear what had happened, though obviously foul play had been involved. Mangano's brother, at the same time, had been found murdered. It was known to us that there had been a festering problem within Mangano's Family around the question of alliances. Mangano, a "Mustache Pete"—a reference to an old-world, non-Americanized Italian—had been uneasy about a growing relationship between his second in command, Albert Anastasia, and Frank Costello, the leader of the former Masseria Family. Both Albert and Costello were Americanized members, though they were knowledgeable about and respectful of old-world traditions. It was assumed, over time, that Mangano's disappearance somehow had to do with the ambitions of Anastasia.

While everyone had their suspicions, no one could really prove anything. And while Albert was never accused of anything, he knew enough to place himself at the disposal of the Commission—without admitting anything—as it looked into the murder. This was an internal matter within his Family, Anastasia argued. The Commission, whatever its suspicions, went along for the sake of peace and accepted his logic. Ultimately, his elevation to leadership of the Mangano Family was accepted by the Commission.

Albert's murder, however, was entirely different. Every person in the country could see the gory photograph of Albert in the next day's newspapers. Whoever was behind this killing was making a statement, not trying to conceal anything except the identity of the murderers. This was an act of open warfare, and within the Families no one could immediately say who was fighting whom and when the next killing might take place. If the pot had been simmering all these years, it had now boiled over. It was mandatory to take strong and forceful action to preserve the peace that had permitted all the Families to prosper over the last three decades.

My father arrived back in the States from Sicily two days after Albert's murder. He has told me many times since then that his presence on the scene might have been enough to make Albert's killers think twice before acting. He also has carried with him to this day Albert's haunting words, "My life is in your hands"—when Anastasia yielded to my father's request to take no action against Vito Genovese.

Immediately following Albert's murder—and before my father arrived in the country—there were hurried calls to arrange a meeting of New York Families, especially involving factions within Albert's Family, to see what could be done to get to the bottom of what had happened. At the same time, rumors of a power conflict between Albert and Vito Genovese had prompted a call for a national meeting, originally proposed for Chicago but now changed to Apalachin, a small town in the Catskill Mountains of New York where the Commission had had its regularly scheduled once-in-five-years meeting the year before. The call for this other, national meeting had been the brainchild of my father's cousin Steve Maggadino, a Commission member from Buffalo. My father had told his cousin to keep his eyes open for him while he was in Sicily, and Steve had taken it upon himself to call a big meeting—probably for no better reason than that he wanted to be a big shot. Steve had a "short man's complex," especially in relation to my father, whose power and influence he resented, and here was the chance to strut and swagger a little. Steve and my father were cousins through marriage. After Maggadino had helped my father, at the time he had been jailed by immigration authorities in Jacksonville, Florida, in 1926, Steve expected him to live in Buffalo. My father had other ideas; instead, he went to Brooklyn, and Maggadino never forgave him for abandoning him. They had no real issues between them until the murder of Albert, which sent shock waves from one coast to the other. Suddenly, this "national" meeting took on national significance.

The really crucial meeting, however, was not the meeting that Steve had called, but one that was convened earlier by the heads of New York's Five Families. This meeting, prior to the Apalachin get-together, was solely devoted to the urgent business of trying to prevent further bloodshed. More than two hundred people from the different Families met at an estate in New Jersey owned by Richie Boiardo, a group leader in the Anastasia Family.

It was clear at this meeting that a lot more than internal discussion was behind Anastasia's death. Yes, it turned out there was real division within his Family and disagreements over Albert's leadership. One of his group captains, for years, had been selling memberships in the Family—at fifty thousand dollars a pop. That had been an incredible violation of our tradition, a cancer that had to be eradicated. Albert, however, when he found out about it, had this group leader eliminated. That was not the problem.

Albert's murder, everyone knew, came from the outside. No one knew for sure on that day who had done the killing, though clearly Genovese was the prime suspect. (Later on, many months later, it was learned through informants that the killers were from the Gallo faction of the Profaci Family—the Family closest to ours. They were part of a dissident group within the Profaci Family that wanted a bigger share of the Family's profits, but they were looking outside for leadership, to people like Vito Genovese and Tommy Lucchese, leaders who had seen Albert as a threat to their own interests.) The focus at the New Jersey meeting, however, was on Genovese's quarrel with Albert. And that basic quarrel was political. With Costello out of the way (he had "retired" after the attempted hit on him), Genovese quickly had taken control of the old Luciano Family. With Albert dead, Genovese, along with Tommy Lucchese, had acquired power within the Commission to lead a bloc of liberals against conservatives who were very much influenced by the thinking and philosophy of Joe Bonanno.

My father had been asked to chair this emergency meeting of the Five Families, just as he had been asked to chair the 1951 and 1956 Commission meetings. There was real anticipation of an explosion, my father remembered.

"You could feel this in the air, see it in the eyes of everyone there," he told me later. But my father, first, was a strategic thinker, even before he was a warrior. If I have learned anything from him over the years, it has been this sense of surprising one's enemies not by doing the obvious but by thinking the unthinkable.

My father proposed that Albert's replacement as head of his Family should be Carlo Gambino, a known ally of Genovese and Lucchese. On the surface, his thinking seemed baffling and even crazy. Gambino, at that moment, was actually thought to have been involved in Albert's murder. Another faction within Albert's Family, headed by Tommy Rava, had even been preparing to go to war against Gambino. But my father argued passionately (some people thought even a little long-windedly) on the absolute need to preserve peace among the Families. Gambino was a good, popular choice, my father argued, because he and Lucchese were already related through the marriage of their children, so harmony would be more likely. Why not have Gambino named provisional head of the Family for three years, see how things would work out, see if peace could be maintained?

Who was going to argue with him? The people who thought my father was crazy were either too glad to go along or too close to him politically.

But the real reason my father proposed Gambino, had nothing to do with lunacy or cloudy political thinking. In his own mind, Gambino was weak, too weak to be a threat to anyone. Gambino, though he was favored by Genovese and Lucchese, was a person who exhibited no qualities of leadership. In private, my father referred to him as a "squirrel." He was servile and fawning around those whom he regarded as more powerful.

"I will tell you a story about Albert and Carlo," my father told me sometime later. "We were in a restaurant one night in Queens, a lot of us in a private dining room. Albert was in a terrible mood that evening because Gambino had botched an assignment over something or other. When Carlo came into the room, Albert got up from his table, walked over to him, and, in front of everyone in the room, slapped him across the face. It was shocking—and humiliating. But you know what? Gambino laughed it off. A stronger man instinctively would have shown some sign of anger or maybe just left the room. Carlo was simply afraid of Albert—then and afterward. He was a coward, a squirrel."

It was just that kind of cowardice that my father was counting on when he put Gambino's name forward. A squirrel would in all likelihood have a similarly evasive approach in dealing with hot-button issues likely to divide the Commission and split our world. He would be more—not less—likely to keep himself out of controversy and harm's way.

The meeting ended on a note of amity and unity, with praise and back-slapping all around. Carlo was selected as head of his Family—on a provisional basis for a period of three years, at which point his nomination would be reviewed by the Commission again. But with this meeting out of the way, the big clambake at Apalachin was next—and this one, my father really wanted no part of. If he had simply had his way, he would then have gone on to Tucson to lie in the sun and recuperate. But he could not do this. His aides pressed him to attend and other Family leaders urged him to go, and so he did.

"When the music is playing, the only real choice you have is to join the dance or become a wallflower," he grumbled later. His original intention was to show up for a cigar and cognac, and to have a little one-on-one sit-down with his cousin Steve Maggadino, just to make sure who was—and was not—going to be calling the tunes. Steve was the reason my father ultimately could not simply ignore Apalachin.

In my father's mind, Steve was now connected to the shifting winds of intrigue and betrayal blowing through our world. There wasn't anything he could really put his finger on, but it made no sense for his cousin to put himself forward so boldly by calling the meeting when my father was out of the country. He could not believe that Steve could be plotting against the Bonannos. He was family, after all, a first cousin. But my father was alarmed by the obvious need Steve had to expand his own prestige. For the first time, he asked himself some larger questions—ones he could not answer—like whether or not Steve was somehow thinking of shifting his support away from the conservative bloc, led by my father, to the liberals, the Americanized leaders.

The big question my father had was about drugs. Was Steve in favor of or opposed to the consensus agreement among Family heads that had been worked out in 1947? My father now had all the information he needed to know that the liberals, led by Tommy Lucchese and Vito Genovese, though they had professed a willingness to accept the ban, were ignoring it. Any effort on their part to change the balance of power in our world, he knew, was in large part about changing the policy on drugs.

The two men met in a hotel in Binghamton, New York, a town about twelve miles away from Apalachin, and spent the better part of a day going over different issues. Over a leisurely breakfast, they talked about mutual relatives, about the old country, the tombstones of the Maggadinos and the Bonannos, then about business: Albert Anastasia's murder. And drugs.

My father could not read his cousin. Was Steve in favor or opposed to trafficking? The question could never be put to him directly. Like my father, Steve was Castellammarese and a master at disguising his real thoughts. He was a bull of a man at five nine; everything about him radiated power—from his massive shoulders, short, thick arms, and stout body to his deep and rumbling voice. He was a presence and a peasant both. But he had fugitive eyes, shiftier even than Tommy Lucchese's. And despite the power of his appearance, there was nothing fixed about him.

The two men had a shared history that went all the way back to those first days in Brooklyn in the 1920s. Both men were steeped in tradition. My father could not see in Steve's eyes or in his body language any of the signs of betrayal that might have given away a less experienced man. Of course, Steve said, he was for the consensus of 1947; of course, he said, he understood the importance of keeping peace in our world. The meeting satisfied my father that Steve's motives for calling the Apalachin meeting were, as he had thought, in the end about nothing more treacherous than ego. Later, much later, he would learn how wrong he had been.

As my father and Steve Magaddino were preparing to drive on to Apalachin, to the estate of Joseph Barbara of the Barbara Family, who had hosted the previous year's official Commission meeting, a state trooper dropped by a local motel to check out another matter entirely. While he was there, he happened to notice Joe Barbara's son, Joe junior, at the reservations desk. After Joe junior left, the cop went over and saw that he had booked six or ten different rooms. Immediately becoming suspicious, the trooper checked with some other motels in the area and learned that they, too, had multiple bookings in Joe Barbara, Jr.'s, name. In the time that it took to put two and two together, roadblocks began to get set up all around the Barbara estate.

What followed was right out of a Marx Brothers movie. When someone in the main house reported seeing police outside, the guests, dozens of them, huddled together to decide what to do next. Vito Genovese volunteered to go out and see what was happening. He got in his car and went down the hill, where he was stopped at a roadblock and asked for identification. After being checked out, he was permitted to proceed. When everyone inside saw that he was allowed to go, they then started leaving. They all went down the hill in their separate cars and were checked just like Genovese had been, then allowed to proceed. Some of the people in the house decided to leave on foot, so they cut through the woods. They were apprehended by the authorities, checked for identification, then let go.

The papers the next day had screaming headlines about the national Mafia convention that had been broken up. Here, at long last, was not only proof that this shadowy organization existed but also that all its members, it seemed, had come together in the same place at the same time—and for what nefarious, sinister purpose? The papers took particular delight in printing the names of the top hoodlums who had been caught in the dragnet. Among the most prominent, they said, was one Joseph Bonanno. It was amazing. Dante himself could not have drawn a more fanciful picture of a conclave in hell.

Only there was no conspiracy involved in this "convention." As the issues surrounding Albert Anastasia's murder had been worked out beforehand, the only real business was to ratify the peace that had been agreed upon by the Five Families at their meeting earlier in New Jersey. In that sense, it was, exactly as many of the people who had been arrested said it was, a social occasion. The inaccuracies in the media were stunning. My father, for example, listed as one of the cops' top prizes, never was in the hands of the police. He was not on the grounds at Apalachin; at no time did he ever attempt to flee, for he was never there. He was in Binghamton, preparing to go to Apalachin. When he got the news of what had happened, he obviously decided to skip the trip and return home. It was as simple as that. The reason his name was cited was a little more complicated—but perfectly in keeping with the irresponsible way in which the media handled the story.

Gaspar DiGregorio, one of our group leaders, happened to be carrying my father's driver's license with him. Why? My uncle Frank had given it to him. Before my father had left for Sicily, he had asked my uncle to make sure his license was renewed. Frank, who wasn't going to Apalachin, asked Gaspar to take it to him. Gaspar had the new license with him, waiting to give it to my father, when the raid occurred. Gaspar was one of those who took off through the woods and was hauled out of the fields and mud looking like he had been fleeing the scene of a crime. At the police barracks, when he was asked to take everything out of his pockets, there was Joe Bonanno's New York driver's license. The cops never asked—and he never told them—who he really was. He had enough presence of mind to know that later on, if he was challenged in court, he would have had no trouble proving that he wasn't Joe Bonanno. Actually, my father had hoped to take the stand when and if this case ever came to trial—because he would have had an even easier time proving that he wasn't there—but all of that was really beside the point. The inaccurate reporting, the story-spinning, none of it mattered. What really counted was that the lid had been blown off our world and there was no way to put it back.

For all of us, particularly my father, who had so carefully kept himself from public view over the years, the situation was terrible. For the first time, his name was synonymous in the public mind with organized crime. Not only that; columnists now began calling him "the Boss of Bosses," and "the Godfather." Overnight, he had become a target for any public official from the local sheriff to congressional committees to the attorney general, for any lawman or politician who was seeking to make a name for himself by going after the mob.

As it had been for my father, so it was for me. This meeting, though I was as far from it as I could have been, changed my life. During that week, I was on a hunting trip with a couple of friends in an area north of the Grand Canyon. My mind was filled with sunsets and the look of long shadows on canyon walls. I hunted deer during the day, and at night around a campfire, my friends and I talked about Hopi legends, which we were all interested in.

I had left home that week on a Thursday—two days before Apalachin. I was gone till that Sunday. When I arrived home, Rosalie was waiting for me. I could see how upset she was. Everyone was looking for me, she said. Then she handed me a stack of newspapers, all of them filled with stories and banner headlines about what had happened.

"They want you to call New York right away," she said. That seemed pretty obvious. What was harder to take in but soon became obvious enough was that Apalachin marked the end of an era and the beginning of another in our world, one that was far darker, far more ominous than I ever could have imagined.

7

The first person I called was my uncle Frank in New York City, who assured me that my father was okay. I was instructed to sit tight until someone got back to me. For two days, I did not leave my house. There were hours at a time when I think I did little else but sit with my hands in my pockets or pace the room waiting for the phone to ring. Finally, the call came. Frank told me to stay in Tucson and wait for my father.

He arrived a day later. Though he was a vigorous man then in his mid-fifties, strong through the shoulders and chest, with a sculpted, powerful jawline, he seemed almost frail to me when he stepped off the plane onto the tarmac at the airport. He looked drawn, almost colorless, as though blood had actually been drained from him.

He told me about the meetings back east, in New Jersey and upstate; he told me about sitting with Steve and then as much as he could about the fiasco at Apalachin. He confided in me not so much because he mistrusted his closest aides but because I could help him as they could not. I was his son, his strong right arm. Whatever my inexperience, my loyalty would never be in question. And there was more.

My father had decided, as a result of all the headlines, incipient prosecutions, and general chaos throughout our world, to remove himself from New York—to remove himself and yet remain in control of his Family. To do this, he needed someone whose face and voice would be his, who would be able, just by being present, to allow him to be present. He wanted me to go back and forth to New York, to spend time there, to be his eyes and ears, to lend, through my person, the full weight of his command.

I don't think my father anticipated that he would be out of the picture for very long, but he soon had a heart attack, which forced him to remain behind, in the West, away from the swirling and bubbling eddies of lava spilling over from the volcano that our world had become. I went back and forth to New York, carrying messages from him, taking messages back to him. But, even more, I increasingly became my father's stand-in, his presence in an environment that was as strange and alien to me as it was familiar and threatening to him.

He told me what to watch for, who the players were. It was strange. We would sit on his patio, which looked out toward the mountains ringing Tucson. At dusk, watching huge dark sun-shot clouds gathering above the mountains, listening to the coyotes howling from hills, we would be talking about New York. I told him about a meeting I had gone to out on Long Island at a restaurant called Ferdinand's. At this meeting, Tommy Lucchese and some of his friends were sitting across the way from me and I said something lighthearted about people from Palermo, *palermetanos*. Before I knew what had happened, I got a shin-breaking kick under the table from Johnny Morales, our Family's underboss.

My father laughed. He said to me in Sicilian, "Sicilians think that when you make fun of their town, you are making fun of their fathers! We are crazy people."

"I was taken to the bathroom by Uncle Frank, who told me I was the one who was crazy for making jokes."

"So you were," said my father, laughing into the western sunset, enjoying himself immensely.

While I knew nothing, I learned a lot. I did not have the burden of dealing with other Families then; that was left to senior leaders in our Family—Nick Alfano, Gaspar DiGregorio, John Tartamella, Johnny Morales. But I'd go to these meetings with them and sometimes I could feel how necessary my presence was. Joe Bonanno, though he was absent, was still present—my words were his; my thinking and even my gestures carried a weight and force I felt humbled by and totally responsible to.

I was also getting from my father and his men a crash course in learning the table. This was a very strict and formal thing. TV and the movies make a mockery of Mafia meetings, but the table was as important to us as it was to diplomats or political leaders anywhere in the world. Take the shape of the table. Sometimes it would be round, sometimes rectangular, but always there was a real and symbolic circle that could not be broken until the meeting was over. I was at a meeting once where a guy had a heart attack. They carried him out, another guy took his place, and the meeting went right on. Meetings could go on for two hours or fourteen. There was no smoking, no drinking except for water. There were no recesses, bathroom breaks aside.

There was an order to where people sat and stood, even to who was allowed into the room. The main people, the leaders and their advisers, were there, of course. The leaders sat at the table; their advisers, like aides at a congressional hearing, were seated behind them and sometimes would lean over so things could be whispered back and forth. It was a privilege to be in the room. It was the inner sanctum. The adjoining rooms, all the way to the outside, were filled with lower-ranking people in the organizations, the bodyguards, selected crew people, and so forth—like the courts of the Sforzas or the Medicis. If this all sounds overblown, it wasn't; it was all about protocol. Protocol was essential in a world where respect was everything and where the slightest variation might reveal true intentions.

"Listen to their words but watch their eyes; always be the last to speak but never the first; watch Lucchese's eyes when he smiles—they will tell you more than his smile," my father said to me—I don't know how many times—reminding me over and over again that in our world nuance and subtlety had ever so much more to do with survival than brute force.

What I saw going to these meetings, what I learned going back and forth, was that the trouble in our world went far deeper than newspaper headlines and bad publicity. I saw the liberal-conservative split up front and personal, in ways I might otherwise have missed. For instance, there were any number of remarks made in meetings where the speaker's mood, his tone, conveyed indifference when there should have been concern, approval when there should have been discomfort and distress. The way people talked about the murder of Albert Anastasia, for example, told me more about where they stood than the position they took. Vito Genovese called Albert his brother one day. The phrase was tinged with insincerity. When he spoke about "poor Vinnie," as though "Chin" Gigante somehow was an unfortunate who had been caught up in something he shouldn't have been involved in, you could pick up the hint of admiration and gratitude in his voice.

My father had a second heart attack in 1959 and so continued to remain in the background. He talked more and more about getting out of New York entirely, even of retirement.

"I don't want it anymore," he told me one day. "I'm too old and too tired for all this. I don't recognize half the people in our world. Who are they? What are they thinking? It's my responsibility to make peace. When I do, that will be that."

I did not really believe my father then. I was too full of the energy and commitment he had passed on to me. I ascribed his feeling to the battering, physical and emotional, of the last months. I was sure he would soon recover and be back in New York.

I was wrong.

What next surfaced was the Gallo revolt against the Profacis. The Gallos were from the Red Hook section of Brooklyn. Larry was a well-dressed, levelheaded man who could pass as a Park Avenue lawyer. Joey, on the other hand, was the vulgar one of the two brothers. He was an outspoken street smart alec who proudly carried the nickname "Crazy Joey" because of some of his outrageous antics. It became clear after a while that the Gallo brothers had been the actual shooters in Albert's assassination three years earlier, in 1957. When this knowledge became certain and the brothers themselves all but admitted it, no action was taken against them. Albert's death was in the past; the future was all that mattered.

But the fact that none of the conservative leaders, including my father, wanted to take revenge only emboldened the Gallos. With the obvious and tacit approval of Vito Genovese and Tommy Lucchese, they began more openly asserting their own independence within the Profaci clan. They muscled into territories that were closed to them, leaned on jukebox routes that were run by members of other Families. They not only accused their boss, Joe Profaci, of hoarding profits for himself; they took other direct actions against his leadership. At one point, Profaci's number-two man, Joe Magliocco, and four group leaders were kidnapped and held for a period of days while demands were made—but not acted on—to spread more money and authority to the Gallos. Profaci himself, in the midst of all this, was in Florida.

The Gallo revolt should have been instantly and forcefully dealt with, but it could not be because the aftereffects of Apalachin continued to make coordinated action impossible. All the signs of a situation spiraling out of control, leading to war and a breakdown of the system that had sustained us for more than twenty-five years, were there—but so far, all of it was noise and rumbling.

Ironically, the law may have had a real hand in preserving the peace then. Apalachin spawned a slew of grand juries that inevitably kept an intense spotlight on the comings and goings of the different Families. Too many leaders—my father included—were suddenly too preoccupied with what the government might do next to plan what their own next steps might be. Instead of war in the streets, there were writs, subpoenas—and prosecutions.

The most damaging of these early court cases involved a low-level drug pusher by the name of Nelson Cantellops, who was arrested in a street-corner bust in New York and did a lot of talking in the hopes of cutting a deal for himself. He knew just enough to set the entire machinery of law enforcement into motion. Cantellops was wired and sent back out on the streets, and as a result both of what he had said and what he then brought in with the wire, the government brought a slew of narcotics trafficking indictments against others in our world—including Vito Genovese.

For a Vito Genovese to be prosecuted was an earthquake. Never mind the irony that his arrest and subsequent conviction were over drug dealing; no leader in our world, even a conservative, could feel comfortable with one of the pillars of the house coming down. But, in retrospect, the general threat did not come from going after one of the heads of the Five Families, but from the minnows swimming in their wake. One of the street-level guys arrested in another case around the same time as Genovese was a soldier in Vito's Family, Joe Valachi. The arrest of Valachi eventually proved to be an earthquake of far greater magnitude.

Another person who was indicted and sentenced for trafficking was Lilo Galante, a group leader in our Family since the early fifties. For us, this was the cruelest blow of all because it meant that trafficking had been occurring in our own Family for some time. My father was heartbroken by this, although unwilling to do anything about it. There was a standing death sentence for anyone who openly defied an ironclad rule of the Family—such as the one against dealing drugs.

"Leave him alone; doesn't matter now," my father told me and those in the administration of the Family. When I asked him about this, his manner and his words were almost gentle, but what he was saying was not.

"If we have reached this point, where leaders in our Family are into this dirty business, they deserve to die, but you will not kill the problem by killing them—that is obvious." I could read the shame, sorrow, and anger in the slump of his body, hear it in the almost bloodless whisper of his voice. For Genovese to have betrayed an agreement among the Families by involving himself with drugs was one thing, but for a person so close to my father, someone trusted and powerful, this was very different. Whatever the government was doing to destroy us was nothing compared to what we were doing to ourselves.

My father's reaction to these drug arrests, and particularly to Galante's, remains a puzzle to me to this day. I would have struck out in retaliation. But he did not. He talked more and more about the ways in which money seemed to determine everything in America—what had been lost was the sense that money was only a means to power, not an end in itself, he said. That was what was so crushing and what could not be fixed by anything like revenge.

I know now that my father viewed all of this not so much from personal disappointment as from a sense of a world being lost. The heartbreak he felt was over a world coming apart, a world in which a certain type of political leadership, which he represented, translated into order, efficiency— and power.

It has to be understood that by the late 1950s, when these fractures in our world began to show, we were at the height of our power in this country. It is hard to fathom and all too easy to caricature the kind of strength we had. Yes, it is true that illegal businesses flourished. There were empires and fortunes that had been built in places like Cuba, Las Vegas, Haiti, places far beyond the urban ghettos where the Mafia began in this country. At that point, before state governments got into the act and legitimized gambling, the industry was like bootlegging in the old days—there seemed to be no end to its growth. There is also no question that during the same period, drugs became increasingly more important.

But power in our world had grown far beyond illegal businesses. Power was about influence even more than it was about money. Over the years, my father and other Family leaders had carefully built up legitimat businesses that were extremely profitable. Joe Profaci, for example, was the largest importer of olive oil in the country. My father had clothing and trucking businesses in New York, cheese factories in Wisconsin and Canada, as well as different businesses in the West. It was not necessary for men like these ever to involve themselves personally in risky, illegal operations—like drugs—whose sole purpose was to gain more money. We were players at the table because these businesses were intricately tied to unions and local governments, so that, literally, the highways, airports, roads in and out of cities, the trash in people's backyards, the buildings that were built or not were all, in one way or another, influenced by or controlled by us. Take the Teamsters. In those days, cooperation between the union and the Families was as natural as breathing. I remember visiting Teamster president Jimmy Hoffa in this period to get his help on a labor problem we were having in the West. A Progresso food plant in Anaheim, California, in which my family had an interest, was being organized by the Teamsters. My father wanted it stopped. I met Hoffa in a hotel in Detroit. We sat around for an hour chatting, laughing like old friends, though we had never met before. Then I told him what my father wanted, an end to the union problems at the Progresso plant. Within days, a contract was signed between Progresso and the Teamsters so that, on paper, it looked as if there was a union in the Anaheim plant—only there was not. Labor issues never again came up at that site.

Money was only the means to an end. When you were a player at the table, you had a say in what happened; when you weren't, you were dependent on what others said. It was as simple as that. But in our world, this understanding was never written in any charter. Families were always free to run their own businesses as long as they did not encroach on or bring harm to the others. The basis of unity we had was built on a respect for the sovereignty of the different groups. The basis for war was the breakdown of that bond of respect.

My father, because he had been the head of a New York City Family longer than anyone, was looked up to and respected in a special way. His opinions and thoughts carried special weight He naturally became the focal point for that group of leaders—the conservatives—who saw in him a reflection of their own values and thinking. His prestige, not his muscle, was what counted. His ideas and his political savvy, rather than his weapons, were his real strength. In any kind of meeting, from a local sit-down to a Commission meeting, the votes of Family heads were never weighted. Each leader's vote counted the same. If a boss from San Jose, whose Family consisted of two crews totaling twenty-five people, was in a room with my father, whose Family consisted of fifteen crews and almost five hundred men, his vote would be given equal weight—same as in the U.S. Senate, where the vote of a senator from North Dakota is equal to that of a senator from New York. But it is just as true, in our world as in the Senate, that the way someone from the big, populous center voted was likely to influence the way the guy from the smaller place voted. If my father said he was in favor or opposed to something that came up at a meeting, the chances were pretty good that the leader from San Jose would wind up going along. That same prestige also came into play with important leaders, too—because my father went so far back, because he was the unofficial custodian of the values and customs of our tradition. It was inevitable, then, that people in our world looked to him for guidance. At that point, even if he had wanted to call it quits and spend the rest of his days on his front porch in Arizona, he could not have.

There was no call for war, no cleansing even within our own Family. The word my father sent out was to preserve the peace, to find reasons for conciliation rather than conflict. This was a strange time in our world. Because grand juries, commissions, committees, trials, and lurid headlines were proliferating, the leaders of the Families were increasingly wary about any kind of contact with one another. Suspicion, mistrust, and ignorance deepened, where what was needed most was communication and negotiation. Yet, at the same time, the profits kept rolling in. The contradictions were total and complete. My father said our world was falling apart. But for the first time in memory, the White House itself seemed to be within reach. In 1958, Joe Kennedy's son began openly campaigning for the presidency. John Kennedy, whom we all knew, happened to be on his way to Washington right around the time Vito Genovese was on his way to a federal penitentiary in Atlanta, Georgia. My father saw this as a last opportunity to unite our world—and he pounced on it with the speed and smoothness of a mountain lion.

8

Sometime in 1959, Joseph P. Kennedy, the paterfamilias of the Kennedy family, had an intermediary of his, Skip O'Brien, a Kennedy gofer, contact an intermediary of my father's to say that JFK was going to be on a fund-raising tour through the West, looking to bolster his upcoming campaign for the Democratic nomination for President. He wanted our family's help.

My father told O'Brien, who told Joe Kennedy, that he'd do what he could to help. As in the past, he arranged to have a number of big fund-raisers for Kennedy with all the state's top Democrats and leading businessmen attending; JFK, his father, my father, and many of our friends enjoyed a couple of days together in the late winter sunshine—and then the real business began.

I was instructed to go back to New York and sound out other leaders about a concerted effort to back JFK.

"There'll be resistance. Old man Kennedy has enemies. Little Bobby is a bone in the throat, hard to swallow," my father told me.

I went to New York and quietly spoke to Joe Profaci, Tommy Lucchese, Carlo Gambino, and to my father's cousin Steve. The divisions over Kennedy were deep. Joe Profaci, for example, said that he just didn't trust Kennedy. Midwestern leaders—in Cleveland and Michigan—had let it be known that we should get behind someone who was more rooted in the unions, where we had more influence, someone like Hubert Humphrey. I was told by Lucchese and Profaci that Santo Trafficante of Tampa, Florida, favored Lyndon Johnson because he was known and dependable, but he wouldn't really be opposed to Kennedy, either, because he had taken a strong stand against Castro. As everyone in our world knew, Santo was one of those who had taken an especially big hit when Batista was overthrown. Other leaders, I learned, like Carlos Marcello of New Orleans, were vehemently opposed to Kennedy—mainly because of his brother Bobby. In Marcello's case, there was a particular reason. As an attorney for the McClellan antiracketeering subcommittee, Bobby had been aggressively pushing to have him rounded up, prosecuted, and deported. Sam Giancana, on the other hand, favored JFK—ironically because he was a playboy. "Throw him a broad and he'll do anything you want," he told me jokingly—not forseeing the complications that would arise when Judith Campbell was one of the morsels fed to Kennedy.

I reported all this back to my father. He took the news of the political divisions stoically. What could be done? There was no way to force anyone to see anything. We, like everyone else in the country, would simply have to wait to see how things were going before commitments were made. But my father by no means gave up the idea of getting behind Kennedy. Beginning in the early spring, Tommy Lucchese sounded out members about the possibility of a special national meeting—a convention—to be held at the site of the Democratic National Convention itself for the express purpose of taking a unified political stand behind a candidate favorable to us. To his surprise, there was agreement that this was a good idea.

For many reasons, this was a significant step in our world. First, and most obviously, there was the notion of hobnobbing with Presidents. Normally, the guy who ran for the White House was someone at seven or eight removes from us even when we knew we would not be impeded by his administration There's a funny story my father told me about meeting Franklin Roosevelt. It was around 1933, the first year Roosevelt was in office. Because FDR was so beholden to Tammany Hall, my father, then the youngest Family leader in the nation—and a friend of a Tammany politico named Albert Madinelli—was invited to a private party to meet FDR. When he finally got to shake his hand, my father literally didn't know what to say. Madinelli walked up to Roosevelt, whispered something to him, and, my father said, FDR just lit up like a Christmas tree.

"So, you're the handsome guy they told me about," he said, loudly enough for everyone in the room to hear. FDR collared a photographer who was standing nearby. He ordered the guy to take a picture of my father and himself together. My father said he felt more like a kid than the leader of a Family, but, in a way, that perfectly epitomized the distance between life at the top and life in our world at that time.

The fact that we could now comfortably rub elbows with a presidential candidate was a sign of just how far we had come, how much power we had acquired—and how much was at stake in our coming together or falling apart.

But a second and more important purpose in having this shadow convention in Los Angeles was in just getting together. Since Apalachin, the everyday routine of keeping the peace, of maintaining unity among the Families, had become increasingly difficult. With headlines, investigations, grand juries, it was harder than ever to mediate disputes, to forestall divisions, to maintain the peace. Here was a chance, once again, to assert the strength of consensus—if it could be found.

All through that spring, planning for our convention unfolded. Over the course of months, different scenarios were informally discussed, revised, presented again. There was never any time that the Commission sat down and approved a proposal for the meeting; it was simply understood and accepted that we were going to come together. When we got to Los Angeles, we spread out all over the city. Whatever happened, this was not going to be Apalachin II. We made arrangements to stay in constant contact with each other by phone, messenger, and private meetings. The different leaders were also in a position to communicate with their people who were in the hall. And there were plenty of them—labor union officials, guys from Teamster conferences, big-city machine people from New York, Illinois, Pennsylvania, state officials from the West—Arizona, Texas, California.

My father chose to stay not in Los Angeles but in Ontario, outside the city. Families used to meet at the Bel-Air Sands in Beverly Hills. Other Families had their headquarters at the Beverly Hills, the Beverly Hilton, even the Ambassador. Getting around always seemed to involve major problems of logistics.

Kennedy remained a hard, almost impossible sell. There were stormy meetings where, for a time, it seemed certain that no consensus would ever be possible. More people in our world were behind Lyndon Johnson than Kennedy—at least when it came to sentiment. And why not? Johnson, in our terms, was a street guy even though he had spent a lifetime in government. He was a guy who had always been willing to do business. He was the oil companies' boy. But the oil companies, the big ones, were our friends. Oilmen like Clint Murchison and H. L Hunt had worked with Marcello and others for years. We all knew that with the right amount of cash, LBJ would break bones to get the right bills passed. There was a fellow who worked out of Texas, Jack Halfen, a street tough who set up a gambling operation in conjunction with local Families. Halfen constantly gave money to Johnson and, in exchange, Johnson, when he was the majority leader in the Senate, obliged by deep-sixing any antiracketeering legislation that came before him. After Halfen slipped up, got caught, prosecuted, and went to jail (resenting the fact that LBJ didn't step forward to save him), he told one reporter that he had kicked in as much as $500,000 in cold cash to Johnson while he was in the Senate.

Still, JFK had his supporters, too—and that made for a few lively evenings. At one meeting at the Sands, Marcello, Trafficante, and Giancana got into a shouting match over the role Bobby Kennedy might play in a Kennedy administration. I remembered something Joe Kennedy had said when he was down in Arizona with us—and so I added my two cents. "The old man specifically told us that if Jack was elected, he was gonna make Bobby ambassador to Ireland or something like that." The dissenters weren't convinced.

At another meeting in the Hilton, where Tommy Lucchese was staying, we got a direct call from Joe Kennedy, who was staying at the home of actress Marion Davies. We were all surprised that Kennedy would contact us so openly. Silence prevaded the room while Lucchese spoke to him and told him that no decision had yet been made. When he got off the phone, he said that Kennedy said he would make any reasonable gesture, do anything he possibly could, if it would put his son over the top.

It was Tommy Lucchese, of all people, who got us behind Kennedy. Lucchese had firmly allied himself with my father. He argued strenuously— on behalf of the New York Families—that there should be a united stand behind JFK.

"We came here to reach a consensus," he said, "a united position on the convention floor. If we are split, we'll all be working against one another. What's the point of that? What do we get outta that?"

Lucchese was not just talking. Whatever else he was, he was a politician of the first rank. "Suppose Kennedy named Johnson as his vice president?" he said. "The old man said he'd do anything. How 'bout that?"

The proposal was startling enough to silence the room completely.

"I'll go to him; I'll put it to him straight. If he don't go along, he don't get our support; if he does, everybody's happy, right?"

There were nods of assent—or incredulity (I've never been sure which), but there was agreement in that room. If Lucchese could get Kennedy to name Lyndon Johnson as his running mate, there would be consensus support for JFK's nomination on the floor.

So the next day, a day before the balloting began, Lucchese and I drove out to Marion Davies's estate in Beverly Hills. Lucchese had called ahead, and when we arrived at the front gate of the estate, our car was quickly allowed to pass within.

We found Joe Kennedy sitting out by a swimming pool, all by himself. He was waiting for us. There were others at a distance, on the grounds— security people in white shirts, friends, staff people—I thought I got a brief glimpse of JFK himself at one point stepping out of and then back in behind a pair of French doors. Joe Kennedy got up to greet us. When we sat back down, Lucchese put our proposal to him.

"I think we're in great shape if you go along," he said, "but we need to know what you think. We think Lyndon Johnson would be an ideal running mate for Jack."

There was the briefest pause. Whatever he was feeling, Kennedy's expression did not change. His eyeglasses had droplets of water on them, but the hard unblinking blue of his eyes remained steady as steel.

"I think it's a terrific idea, Tommy," he said. That was it. He stood up, extended his hand, and smiled that broad, raffish, crooked-toothed smile that he had managed to pass on to generations of Kennedys. The deal was done.

Immediately afterward, I drove Tommy out to Ontario so he could tell my father and some other people there the news personally. I never before saw Lucchese so completely at ease. Lucchese, a small, tightly wound man, elegantly dressed at all times, who never had a hair out of place, seemed to let go completely. It was like the razor-sharp creases in his trousers magically disappeared. He sat back in the passenger seat of the convertible

I was driving, sticking his hand out to let the air rake through it. His face was tilted to the sun; he was laughing and singing. From time to time, he'd drift off and then come back to life, singing, talking. He asked me, as though he was a long-lost uncle, how things were going in Arizona, how the cotton farm was, the nightclub I was involved in running. Soon we were in the small, elegant bedroom community where my father was staying. He and Tommy embraced, shared espresso together at a kitchen table, chatted like old *paisans* as they went over the good news. Tommy, however, had two more bits of business to bring up and take care of. First, he wanted to give my father the wedding envelopes from people in New York for his daughter Catherine's impending marriage. Second, he wanted to bring up the fact that three years had elapsed since the meeting in New Jersey following Anastasia's death. At that meeting, it had been decided that there would be a three-year probation period imposed before Carlo Gambino would be officially designated as the head of his Family. Tommy wanted to confirm that there had been peace and tranquility the last three years and wanted to know if my father had any objection to ending the probation period and making Gambino the head.

"I have no problems," my father said, "if you have no problems. If everyone's at peace, then fine."

Gambino was thus the new head of his Family.

With the agreement, the nomination was settled. Whether the concerted support of the Families, relayed to delegates on the floor, was decisive or not, I cannot say, but I do know the convention, which seemed to be in doubt for a while, decisively turned to Kennedy and that the deal struck the day before held. Lyndon Johnson, to the shock and surprise of many, was selected by Kennedy as his running mate. There has been a lot written about Bobby and Jack agonizing over the vice-presidential nomination. There's a famous photograph of the two brothers huddling in intense conversation—supposedly over the VP choice. The photo is accurate, but the story behind it is bull. The intensity of the brothers' conversation was over Jack's telling Bobby the bad news. There was no pondering of anything. Johnson was already on the ticket. At that point, perhaps within a day of our meeting at Marion Davies's estate, old Joe Kennedy had left town, away from the cameras and the limelight, his work done, his own power more secure than ever.

Our man (not to mention his running mate) was the Democratic nominee. The future should have been as wide open for us as for the Kennedys. And in a sense, it was. The opportunities, the connections were all there. But like Camelot, it was all a dream. Just as it was for the country, so it was in our world. The New Frontier was only a fantasy waiting to come apart. The divisions in our world were for a time covered over by this significant step toward unity. The national consensus we fashioned there, though a powerful restorative, in the end was only one brief summer party set against a long and ongoing season that could never be turned back. The divisions and fissures that had been going on for quite a while were beginning to show in our world. They were deeper than anyone cared to admit. A world of distrust and disloyalty had begun to overcome the traditional Families. These could not be resolved and, in the end, were only complicated by presidential politics. Though no one could have predicted it then, our political "triumph" was a double-edged sword, hastening, not slowing, the process of destruction. The election of John Kennedy in 1960, more than anything, represented the beginning of the end of Mafia power in this country.

9

The election of JFK made me think again about the two Joes. Who was JFK, after all? He was the son of Joe Kennedy, who came from the same world my father did. The Kennedys and the Bonannos, seemingly so different on the surface, were more like each other than not. I remained fascinated by this pairing. Joe Kennedy and Joe Bonanno both learned the principles of their ancestors in order to give them strength in the face of adversity. Like Joe Bonanno, Joe Kennedy grew up in a powerful family, organized around a system of bosses. Both Joes, the sons of immigrants, were men of courage and daring who attempted to create in the new country principles from the old, not realizing that those principles were in direct conflict with what they found here—namely, the law and contempt for their traditions.

Both men made their way from bootlegging to real estate, the stock market, and movies; both acquired enormous wealth, which they always regarded with a kind of disdain, not as an end in itself but as a means to influence and power. Each man, in the deepest part of his psyche, understood that money earned, no matter how much, would never be taken for granted and never surrendered to the next generation in such a manner as to spoil them. Both men regarded their firstborn sons as their strong right arms, heirs not to privilege but to a traditional life in the service of something larger than oneself. After the death of Joe's eldest son, selected for a life in politics, JFK, the next oldest, became, in effect, the next firstborn.

As with the father, so with the son. When I looked at JFK during those days, there was something I knew about him immediately. I knew—even if Sam Giancana and others in our world did not—that he was far more than a playboy. He was as obligated to his father as I was to mine; he knew, more than any of his critics, that becoming a man of respect, a man of power, was not something earned by right of birth, but by performance. There was something cold and hard in his eyes—same as in his father's— and behind that hardness, you could see quickness of mind, the wit, the easy charm, all working toward an end, an end of power and performance. I wonder if he had seen the same thing in my eyes when we met.

Kennedy won by the thinnest of margins and with our help in the crucial state of Illinois. It is no secret now that Kennedy's nine-thousand-vote win in the state was accomplished with more than the usual "graveyard vote," regularly employed by big-city machines. Sam Giancana strutted for a while, bragging that in wards controlled by his Family, Kennedy's margin of victory was more than 80 percent—considerably more than the totals piled up in other wards of the city. Republican party officials in the state, after an unofficial canvas of votes, came up with enough phony votes to show that Nixon had actually taken the state by about five thousand votes. According to Sam, and others, Nixon, who had his own friends in our world, was persuaded not to challenge the outcome. Nixon conceded defeat the morning after the election, forgoing the opportunity of having an official recount in Illinois.

My sense of the two Joes prepared me for the shock of the winter. JFK, far from naming his brother Bobby as ambassador to Ireland, appointed him attorney general of the United States. If Kennedy had wanted to, he could not have sent a more alarming signal to our world. Those who opposed Kennedy from the start, men like Carlos Marcello and Jimmy Hoffa—who all the while had been another target of Bobby's—were especially vehement in denouncing the appointment. But there were others, like Angelo Bruno from Philadelphia and Steve Maggadino—men who had either supported Kennedy or been "neutral"—who saw something far more sinister. In their eyes, Joe Kennedy was still the boss, still the man, according to tradition, who called the shots. And that meant, in this case, that he was going to use the Justice Department, with all the power of the federal government at its disposal, to get rid of anyone and everyone who could ever step forward and dirty the name of Joseph P. Kennedy. What a coup, these people said.

"The other possibility," Tommy Lucchese told me, "is that Joe Kennedy will now control the Justice Department and see to it that things do not get out of hand. He has been a friend for too long."

"No," my father said, "I do not believe this. He is not and never was a man of our tradition. So you cannot count on his loyalty. We will just have to wait to see what this means."

But my father then took action. Because he felt personally responsible for helping engineer support for Kennedy in our world, he felt free to go back to Joe Kennedy and remind him of that support. We sent a captain in our family, Smitty D'Angelo, to Palm Beach to meet with Kennedy and tell him about our concerns. Smitty went there sometime in the late summer or early fall of 1961. He specifically told the old man that there were people in our world who felt betrayed, who had looked to him as a friend, only to be disappointed. Kennedy then told him not to worry. Smitty reported back to us.

"He said to me, 'There's nothing to worry about. The boys will be home with me over Christmas. Wait till after Christmas.' "

Well, Christmas never came that year. Less than a week before the holidays, Joe Kennedy suffered a massive stroke and thereafter, till his death on November 18, 1969, was never involved, even remotely, in the activities of his sons.

There was another jolt in that period. In April 1961, a long-awaited U.S.-backed invasion of Cuba failed on the beaches of the Bay of Pigs. By failing to provide needed air cover—as he had promised—JFK was seen by many in our world as a Judas, especially by those who had had strong financial ties to the island under Batista. It was suddenly clear to many that any allegiances Kennedy may have had to us were nonexistent. JFK would do whatever he needed to cover himself and his administration, regardless of commitments and promises made.

I have to say that for me, all of this seemed remote. My own life and commitments had nothing to do with what the Kennedys did or did not do. My tradition placed me at the service of my Family. Our way of life was what mattered. The interests of the Bonanno Family were what I had devoted myself to before the arrival of the Kennedys, and they remained so. As far as I'm concerned, the difference between the two Joes and their very different families and destinies had left me on a quite different path, out of the spotlight, away from headlines and reporters. The Kennedys had their problems, and we had ours. I have to admit that my chief worry then was what was happening in our world.

My father's increasing talk of retirement was a matter of real concern to me. I had no idea who would replace him if he stepped down—and I know he had none, either. All of the high-ranking people in our organization were as old or older than he was. Newer leaders had not been sufficiently groomed. There was, increasingly, a vacuum between old leaders and newer members, who were unfamiliar with the traditions that had shaped the Family. In the Profaci Family, the same problem of not bringing along newer people had already led to serious and dangerous divisions.

If my father did step down and was replaced, where would I stand? The tale of the two Joes didn't yet extend to the tale of the two sons. I looked at other possible leaders of our Family, unsure of where I fit into the scheme of things.

There were any number of men I liked and admired, people like our consiglieri John Tartamella, Gaspar DiGregorio, Natale Evola, John Morales, but they seemed to me to be far less able than my father to bridge the gap between the Old and New Worlds. I was comfortable around a lot of the older men because I had been so schooled in our tradition that it was really a part of my own makeup. But I also felt comfortable around the newer people, guys who, like me, had been born and raised in this country, who had learned its idioms and rhythms as a natural part of growing up. I knew I still had much to learn from the older men. I would gladly have placed myself under any one of them, but the question for me was where our Family would be without my father at the top—and I could not answer the question. I felt like I had plenty to give in this situation, but I felt utterly hamstrung. I was my father's servant at a time when he was readying himself to stop serving.

In this period, I was also preoccupied with troubles at home. Rosalie had become pregnant in the year after we were married, and when she gave birth to a daughter late in 1958, the child died. We were both devastated. Though we were determined to have children, Rosalie could not become pregnant for some time afterward and she eventually became convinced that she was unable to have children, which was not the case. Her depression deepened to a point where she seemed inconsolable. I know the life she led was not the one she had envisioned when she married me. I think in all likelihood she had imagined that getting out of Brooklyn and living in Arizona would mean an escape from the very world she found herself in and which she could not understand. I was not—nor ever would be—the kind of man who would leave in the morning, kiss his wife on the cheek, and say, "Be home for dinner, honey." There were times when I did not come home at all—when I said good-bye in the morning and went to sleep that night in New York or California. I wasn't able to tell Rosalie when, where, or why I was going. I don't know if Ro resented my father or not, but she had to have seen in my relationship with him that there was more, much more, than the ordinary obligation of a son to his parent.

I thought that Rosalie's spirits would pick up if she had a child. We had briefly talked about adoption and I knew from those discussions that the idea was acceptable to her. But I did not tell her, for a variety of reasons—not the least being that I didn't want to make her more anxious than she already was—that I had actually made a decision to go ahead and locate a child. There was also no way I could explain to her that normal channels were impossible in this process. Adopting through licensed state and private agencies meant, inevitably, that there would be background checks. That was simply out of the question.

So for months, I scouted around. I knew people in the right places, in the state departments of health in both California and Arizona, in many of the different hospitals. There were a number of possibilities before I finally got a call telling me about a young lady who had come to Arizona from Virginia to have a child that she wanted to give up. She was in turmoil because the idea of losing a child to a "system" was too much. She wanted her child to have a really caring home, where both parents would be sure to love the child and have the means to raise it properly. I met this young woman and I was able to convince her that Rosalie and I were the parents she was looking for. I arranged for her to have the child out of state, at the University of Colorado Medical Center in Denver.

A week after the child, a boy, was born, I traveled up to Colorado. Rosalie did not know where I was going. When I got to the hospital in Denver and saw the child looking up at me with big green eyes, I almost had to laugh. The kid's background was Scots-Irish (he had more Kennedy than Bonanno in him). I waited outside the room where the mother said her good-byes to her infant—that was a scene I didn't want to be part of—then the child was placed in my arms by a nurse. I had a little basket waiting and I carried him all the way to the airport, where I caught a flight for Tucson.

When I got home, it was after midnight. Ro had gone to sleep; the house was dark. I went into the bedroom and, as gently as I could, placed the child down next to her on the bed. Then I turned on the light on the nightstand and woke Rosalie up. She opened her eyes and there was the kid lying alongside her. I didn't say anything.

"Whose is it?" She said it as if I had kidnapped the Lindbergh baby.

"Yours," I said.

She seemed to think I was nuts. "Get outta here!"

"He's yours. He's ours. Don't ask any questions; just love him like you gave birth to him."

With that, I got up and went off to the bathroom to wash up. When I got back, Ro was holding the baby as if it had been hers all along. We named him Charles, after my grandfather on my mother's side, Charles Labruzzo.

As far as I was concerned, that was it. She was full of love for the baby, gave everything to him. But the real problem all along was our lifestyle in Arizona, which no number of children could have fixed. I was my father's son. I was a Man of Honor.

And I had business to take care of.

10

For me, Arizona was home. It was where I spent most of my childhood, where I felt most comfortable, best able to function. I continued to go back and forth to New York, to stand in for my father when I had to, but the major part of my life then was in Arizona. I did not think of New York, the centerpiece of the Bonanno Family, as a place where I would eventually wind up, any more than I thought that national politics really had anything to do with me and my day-to-day life.

In Arizona, I had my crew. And that was enough. There were about twenty-five or thirty people, some local, some who had relocated from other areas, for whom I was responsible. In Arizona, a Mafia crew was a little different from in New York. There, everyone knew everyone, there were endless get-togethers and meetings, and everyone seemed to be bumping up against everyone else. In Arizona and the West, it was common for members of a crew to see little of one another, maybe meeting once a month. Each individual member, as in the East, had his own business to take care of, his own life. Most of the activity in any crew anywhere was legal. Of course, crews were also involved in illegal activities. The idea in either area was that the members of the crew were there to aid one another; their loyalty was to the crew and to the Family. The crew chief or captain was there at all times for his men. The envelopes they gave him at the end of a month—at least in my Family—were never compulsory and were set at no fixed rate (that was as my father insisted—and it worked). So long as the tradition held, the money kept coming in. When a crew member did not submit an envelope at the end of a month, or six months, there was no pressure, no retaliation. The key, always, was the willing bond of loyalty.

Most of the people in the crew were into small businesses, farming, operating convenience stores, gas stations, even newsstands. We were into gambling and shylocking, and especially into sports betting. That was where the big money was, because a lot of people in Arizona, as elsewhere, were addicted to wagering on sports.

We had an establishment on the second floor of an office building at Tucson Boulevard and Broadway. The building was owned by Judge Evo DeConcini, whose brother-in-law had a beauty salon on the first floor. We had bank of seven phones in a back room upstairs—and we were as safe as we could be. Judge DeConcini was our friend; he knew everyone in the state, from the local cops on the beat to the governor. We needed no more protection from the law than his ongoing friendship. We were so secure in our thriving, wired den that we hoisted a sign up over our windows: B&P PUBLISHING CO., ARIZONA'S OWN BOOKMAKERS. It was a lark. We actually had a visit one day in 1961 from local cops. We showed them what we did: We published poetry (not in the back room, but the front). We had two titles in print that year: a book of poems, *Wolfwind in the Arroyo*, by a young Navajo, and another, *White Bones Bleached*, by a local grade-school teacher.

Sometimes, I took members of my crew with me to settle disputes elsewhere. There was one time in the early sixties when I got a call from a group captain in L.A., Frank "Bumps" Bompensiero. He was having trouble with someone in the area who had muscled into the gambling and bar businesses his crew was running. According to Frank Bumps, any action taken against this guy by local people would be impossible because they were too well known. He needed to be "persuaded" by outside people. So I volunteered. With intelligence supplied by Frank Bumps's people, we were able to find this guy and convince him—I don't know a better way of putting it—to take a vacation and not come back. He listened to us; the problem was cleared up. So far as I know, he's still on vacation.

I mention this only because I was a little too full of myself in those days, a little too sure that anything I did would turn out all right. Too much of the time, I let myself come and go as I pleased. So long as I was there for my father, and my crew, things were okay. I did not see that there could be consequences for my actions that went far beyond my backyard, that could throw me, whether I wanted it that way or not, right back into national Family politics. Ironically, that was especially true when it came to my personal life.

Rosalie and I were having problems that I continued to overlook. She had the baby and was more or less pinned to home. Tucson was a small town to her and there weren't enough friends her own age and not enough to do. I think she was bored a lot of the time, and it carried over into our relationship. She couldn't understand why I was willing to live like a big fish in a small pond, why I was so willing to be at my father's beck and call. We never got into arguments over any of that, because fighting was out. I had a temper, and Ro was withdrawn. Instead, there were just comments back and forth, little things said and implied. Sometimes we would stew in silence until one of us simply left the room, went to bed, or got in a car and took off.

I had neither the patience nor the humility in those days to step back and see what Ro might be feeling. I thought things were fine. In my mind, you got married, gave your wife a home and a kid, and that was that— what more could your partner want? It wasn't the kind of thinking that made for a good marriage, but in the male-dominated tradition I grew up in, that was the standard. The men went out and did their thing, the women stayed home and looked after the kids, and because of the nature of the men's business, there were never any questions asked, or answers volunteered.

What was missing from that model, of course, was what happened when partners did not share the same view. In the world both Ro and I had been raised in, when a woman dared to criticize or question her man, she risked humiliating him, taking away his manhood. In private, the strongest marriages were able to get past that barrier; criticism and questions were allowed and even necessary. I know my parents had that kind of marriage. I never knew specifically what my mother said to my father in private, but she was the only person on the planet who was able to tell him that his hat size was too large and that what he thought was wisdom wasn't necessarily so.

In those early years, Ro and I did not have that kind of bond. Our temperaments were too different, our lifestyles too widely divergent. I knew that in her heart of hearts she judged my way of life and was turned off by it. She wanted "a regular marriage" and I did not, could not provide that for her. In turn, what I got from her was a kind of distance that became an unspoken agreement to keep our lives emotionally separate. When I left in the morning, I had my Cadillac, and she had her Oldsmobile convertible to take her to the swimming pool. She had her day; I had mine. In my heart, I was fulfilling my responsibilities simply by providing for her. But, of course, more, much more, was going on under the surface of what was, for both of us, a marriage that was not working. The fast pace of my life, coupled with the tension of all that was unresolved and not even spelled out at home, made it almost inevitable that I would wind up becoming involved, deeply involved, with another woman.

There was a waitress at the lunch club I went to in Tucson with whom I became friendly. Helga was twenty, a German national who had married and then separated from an American GI. She was physically quite attractive and a very sweet person, as well. In the beginning, our relationship was strictly casual and platonic. On her days off, I sometimes took time to have lunch with her. As I got to know her, I began to feel sympathy for her more than anything else.

Helga was divorced, had two children, commuted to work from San Manuel, about an hour's drive from Tucson. Sometimes she would have to stay in Tucson, and her kids would have to stay with an elderly lady who baby-sat them. Her marriage, she said, had been a nightmare. She told me how her husband used to come home drunk night after night and one night tied her up, beat her, and left her. The more I knew about her, the more feeling I had for her. It particularly bothered me that her job forced her to be separated from her children, though it was obvious that she was a good mother.

It started out by my giving her my car to go and visit her kids. I just gave her the keys one day and said, "The car's downstairs; go see your sons." She was overwhelmed by that and couldn't thank me enough. In turn, I was curious about her kids. I told her one day I wanted to meet them, that we'd take the car and have a picnic, all of us. So one Sunday, Helga and I and her two small sons sat around her apartment swimming pool for the better part of an afternoon. I played with the boys, asked them all kinds of questions about how they liked where they were living, what they did when their mom wasn't home. It bothered me to see kids who were so innocent and small with such obvious hurt hiding in their eyes.

The more Helga seemed beholden to me, the more I wanted to do for her and her family. I had her move the boys down to Tucson so they could live with her every day. I found a new apartment for them and located a day school for the boys. I had been with her for three or four months before I ever touched her. She later told me that, more than anything, my being a gentleman made her feel attracted to me; she couldn't get over it. When I kissed her that first time, she said she had been wondering when I would finally get around to that.

It was really strange. Sleeping with her was not on my agenda. It just wasn't. From the time she became a real person to me, rather than a body to look at, I had been much more interested in seeing that her life worked out. I almost surprised myself by discovering that all along I had been attracted to her. I asked her one Friday if she wanted to go down to Mexico for the weekend, and she said yes—and that was that.

I mention all of this because the affair finally had very much to do with who I was and where I was going in my world. It was 1961, Kennedy was in the White House, his brother at the Justice Department, and the worst fears of people in my world were beginning to materialize. There was an ever-increasing barrage of criticism directed at organized crime coming from government officials and the media. The aftermath of Apalachin was continuing with a vengeance. It was now almost mandatory for prosecutors, big cops, people running for office to say and do things to show that they were macho when it came to crime.

I ran into this at home. Sometime in 1961, largely because I had new business interests, I moved my family to Phoenix. Rosalie welcomed the move because it meant living in a bigger city, a better chance, she thought, to have a social life, to raise a family. More than anything, she wanted company, company for herself and for the children. We had a second child, Joseph, that she had given birth to, and she was excited by the move—for a while. I, too, thought the move might be good for her, might get her more involved in her own life and less concerned with mine. I was a part owner of a supper club, the Romulus, and I did a lot of business out of the club. I knew what I wanted.

I moved Helga to Pheonix, too. I got her her own car, a place to stay, and a job at the club.

But the newspapers soon started running stories about "crime figures" being involved in the ownership of the Romulus. As a result of the stories, authorities started hanging around the place. And then because they were hanging around, it became harder to manage each phase of the business, from taking care of licenses simply to attracting patrons. There was nothing I could do. Our connections couldn't help because all of this was out in the open. The authorities actually stopped people coming in and out of the club, questioned them, even checked their breath for excessive alcohol consumption. I wound up suing the Phoenix Police Department for violating my constitutional rights to run a business. The suit dragged on for a while and went nowhere. And it was only the beginning of an avalanche of troubles, the personal ones somehow always mixing with the larger political ones.

I continued to see Helga, I spent a lot of time at her place and found her to be consoling at a time when I badly needed someone willing to listen without judging or asking for more. I had told her something about the tradition I came from and she had seemed fascinated by it, as if it was part of an adventure story. Although I obviously couldn't disclose secrets to her, it was just a relief to share anything about myself with her. It was a new and different experience for me because I had been so used to keeping everything in my life so close to the vest. I had never been able to share my world with Rosalie, even though she had been born to it herself. She neither understood nor sympathized with my "profession," as it was unpredictable, risky, and obviously provocative as far as the law and the media were concerned. What Rosalie wanted was an ordered, structured, dependable family life. I, too, in my way, wanted that, as well. It was part of my tradition. It mattered to me—to spend time with the children, to be there on Sundays when we had our traditional dinner at three o'clock, to insist that we do things together as a family, that the children always had a sense that we were a unit, that each of their parents was always there for them.

But I suppose I was like many other men who had relationships outside marriage. I never felt I loved Rosalie less because of my being with Helga, but I couldn't bring myself to leave either woman. I had two households, two women, and double the trouble.

One day, Helga told me she was pregnant. Obviously, this was not something I had planned or wanted. But I did not then, and do not now, believe in abortion. Neither did Helga. I honestly did not know how I was going to deal with this, other than by making sure, no matter what happened, that I would be responsible for the child I had fathered.

Of course, I had not planned to tell Rosalie about any of this, either. But she found out anyway, some months after the child was born. Rosalie came into the club one day and noticed this girl who was working there, noticed the way Helga looked at her and also the way she looked at me— and she just knew. Now, many years later, she has let me know that she knew by the way I smelled when I came to bed. I smelled clean, she told me; that meant, in her mind, I had showered before I had come home. Only one reason for that. And I never saw it or imagined what she might be feeling lying there next to me.

In any case, Helga told me one day that she had received a telephone call from one of Rosalie's brothers in Brooklyn, asking her to break off her relationship with me, offering her money and plane fare back to Germany if she would do it. She hung up, she said. Before I could figure out what steps I could take next, Rosalie herself took the biggest one of all. Helga phoned me one night and I noticed immediately that her voice sounded funny.

"Your wife is here," she said, almost in a whisper. I couldn't believe it.

When I hung up the phone, my heart was pounding. I didn't know what to do other than go to Helga's house immediately, which was about the last thing I wanted to do. But I got in my car and drove there anyway, all the while dreading what I was going to find. At the same time, I almost felt like laughing. The idea of Ro barging in on Helga was like something out of a bad soap opera—one that I had written, directed, and produced. But then, when I got to the apartment, what greeted my eyes went beyond anything I could have imagined. There in Helga's small and neatly furnished house, both women were seated on couches facing each other on opposite sides of a coffee table. But what was completely crazy was that each of the women had their three small children next to them and in their arms. Chuck, my oldest, was standing next to Ro at the side of the sofa, Joe, who was about two, was nestled next to his mother, who was holding Tore, recently born, in her arms; Helga had her two small children at her side and was holding Billy, our newborn son, tightly in her arms.

The women were staring at each other with stone faces that might have exploded or disintegrated at any second.

I did not pause for discussion or analysis in this situation.

"Come on, Ro, we're going home, right now," I said. I took Chuck with one hand, Joe with the other. Rosalie got up, holding Tore, and followed me. Helga and her children remained frozen in place, just watching. At the door, I turned my head and nodded good-bye. I felt numb. I simply kept following my feet as I led Rosalie and the kids to my car and drove them home. In the car, we said nothing. The tension between us was like an extra passenger, sullen, silent, and hostile. I kept my eyes straight ahead, on the road, occasionally checking in the rearview mirror to be sure Chuck and Joe were secure in the backseat. I made a little joke, something innocuous, just to let the kids know everything was all right.

When I deposited them at home, I phoned a friend of mine to go back to Helga's and drive Ro's car home.

I did not know how to resolve this situation. I could not break off my relationship with Helga, yet I knew what damage it had done and was still doing. I never wanted to hurt Rosalie, but now the hurt had gone beyond the circle of our personal lives. The damage reached into my larger Family. From the moment Rosalie's brother knew, it was clear to me that people in our world also knew. You could not keep something like that contained for very long once one relative knew about a wrong done to another. News of the wrong spread like wildfire, or at least like malicious gossip, because in this case, the Bonanno-Profaci alliance was involved, and there were relatives galore on both sides. This is a perfect example of what I said earlier about it being impossible to understand my world without first understanding the blood connections linking people, and the very strict code by which people lived. Yeah, men had women on the side, but it was always private and it was never something that blemished the honor of a Family.

Two of Joe Profaci's daughters, Rosalie's first cousins, kids she had grown up with, who had always been around the house, were married to members of the Zerilli and Tocco Families in Detroit. There were also blood ties between the Profacis and California Families. So what would have otherwise been a private domestic dispute became, with one whispered word, a political bombshell.

My father came to me one day and said, "Don't dirty our family's name, don't be the first to do that." His words were not spoken in anger, but they did not have to be. They were not offered as a judgment of me as a person, but as someone who knew and understood the traditions that governed life in our world.

I did not know what to do. My father made me feel ashamed of myself on the deepest level, but still I did not know what the best course of action might be. I understood intellectually that I had to break my relationship with Helga, but that was not enough. I had feelings for her that I simply could not turn off. Yes, I knew I was creating a problem and that I was causing pain to someone I loved, but I was also deeply involved with a person who had borne a child of mine. For the first and only time in my life, my will, my training, my feelings for other people, my ability to control what I did, my awareness of the larger world I belonged to were not enough.

In the meantime, however, I spent more and more time going back and forth to New York. No matter what was going on in my personal life, the increased responsibilities I had there at a time of increasing turmoil had the effect of physically removing me from my problem—at least for periods of time. I welcomed that.

What was awaiting me in New York, however, was far from comforting. The Gallo uprising within the Profaci Family was still ongoing. There was no question that it had wrought damage that would be hard to overcome. Even when the revolt was finally—and inevitably—put down, it was already clear that the Profaci Family had been weakened and that, as far as the Bonanno Family was concerned, our strongest ally in maintaining a viable conservative bloc within the Commission had become less effective. When the Gallo revolt was finally over, the main result was utter turmoil within the Family. Who could trust whom? And who had the power? These were the questions burning in everyone's mind. The Gallos themselves faded into obscurity, with Larry dying of cancer in the mid sixties and Crazy Joey, after going to prison for extortion, being killed in the seventies at Umberto's Clam House in Little Italy, a section of Manhattan.

There was a kind of drift now in our world that seemed as dangerous as it did aimless. Nineteen sixty-one was a year for a regularly scheduled Commission meeting. The meeting never took place. The miniconvention in Los Angeles the year before was as much as anyone had dared risk. Top leaders still were divided about the wisdom of risking a big Commission meeting that might create another Apalachin.

But events always had a way of moving beyond anyone's control. In

1962, with the Gallo revolt in its last stages, the question of Joe Profaci's leadership in his Family came up once again, this time from outside. The matter was so urgent, it became the basis for a hastily called meeting of the leadership of the different New York Families. The leaders of the Five Families, because they were all Commission members, declared themselves a quorum (five out of nine standing members) and conducted what they called "a Commission meeting"—I think out of desperation—to see if they could do by legislative fiat what had not been done by the Gallos in the streets. (Later on, this meeting became the subject of an even deeper controversy, when legitimate questions were raised about accepting the deliberations as an actual Commission meeting. Nineteen sixty-two was an off year; the Commission should have met in 1961. Without the 1961 meeting, the Commission, in reality, had gone out of business.)

The instigator of this meeting was Carlo Gambino, that squirrel of a man, who was close, too close, to Tommy Lucchese. It was immediately apparent that Lucchese himself was the actual force behind the get-together. But as form was strictly followed, it was Gambino, the bringer of a specific complaint, who first addressed the different leaders.

What was on his mind, he said, was that Joe Profaci, a wonderful man and a great leader, who had served all of us so well, had unfortunately become the cause of too much dissension within the ranks and that for the sake of peace and tranquillity, which everyone wanted, the time had come for him to step down as a leader.

My father, as in the past, had been asked to chair this meeting. When Gambino was finished, my father's expression was without emotion, although I knew what he was feeling. His features were calm and composed; he looked almost serene. Profaci was asked to leave the room so that the question raised could be frankly aired. Without a word, Profaci withdrew.

I am sure that everyone in that room was waiting then for my father's reaction, for our Family's response, to what was an obvious assault not only on Profaci but on us, too. My father still betrayed no emotion. He seemed more interested in what others had to say than in saying anything for himself. But I knew that ploy well by now. Speak last, draw others out, watch, listen, gather information, and then, only then, close the trap.

After some general comments, my father leaned forward and ever so gently looked in Tommy Lucchese's direction.

"Would you like to talk first, Tommy?" he asked. In the way my father addressed that simplest of questions to Lucchese, anyone in the room might have believed that he was deferring to someone he felt sympathy for. Lucchese was getting old. The years wore on his face now; he had been through all the wars my father had been through, going back to Maranzano. Tommy's face was almost ghostly, his manner weary and listless. Sympathy, in this case, was a fox's invitation to feel at ease, to step forward with no fear of penalty.

Lucchese, like Gambino, was full of oily smoothness. But where Gambino had been blatant in his hypocrisy, Lucchese was far more skilled, far more potent as a leader. He, like my father, knew all the tricks of the table.

His speech was about disunity and, even more, about the requirement in our ranks for strong leadership. Lucchese was making the subtlest of appeals based on the sympathy my father had expressed in his manner toward him. We all had been damaged by time. Age had taken its toll on our best and brightest leaders. If we were going to renew ourselves—as we had to—inevitably we needed the sort of leadership that would have strength enough to deal with dissension and division. When Lucchese spoke about Profaci, he emphasized the years of service he had given and his right to a decent and peaceful retirement. It was a beautiful presentation, full of modulated restraint disguising its sharp edge: the betrayal of Joe Profaci. How could anyone step forward now and harshly argue with the sentiments expressed? They were unarguable, the praise for Profaci perfect.

There was a heavy silence in the room. No one indicated that he wanted to speak. My father looked from face to face around the table. He looked to Joe Zerilli from Detroit, the Commission member he most expected to support him. Heads were bowed or held at an angle where eye contact was impossible. I did not know what my father would say or do. There was a glitter in his eye that I recognized, a lit fuse of feeling; that was all. Suddenly, he barked out, "Don Piddru should stay!" In the silence of the room, these words sounded like thunderclaps. Everyone came to attention. My father now looked from face to face and this time eye contact was unavoidable.

"The real issue here is not old age," he said; "all of us are getting older. The real issue is trust. Do we trust one another in the managing of our affairs or not? If the answer is distrust, then it is obvious that as night follows day, every person with a grudge or a secret desire for advantage will come out of the woodwork and we will never be able to control the consequences.''

This was not speech making. My father had drawn a line in the sand in the only way he could. The strategy he had used in drawing out Gambino and Lucchese, only to snap them up in a powerful defense of Profaci, made it absolutely clear that the Bonanno Family would go to war over this rather than stand idly by and see their closest ally eliminated. That was what was communicated, and the effect was that Lucchese and his allies backed off. For the time being, order was restored.

The ironic part in all of this was that there were forces far beyond anyone's control or political skill at work in this room. All of the Family leaders gathered around that table, jousting this way and that, were older men, men in their fifties and sixties. There was the usual division between conservatives and liberals. One group of old men spoke Sicilian and knew tradition and custom; the other group of old men poked fun at the Mustache Petes, knowing all the while that money ruled the roost. In any case, the real ruler of this parliament was age. Joe Profaci's problem was not the Gallo uprising or someone looking to push him aside, but the fact that he had cancer. My father had the ability to get Tommy Lucchese to back off, but he did not have the skill to contain the uprising in Profaci's own body. What politics had been unable to do, cancer accomplished.

Profaci's cancer was, at first, a surprise and then a nightmare. It was incurable and fast-spreading, coming on with the speed of summer lightning. He became a shell of a man within months and died in that same year, leaving a vacuum in his organization's leadership that simply could not be adequately filled. Profaci's successor was his number-two man, Joseph Magliocco, a longtime friend, but a man who was not really ready or prepared to lead a divided Family. He was well-intentioned but had little administrative ability and even less when it came to dealing with difficult internal problems like the Gallo revolt.

The Bonanno Family, of course, supported him, but with the clear sense that the alliance that had so long been a backbone of strength for both Families had been seriously altered.

There was still no real connection in my mind between my personal troubles and these other ones. I knew, of course, that everyone now knew about my relationship with Helga—and that made things uncomfortable. But so long as no one made an issue of what had happened, there was no problem. In Brooklyn, around the Profacis, silence reigned, and as far as I was concerned, that was all right. But it was wishful thinking on my part to hope that all of this would simply disappear.

Back in Arizona, my problems with Rosalie and Helga continued. There was simply no balancing any of this. It was a situation out of control. One night, Rosalie accidentally took an overdose of sleeping pills. She came home one evening, tired but unable to fall asleep. So she took one pill and then, when that did not work, a second and then a third. When I turned up later and was unable to wake her, I did not want to call an ambulance and risk alerting the media. I took her to the hospital, which was just a few blocks away. Nevertheless, by then, reporters somehow were on the scene and got enough from attendants in the emergency room to conclude that Rosalie had attempted suicide. There were headlines about it the next day. And the headlines inevitably blew our domestic problem right out of the water.

Within hours, it seemed, Rosalie's mother was at her side in Phoenix, as was my sister, Catherine. When Rosalie returned home from the hospital, the two women were there with her. There was tension in the house every minute. It was unavoidable. I was the cause of this, I was the one who had brought my wife to the point of killing herself, and I was the one who had made her life a living hell.

There was one evening when the tension at the dinner table became too much and Rosalie's mother got up in tears and left the room. She went to be with Rosalie in her bedroom and locked the door after her. I followed, and when I realized the door was locked, I began pounding on it, demanding to be let in. I heard Rosalie scream. In my mind, I felt I was being shut out not by Rosalie but by her mother, who had no business coming between us. Catherine tried to pull me away from the door, but I was so blinded by anger that I raised my fist to her. I could not believe I was doing this; it was like someone else acting in my skin, against my wishes, against my mind. I did not strike Catherine. I could not. Instead, I slammed my fist as hard as I could into the wall next to the door, shattering my knuckles, permanently injuring my hand. Catherine sat with me, put her arms around me, and I wept on her shoulder, as much to let go physically of the storm of feeling that I had accumulated as for the comfort she offered.

This moment was a turning point. The next day, Rosalie said to me that she wanted to return to Brooklyn with her mother and the children. She was careful to tell me that she wanted to go not because she wanted to separate but because her sister was going to be married and she wanted to be there to help her with the arrangements and to serve as matron of honor. I did not object, although I knew the real reason for her leaving.

In the weeks that followed, I was on the phone with her regularly. Our conversations were always about the children, about other people in the family, never about ourselves. I did not want to lose her and I greatly feared I was going to. I honestly did not know what to do. I finally told Helga our relationship was over. I told her I would always support our son and that, if she chose, I would pay for her way back to Germany. She ultimately agreed to this, knowing that I could never leave Rosalie.

But what I did not understand then was that something else entirely was working its way into my life. Rosalie was in Brooklyn. I was in Arizona. To get her back, I had to leave Arizona and go to New York. That was simple. But I had no intention of remaining in the East. My home was in Arizona. My plan was to spend a few weeks in New York and return to my home—with my family.

Instead, I stayed for the next six years, when war broke out in our world and I went from being a crew leader in the West to becoming the wartime leader of the Bonanno Family.

11

In 1960, Vito Genovese began serving a fifteen-year prison sentence in the federal penitentiary in Atlanta, Georgia, for narcotics trafficking. Vito continued to rule his Family or at least have a strong influence over it from jail. There were many other people from our world who had been sent to Atlanta, and the traffic in and out of there was such that he was perfectly able to conduct business from his jail cell.

Vito was sure he had been set up, that someone who meant him harm had talked to the authorities and given them enough information to arrest and prosecute him. He was on the lookout for guys. He suspected Tony Bender, a group captain in his Family. Vito had let others know for some time that he thought Tony was skimming off profits from drug deals that he should have turned over to his Family. One day in early 1962, Tony told his wife that he was going outside for a walk, that he'd be back in a little while. They're still looking for him.

One of the people close to Bender was a soldier named Joseph Valachi. Valachi became the center of the most explosive federal intrusion into our world ever. It was not from anything he knew or later said to the authorities or in public that was so damaging (he knew far less than he pretended to know), but from the avalanche of publicity he brought down on all of us.

Valachi was a nobody with access to no one. He was picked up in 1959 or 1960 on a narcotics trafficking charge, tried, and sentenced to prison. He wound up—you guessed it—in Atlanta, eventually being placed in the same cell with Vito.

Vito suspected Valachi of being an informer because he was associated with Bender. He may or may not have gotten further evidence of that from another inmate, who himself was looking to shake off the rap of being an informer and so laid that label on Valachi. In any case, Vito had a way of coming at people so that they couldn't figure him out. He'd smile and you knew he meant something else; he'd ignore you and you knew he was watching you with eyes in the back of his head. He'd kiss you on the cheek while he had a knife hidden in his hand. As tricky as he was (maybe just because of that), he struck terror in the hearts of people like Valachi.

Valachi assumed Vito was going to have him killed. There's no question that people let him know what they thought of him in the prison yard, in the mess, wherever he went. Valachi became paranoid about Vito. One day, he took a pipe and killed someone he thought was somebody else, the guy he thought was going to come after him for Vito.

It didn't matter that he killed the wrong guy and that the look-alike, just like Valachi, was a nobody. In his own mind, Valachi saw himself more than ever as a marked man. The government saw that, too. We had always thought that Valachi had had some kind of relationship with them before. In fact, one of the things that Vito maintained afterward was that Valachi had been cooperating with the government from the time of his arrest in 1959.

For sure, Valachi began talking in the middle of 1961 and continued to do so for the next couple of years. He talked to anyone and everyone who was willing to listen and who would offer him protection from what he knew would be certain retribution. He turned to the government before there was a witness protection program; from behind that shield, he talked, in public, first to journalist Peter Maas, who would write the best-selling *The Valachi Papers*, and then to the McClellan committee. But what he knew was street-level stuff. At no time did he ever have access to the decision-making levels of his or anyone else's Family.

Because Valachi got headline after headline about the "Cosa Nostra" (where he got that name is interesting: We used the phrase—Sicilian for "Our Thing"—informally, idiomatically, never to designate in any formal sense a national organization or structure), everyone from law enforcement to local columnists turned up the heat on organized crime. Even Hoover could no longer stay out of it. He had been sitting on a black bag wiretap done in 1959 at Sam Giancana's headquarters in Chicago. The Commission had been mentioned and its members all named. But Valachi's revelations were made in public. Though Hoover to his dying day never used the word *Mafia,* he could no longer hold back. He had to let the FBI do its own thing even if personally he was reluctant and even fearful of doing so.

As a consequence, many people in our world ran for cover, some of them wearing wires, which helped provide evidence in dozens of prosecutions.

Because my father was named by Valachi as his "Godfather," who drew blood from him at his initiation ceremony, he, more than ever, wanted to lie low. He began to avoid all those places—west and east—where he might be subject to publicity, arrest, or subpoena. He spent quite a bit of time in Canada, where we had a number of different business interests in Montreal, and he kept in touch mainly through me.

For me personally, this was all crazy. I was honor-bound to serve the needs of my Family, but my own family situation was completely unresolved and, if anything, was even more risky than the chaos in our world. I felt like each step I took then had the potential—literally—of blowing up in my face.

Rosalie had moved into her parents' house with the kids. Visiting her there meant that in order to see her I had to deal with her mother, her sisters, her brothers, who all regarded me as a person who had injured their daughter and sister as well as the honor of the Profaci family.

When I called the Profaci house that first time to talk with Rosalie, she didn't sound particularly glad to hear from me. I was staying with my uncle Frank, who agreed with me that it might be best if I had others in the family visit Rosalie first to convince her to come back to me with the children. I contacted my aunt Rose and my aunt Marion, who went to the Profaci home, but they quickly discovered that Rosalie was determined to stay put.

My uncle and I talked about what might happen if I went over. Our discussion was ridiculous; we both thought the situation was like something out of a radio melodrama. But we decided that if I was actually to visit my mother-in-law's home, it would be best if I went armed and accompanied by someone else—namely, my uncle Frank.

So we showed up at the Profacis' door late one afternoon, both of us with guns as we looked up and down the street to see if anyone might be hiding or sitting in parked cars, waiting to ambush us.

When I rang the bell, it felt as if I waited an hour before someone answered. Rosalie's mother opened the door and was all over me. I couldn't immediately make out what she was saying because she was talking quickly, almost in a whisper, but her words were full of anger and accusation. Out of the corner of my eye, I saw Rosalie's older brother sitting in the living room, pretending I wasn't there. He was staring vacantly off into space. I would like to have made sure I got his attention, but I had more important things in mind. I wanted to see Rosalie. She wasn't home, my mother-in-law said. I knew that was probably false, because just after she opened the front door, I had heard other people moving around in the house, and if Ro and the kids weren't there, then why was her mother whispering to me? I had no idea what to do. Then, all of a sudden, I saw my son Chuck coming down the stairs. I walked past my mother-in-law, took Chuck in my arms, then turned and walked back to the door.

"I'm leaving now," I said, "but I'll be back. And when I come back, I want Rosalie to be here and ready to leave." With that, I carried Chuck outside, my uncle Frank following, and we drove away.

When I got to my uncle's house, I decided to call Rosalie's uncle, Joe Magliocco, the new head of the Profaci Family. I explained to Magliocco what was going on, because I most assuredly didn't want this situation to get any more out of hand than it already had. Magliocco's voice was the one I was looking for. He was an old-world guy; his accent was familiar, but so was his understanding. He came from the same culture that I had been raised in, where for better or for worse, a wife is a husband's property. He did not say, though he might have, that a husband also had an obligation to honor and respect his wife—which I had not done. He was interested, as I was, in reconciliation. He might have, but did not—on behalf of the Profacis—harbor thoughts of revenge.

"Yes, I've heard about what's going on," he told me. He invited me to visit him immediately at his estate in Islip, on Long Island.

When I got there, he welcomed me. We sat together for a while sipping espresso and then I took the matter up again. I told him that I did not want to do anything without consulting him, that I respected his intelligence and his authority, and that I would be only too glad to wait and see if there was anything he might do to help.

Magliocco nodded, then told me that he had already taken the liberty of calling the Profaci home. "I told them to be here this afternoon," he said almost matter-of-factly. "Whatever is going on, I know only one thing: Rosalie is your wife and you are entitled to her."

I felt like I was in luck. The Maglioccos had prepared a sumptuous lunch that we consumed in leisurely fashion. For the hour or so that it took, I felt as if I had no cares in the world. Uncle Joe, who loved food (and who had the weight to show it), made me feel as if this meal was the only business at hand. Finally, after we had more coffee, he got up, went inside, and picked up the telephone. When he hung up and came back out, he was clearly agitated. He told me that his relatives were crazy, and that they had taken off for New Jersey. I did not know what he meant. But Magliocco was not looking for guidance from me.

"You be here tomorrow; I will work this out. You come back tomorrow and they will all be here," he said with gruff assurance.

I had no choice but to follow his lead. The next afternoon, as I had been instructed, I turned up at the estate again. When I entered the house, Rosalie, the children, and her mother were all there. We exchanged pleasantries, then sat around for a while feeling awkward and uncertain. Finally, I asked, "Is my wife coming with me?"

Before Rosalie or her mother could say anything, Magliocco said, "Of course she's going with you. . . ."

But Mrs. Profaci had no such understanding. She was still blazing with anger and resentment, very much the den mother protecting her brood. She turned to Rosalie and asked her to leave the room. Rosalie went inside with the children. When we were alone, Mrs. Profaci confronted me. Her eyes were narrow and hard. I had never seen this side of Rosalie's mother before. Whatever else was going on, I admired the fierce pride and strength in her that would make her a formidable foe of anyone who stood in her way.

"I am warning you, if anything ever happens to my daughter . . ." Her voice was quiet but shaking with rage. Before I could begin to reply, Magliocco interceded.

"Stop!" he said. He moved close to his niece and quieted her down. Only when it was clear that the storm had passed did he usher Rosalie and the children back into the room. We sat around awhile longer, until the tension in the room slowly ebbed. I wanted to make things as easy as I could for Rosalie. I suggested that she return to her mother's house for another night and that I would then come by to pick her up the next day.

The following day, I met Magliocco in front of her house. Rosalie was all packed and ready to go when I rang the bell. We went inside, and instead of immediately leaving, I wanted to do everything I could to put Mrs. Profaci, all of them, at ease. We sat around and talked and then stayed on for dinner, until we actually reached a level of ease with one another that had been missing for months.

When we left, it was late. I had originally thought we would drive somewhere, find a place in the country and stay for a while, getting used to one another again. But it was too late now to drive. I had no wish to spend the night with relatives, and the idea of a hotel in Manhattan seemed dreary and cold. I don't know why—maybe because I loved planes, watching them land and take off, and because I knew that the children might enjoy this—but I suggested that we spend the night at a hotel near Idlewild Airport. It was just a short drive, and when we arrived, I got us the most luxurious suite available, one that had a panoramic window overlooking the field itself, so we could sit there watching the big planes come and go.

Rosalie and I sat up late. I ordered champagne, which she sipped reluctantly, and we talked after the children had gone to bed. While she had made her decision to continue our marriage, it was also clear that we could not go back to the life we had before. Rosalie, most assuredly, did not want to return to Arizona, and I was not about to force the issue.

The next day, we visited her uncle's house in Islip once more. We had dinner and sat around. At that point, Magliocco suggested that we might like to stay with him for a while until we worked out what it was we really wanted to do. We both thought that might work. The estate was huge, and there was plenty of room for our family, so the offer was gratefully accepted.

But in that little twist and turn of finding a temporary residence, there were consequences far beyond the playing out of my marital problems. We moved into Magliocco's home precisely at the moment when his leadership of the Profaci Family became an explosive issue.

Magliocco's elevation happened to take place by an election of the captains within his Family. Because the Gallo revolt had so badly fractured the family, that vote had been called into question by New York leaders, particularly Tommy Lucchese, who had supported the Gallos, as well as by leaders such as Joe Zerilli of Detroit. With the heat coming down because of Valachi, it was harder and harder to take all of this to the table, where it might have been mediated. At this point, the Commission was not a commission. Many members—like my father and others—were lying low, not wanting to expose themselves to investigators or police. In this vacuum, people like Tommy Lucchese, with help from such people as Carlo Gambino, could assume far more power than they might have otherwise. What it all came down to was the political power struggle within the Profaci Family. There was no Commission left; the pure mechanics of the Family's machine was already slowly coming to a halt. In short, there was no strong ideal or leadership, even though many were vying for the position.

Lucchese took the position that the election of Magliocco by his own captains had been illegitimate. The captains, he argued, had, in reality, been divided. The Gallo faction certainly hadn't voted for Magliocco; a third faction, headed by Joe Columbo, had split off and gone on their own—so who had voted for Magliocco anyway?

In fact, the Columbo people had come back into the fold before Joe Profaci's death and had sided with him against the Gallos. So where did Lucchese get off trying to say otherwise by interfering in another Family's election? He was merely pushing the envelope, but there wasn't the usual machinery around now to keep him in check. While it was true that there were many people in our world who had assumed that Larry Gallo would wind up as the leader of the Family after Profaci died, that wasn't the way it worked out. When the dispute was resolved—basically by the election of Magliocco by the captains—there were two factions that had finally come together, and the third, led by the Gallos, was out. The point was, the Gallos had the backing of Tommy Lucchese, but the way this personally affected me was that Rosalie's brother, Sal Profaci, a member of the Profaci Family, now withheld his support from Magliocco. He had turned his back, together with Joe Profaci's own son, Sal, on someone who was not only their leader but their own kin.

One day, Rosalie's cousin Sal arrived at the house in Islip and told Magliocco that he was wanted at a Commission meeting in New Jersey. Magliocco foolishly decided to go. I say foolishly because it was absolutely clear that at that point, the Commission no longer had any standing and was only going to be loaded one way, with too many people being absent. Still, he went.

He came back from this meeting in Camden and told me that the Commission had made an edict that he had been illegally elected. Then they stripped him of his authority, fined him forty thousand dollars, and told him that he had thirty days to hold a new election.

Because I was living in Magliocco's house at the time, I—and my Family—became more caught up in this dispute than was necessary. I happened to be home one night when Joe Colombo, Sonny Franzese, and Carmine Persico came over to discuss the results of the Commission meeting. I knew why they were there—it was obvious. Magliocco was well aware that such a meeting might create a dilemma for me and my Family. In fact, when these men turned up, he came to me and said, "Look, we have to make some decisions tonight, I don't want it to have nothing to do with you and I don't want anybody to get ideas."

I told him I understood and that I didn't want it to have anything to do with me, either. I went upstairs and went to bed. But around 1:30 in the morning, there was a knock on my door. It was Magliocco. He needed to talk to me, he said. So I got up and went downstairs with him.

When we were seated in his library, he said to me that he was sorry he had to mention anything to me but that the time had come where he had to. I really didn't need him to tell me anything. I knew what was happening with Lucchese, and it didn't take much to imagine what had taken place at this decision meeting.

"I don't want you or your family involved in any way," Magliocco said, "but I'm honor-bound to tell you that after what we decided tonight, it would be better for you to leave as quickly as possible." If he had actually come out and announced that there had been a war council, he couldn't have been more direct.

Our tradition teaches that you never desert your friends when they are in trouble. There can be no sense of honor without this most elemental willingness to stand up for one another in tough times. Joe Magliocco and his Family were in trouble. The decision for me was automatic. But I said nothing until I had worked it all through in my mind, until I knew precisely what actions I needed to take.

"Okay, don't tell me any of the details," I said, "I don't want to know them. The only thing you were obligated to tell me is what you've already told me—to be careful. But now the decision to stay or leave is mine—and I'm staying. But you understand, I first have to check in."

With that, I absented myself for the next couple of days while I made a trip up to Canada to speak with my father. I told him what had happened and he asked me then what it was I wanted to do. What I really wanted to do, I said, was take my family and go back to Arizona and resume my regular life, but I now felt honor-bound to stay in New York and support Magliocco.

My father accepted this, but he was flabbergasted at the news of how Magliocco had essentially let himself be maneuvered into a phony Commission meeting where he wound up having to accept a decision to pay a fine and then to hold new elections in his Family.

We decided nothing more at that point other than it was all right, as far as he was concerned, for me to continue living at Magliocco's house, to make what decisions I felt I needed to make, and, above all, to be my father's eyes and ears in what was obviously a dangerous and unpredictable situation.

I returned to New York and continued to live at Magliocco's. I did not get into any extended discussions with him about what was going on. He did ask me at one point when I thought the troubles might start, and I told him that since he had been given thirty days to hold new elections and come up with the forty thousand dollars, he was probably safe till then. But we never went into details. We were, after all, from different Families, we had our own affairs to look after, and it was important for both Families to keep their identities separate under the same roof.

The threat of impending violence, however, was impossible to ignore. Though Magliocco's estate was huge and well protected, he became paranoid about security. There were phone stations all over the place, which he checked regularly to make sure no intruders had penetrated any of the electronic fences. Whenever he was going to use his car, which was parked in an area far below the hill in which the house was located, he first checked it to make sure it had not been wired with a bomb the night before. He did this by turning on the ignition from a remote-control switch he had in the kitchen, which overlooked the driveway.

Magliocco was the kind of person who exuded danger and confidence.

He was an enormous man, weighing maybe three hundred pounds or more, full of energy, and very decisive in his words and physical gestures. He never seemed in doubt about anything, which probably accounted for his foolishly believing that he could walk into a Commission meeting designed to take his hide off and walk out unscathed.

In this frame of mind, he asked me one day to accompany him on a drive he was going to take. I knew that he was not talking about taking a trip to the market, but I didn't ask any questions—you don't in that kind of situation; you rely on the bond of trust and respect that makes words unnecessary. After Magliocco started the car from the kitchen, I went down to the driveway, slipped in behind the wheel, and waited for him. He came out of the garage a couple of minutes later carrying a shotgun. I knew then only that this little trip was a wartime move, but I didn't know if it was offensive, defensive, or whatever. I assumed only that Magliocco wanted my help—that was enough. I asked him if I should go back in the house and get a piece for myself. No, no, he said, everything was fine; there was no problem.

We drove in silence. I had no idea where we were going. Uncle Joe held the shotgun across his lap and I waited for him to tell me something. He directed me to drive to the Brentwood station of the Long Island Railroad and then asked me to pull over. For the next fifteen minutes or so, we just sat there till a train pulled in. We watched the people coming and going on the platform and then, suddenly, I saw someone I recognized, Sally "the Sheik" Musacio, the father-in-law of Magliocco's nephew, walking slowly toward us. For a second, my mind clutched. I thought this was the guy Joe was going to hit. But that made no sense; he was an ally, a relative. What was going on? Just as casually as that, Sally came up to the car and nodded to me as Joe rolled down his window. The two men looked at each other.

"Is everything set?" Magliocco asked him.

"Yeah," Sally said, "everything's set."

Magliocco then said, "Okay, start."

And that was that. Sally turned around and walked back to the station to take the next return train to New York. I knew then—without asking or being told—what had happened. This was a command to go to war— that is, for Magliocco's people, specifically, to hit Tommy Lucchese and Carlo Gambino. In our world, when a decision of this magnitude is made, it is always made by face-to-face-contact, never by phone, or by any other method that might risk interception. I was there as an eyewitness for my father. But the command never was carried out.

Before a shot could be fired, Joe Columbo, who was a captain in Magliocco's Family, went to Gambino and Lucchese and informed them of what had happened. He told them, too, of my presence at Magliocco's side. The war that never was became the conspiracy that still could kill.

Even though I was not involved in any plan to hit anyone, I—and the Bonnano Family—suddenly were in up to our necks.

The thought passed through my mind that Magliocco had implicated me—and my Family—merely by having me at his side when he made this trip to the railroad station. I went with him because he had asked me to go—and he was a friend and my wife's uncle, someone to whom I would not say no. I am sure he believed my presence in the car would not become known. But that was a careless mistake on his part, proof that he was not really up to the leadership role he had assumed; and it was a mistake on my part to have gone along out of a sense of narrow loyalty and rigid responsibility.

But at that moment in time, all of us, the Bonannos, Magliocco, the Gallos, Tommy Lucchese, were caught up in something larger and more destructive than any of us singly or together might have imagined.

Then there was the question of the Bonannos. My father instructed me to talk directly with Tommy Lucchese. I made plans to do this—to visit Lucchese at his home on Royatt Street in Long Beach, New York.

Three of us were assigned to visit him—my father's underboss, Johnny Morales, Gaspar DiGregorio, and me. Before we left, Johnny took me by the arm. "Leave your weapon here, Bill; we're not going to have arms on us when we go in."

I looked at him as if he were crazy.

"Do you know what you're doing?" I said.

"That's the way it has to be," he answered.

We rode out to Lucchese's house in silence, the tension in the car palpable. When we got there, I told Johnny and Gaspar that I wanted to be the last one going in—so if anyone was waiting out in the street, in a car or in a doorway, I would be able to move faster and confuse whoever was there. My mind was going a hundred miles an hour.

We were shown in by a woman, someone I didn't know. But that was a good sign. If we were going to be whacked, cut up, carried out in body bags, there would be no women in the house.

We were shown into a large parlor. A serving of anisette cookies was already arranged on a plate. There was a smell of freshly brewed espresso in the elaborately decorated room. A couple of minutes later, a door opened and Tommy and one of his captains, Carmine Gribbs, and his underboss, Stephen Lasalla, came striding into the room. As usual, Tommy was impeccably dressed.

We exchanged pleasantries. As protocol dictated in a meeting of this kind, Johnny Morales, because he was the highest-ranking member of our Family, did the talking. He explained to Lucchese that there were rumors about me being tied to Magliocco and that they were false. He explained something about my personal problems and about Rosalie and I living in the house. That was the only reason I had happened to be in Magliocco's company, he said.

Tommy smiled in that hooded way of his and nodded. He said that never for a moment did he believe that I would enter into a conspiracy against him. He expressed regret at my domestic situation and he gave a little speech about family values. And then we all embraced—and it was over.

Except that by that point, neither Tommy Lucchese nor Joe Bonanno, nor anyone else in our world, for that matter, could prevent what was coming.

The meeting at the railroad station occurred in the early fall of 1963; the meeting with Lucchese took place shortly after that. On November 22, John F. Kennedy was shot in Dallas, and Magliocco died soon after that.

Uncle Joe Magliocco, getting out of bed one morning, suffered a fatal heart attack. The whole question of his role as a leader was settled by one blow of fate. The leadership of his Family would soon fall into the hands of Joe Columbo.

It had been quite a fall.

12

Like everyone else in the United States back then, I was shocked when I heard the news of the assassination. I was having lunch with Joe and Pete Notaro, Phil Rastelli, and Carl Samari at Mr. Richard's Steak House on Forty-sixth Street in Manhattan when someone came over to our table and excitedly told us the President had just been shot in Dallas. We all got up and walked over to the television set and watched for a while till Walter Cronkite came on and announced that the President had been pronounced dead at Parkland Memorial Hospital, where he had been taken after the shooting. We then walked outside and stood around on the street, stunned like everyone else. It was a bright day, warmer than usual for that time in November, and there seemed to be a lot of people like us just standing there as though they had been frozen in place by a ray from outer space.

That night, I had dinner at Ferdinand's on Long Island with a group of people in my Family: Joe Notaro, my uncle Frank, Vito DeFilippo, and Charlie Battaglia, who had come into town from Arizona. We went there because it was one of the few supper spots that had remained open. We had business to conduct—that came first—but inevitably the subject of the assassination came up. The conversation was general, the kind people anywhere might have been having at that point. Kennedy was by no means a favorite of ours and we were familiar enough with the ways of power to be skeptical that a lone gunman was the shooter.

Then two days later, somewhere around the middle of the day on Sunday, as Rosalie, the kids, and I were getting to ready to go to Salisbury Park in Old Westbury, Long Island, a call came to the house. We were told to turn on the TV. Jack Ruby, right there on network television, had just shot Oswald in the basement of the Dallas County Jail.

As I watched replay after replay of what had just happened, I could not believe what I was seeing. Not because the prime suspect in the assassination had been killed, but because of who had done the shooting. I knew that face, that body, that swift, squat, compact move. Jack Ruby was known to everyone in our world. He was not a made member (he was Jewish), but he was a gofer, a fixer, the kind of non-Family person who was always available for favors, to do some rough stuff, make a payoff, do a job. I didn't know him, but I had seen him around, in Chicago, New Orleans, Cuba, everywhere. He was out of Chicago and New Orleans. He belonged to Sam Giancana like a pinkie ring. He had been living in Texas for some time and had been running in our world for years. There could be no mistaking the meaning of his involvement.

As soon as I could collect myself, I phoned Smitty D'Angelo, who happened to be in Fort Lauderdale, and instructed him to get himself over to Tampa immediately and find out what he could. If he couldn't find anything there, then he was to go on to New Orleans, Texas, Chicago, until he found some answers. He found them in Tampa.

Tampa was the home base of Santo Trafficante; once a Kennedy supporter, he had soured on him after the Bay of Pigs when he saw all his Cuban interests go down the drain. Tampa, everyone knew, had close alliances with Texas, New Orleans, and Chicago. Trafficante wasted no time in telling Smitty all he needed to know. His Family was involved, along with Carlos Marcello's and Sam Giancana's. Jimmy Hoffa was involved, too, but was not responsible for much.

"Santo said it was a local matter, and that everything has been taken care of," Smitty told me the very next day, Monday, November 25. As soon as his plane touched down in New York, we met at a restaurant on Lorimer Street in Brooklyn. We were in the back, sitting in a booth like any two customers in a local Italian restaurant anywhere in New York—except that we were talking about who was actually responsible for shooting the President of the United States. Smitty had not asked for and had not been told about any of the actual details of the killing. But Trafficante told him that Cubans were involved and that there had been a fuckup with Oswald.

(After killing JFK, Oswald had shot Dallas policeman J. D. Tippit later that same day.)

"The cop Tippit was supposed to take him out," Smitty said, "but Oswald got him. Oswald was the patsy. Some patsy. That was why they used Ruby."

"Local matter," I muttered. I understood the words. In our world, those words had meaning. *Local* had nothing to do with geography, only with spillover effect for others. The dispute, in this case, insane as it seemed, was to be thought of as an internal matter, involving only the Families who took part in the assassination. According to Santo, no one else was going to be implicated or affected.

I did not closely question Smitty. I did not want to. Limiting information in our world, as in most clandestine organizations, is fundamental to survival. After I debriefed him, I asked for a meeting of different leaders in the New York Families for the following evening. Carmine Gribbs from Lucchese, Tommy Eboli from Genovese, leaders from the Profaci/Magliocco Family, and Sam DeCavalcante from New Jersey. We met at a restaurant in Lindenhurst, New Jersey, in a private dining room; the rest of the place was closed down.

Smitty repeated to them, on my instruction, less than what he had told me—only the Families involved, that it was local, and that Santo had assured everyone that things "were taken care of"—all that was necessary for people to be assured of their own safety. There were a few murmurs of surprise, but, because people in our world understood the need for less, not more, information, there were few questions. There would be no repercussions. At this point, that was enough.

On the other hand, there was in that room, as there was throughout our world, some awareness of just what it was that might have driven the people involved to assassinate the President of the United States. And that, undoubtedly, did not sit too well.

Everyone knew, for example, that Carlos Marcello, the leader of the New Orleans Family, had, within months of Kennedy's inauguration, been arrested and deported from the country by the Justice Department, headed by Robert Kennedy. We were all familiar with his troubles because he complained about them. He had reentered the country, been rearrested, and been tried for a host of crimes. It was known (and later confirmed in congressional testimony) that a business associate of Marcello's had been going around saying he had heard Carlos, in a drunken rage, threaten to kill Kennedy and that this would be the best way to get rid of the attorney general, as well. Kill the snake by cutting off its head, something like that.

We also were well aware of Santo's feelings of betrayal and loss following the Bay of Pigs invasion, along with Bobby Kennedy's subsequent targeting of southern Florida for Justice Department action against drug trafficking. Trafficante was known to have boasted to friends on at least one occasion that JFK "was going to be hit" for the trouble he was causing, before he had a chance to be reelected. Everyone was also aware of Sam Giancana's bitterness toward the Kennedys, and Hoffa's feelings because of federal probes of the Teamsters were clear, as well.

Hoffa had been the Justice Department's number-one target ever since Bobby Kennedy took office. Hoffa, in recent years, had been almost loose-lipped about his desire to see the Kennedys eliminated. He openly talked up different assassination plots he was thinking about around people he knew, like Ed Partin, one of his close aides, who, in turn, spoke to people in our world. It was beyond belief. This local matter, at least as far as I could see, was as loud and clear as a marching band in full parade dress coming right down the middle of the avenue.

What was also clear (for anyone who had their ears and eyes open) was the obvious involvement of the government. It did not take a rocket scientist to figure out that others beside mob figures, in some very crucial ways, had to be involved. For instance, anyone looking at photos of the Texas School Book Depository building at the time of the assassination will notice that all the windows in the place were wide open. How could that be? The Secret Service and the local police routinely sealed all windows, sewers, storm drains, and other openings along the route of a presidential motorcade (later, much later, at a very different time in my life, I would learn just how consequential that single act of planned negligence turned out to be). Likewise, anyone who watched the killing of Oswald by Ruby had to know that someone, somewhere, had made a decision to let Ruby get into the Dallas County Jail building, where he could then, just by chance, position himself in exactly the right spot to get off a point-blank shot at Oswald's gut.

We also had general knowledge that went beyond the obvious and inescapable. Take the matter of the FBI. In the years since the assassination, it has become clear that J. Edgar Hoover was responsible for any number of decisions to bury, withhold, or divert crucial information that might have prevented the assassination and might have led to an investigation that went beyond Lee Harvey Oswald as the lone gunman.

Hoover, for example, had been aware in the months prior to the assassination that threats had been made against Kennedy's life, including one that involved a possible trip to the Dallas area in November 1963. Hoover chose to ignore the prior warnings. After the assassination, there were any number of evidentiary leads that were apparently ignored or scuttled. Immediately following the shooting, there were reports by any number of eyewitnesses that gunfire had come from the grassy knoll. Witnesses in the area either were not questioned by FBI agents or were hastily deemed to be unreliable. Three derelicts were picked up in the area and ordered released by the FBI before they were fully interrogated. At all times, Hoover personally sought to limit any inquiry into the background, character, and possible mob contacts of Jack Ruby, thereby lending credence to Ruby's ludicrously false statements about how he had killed Oswald on his own out of patriotic motives and for love of JFK and his family. All of this eventually was spelled out in 1975 and 1976 in hearings before the House Select Committee on Assassinations.

In addition, through our own contacts, we eventually learned that Hoover blocked the investigation in yet another important way. At the time of the assassination, there was a group of elite agents finishing a training session in Quantico, Virginia. When news of Kennedy's death was flashed, these agents asked, as a unit, to be sent to Dallas. They had the specific kinds of investigative expertise that would have been crucial in developing evidence in the hours and days following the killing. Their assignment request was turned down cold. I eventually learned about this, personally, from one of the agents who had been in that unit.

But Hoover's hatred of the Kennedys was well known to us at the time of the assassination. Lewis Rosenstiel, an old bootlegger who went on to become the head of Schenley, was a close bisexual friend of the Hoover, a source of information beyond photographs about the director's personal life. Rosenstiel was also close to people in our world. Through New York lawyer Roy Cohn—another mutual friend—Rosenstiel had long ago passed the word that Hoover had blackmailed JFK into reappointing him as director of the FBI after Bobby Kennedy had threatened to remove him when he reached mandatory retirement age. Rosenstiel confirmed what later was a rumor in the tabloids: that Hoover went to Kennedy and told him he would expose his affair with Judith Campbell if he was not allowed to continue in office. Rosenstiel said that Hoover presented Kennedy with wiretaps and other evidence that he was prepared to make public if he did not go along. Kennedy went along. (Rosenstiel, later on, was also the likely source of another story widely circulated in our world: that on the morning of the assassination, Hoover had a telephone conversation with Lyndon Johnson in which he told him, "Your time is coming.")

Everyone in the room that night also had some general sense of the Cuban connection, the relationship of Marcello, Trafficante, Giancana, even Jimmy Hoffa to the Cuban exile community and through them to the CIA. Years before, the CIA and members of the mob had come together over a series of attempts to assassinate Cuban premier Fidel Castro. The people from our world who were involved included Giancana and his most powerful subordinate, Johnny Roselli. Giancana and Roselli had gone along, mainly in the hopes of getting the government to ease up on their Caribbean business interests. No one was ever able to get to Castro, but the efforts were real—they went under the government code name AMLASH. We knew about them because Robert Maheu, a private investigator who had done a lot of work for Jimmy Hoffa and the Teamsters, was the go-between on the project.

The thought that people from our world might somehow have been involved with the CIA in the plan to kill the President was unavoidable and did not sit well with anyone. It certainly did not sit well with me. The moment such a partnership was agreed to, our people—anyone involved, those who in any way possessed knowledge of that involvement—were in permanent peril.

After I briefed these New York leaders, I flew up to see my father in Canada and tell him what I had learned. He listened in dismay. He was not at all impressed by the assurances that had been given, any more than he was by what had actually happened.

"This is the result of no leadership," he said. "With a functioning Commission, this never would have happened; they would have had to come to us like Albert did with Dewey." We were sitting in a home where he was staying. There was an early snow falling outside a huge bay window facing across an expanse of lawn that was now as white as Christmas.

"It was always understood that you don't hit people in government, any more than you hit journalists. These people don't just represent institutions and popular opinion; they are our lifeline, even when we don't like what they do. No one who really understood our tradition could ever have involved himself in this," my father said. "These people are not us. This is an attack against us, too. The bullets they fired were at everything we stand for."

I understood what my father was telling me. I did not feel this in quite the way he did because I did not yet have his experience, did not yet fully appreciate the importance of the tradition as he lived it. I was more preoccupied then with the force of the news itself, with the fact that my father and I, as well as others close to us—now were bearers of information that would forever be a burden.

But what I did not know then, after I had debriefed Smitty and as I was sitting there with my father, was that one day I would be confronted with the heart of the plot: the planning, the execution, and the identity of the man who had actually killed the President. I would learn more than I ever wanted to know and enough to bear out fully my father's judgment that the bullets that ripped through Kennedy were indeed aimed at us, as well.

The irony of the Kennedy assassination was that it was a "local" matter. The national stage remained in New York. The turmoil in our world there continued. Everything in New York was not "taken care of." Our future seemingly had nothing to do with the Kennedy assassination, though we would soon enough find out just how meaningful this moment was for us all—and for me in particular.

Call it fate, call it chance, but it just so happened that through a peculiar wrinkle in time, there was yet another chapter in the Tale of the Two Joes to be played out. At exactly the moment when John Kennedy's time of power had ended, mine was about to begin.

13

All through November, up to and beyond the time of the assassination, my sharpest concerns were increasingly focused on how Rosalie and I were going to live. With Joe Magliocco's decision to strike out at Lucchese and Gambino, it was no longer possible for my family to remain under his roof. His house had become a war zone. There was tension in the air all the time. One morning, after I was gone, my two-year-old son, Joseph, was crawling around on the floor and he came across a shotgun propped up against a wall in the house. He reached out and somehow his little hand came down on the trigger and the gun went off, blasting a hole in the ceiling. Magliocco was sleeping upstairs and narrowly missed getting hit. There were screams in the house. My wife began screaming, too. The whole place was bedlam; we simply had to get out of there.

I believe that if Rosalie and I had been able to work out our personal problems, we would have returned to Arizona. But given all that she had been through, she was simply unwilling to return to the West. Though she had originally welcomed the idea of clearing out of Brooklyn and starting a new life away from her family, she now believed the East represented some kind of safety net. So, at least for the time being, the price of our remaining together as a family meant living close to her mother, brother, and other members of her family. We looked for and finally found a home in East Meadow, New York, on an pretty street in an attractive community. But this decision of ours was really the fateful turn in our lives.

During the late fall and early winter months of 1964, with my father continuing to remain out of the picture, I became more and more involved in the day-to-day running of our Family's interests. And, in the process, I inevitably became more drawn into a struggle that was far more tenacious and subtle than I imagined.

In my father's absence, he had left daily operations in the running of the Family to three people: Johnny Morales, Gaspar DiGregorio—both group captains—and me. All decisions affecting the general standing of the Family required a vote; no one could decide anything on his own. The reason I became part of this temporary triumvirate was not only because I was the most secure connection to my father but also because, in practical terms, it made sense on the street.

Johnny Morales was a good unofficial number-two man, but because he was a fugitive, wanted by federal authorities due to his failure to report for military service, he was someone who constantly had to limit his contacts. He lived under an assumed name; only the closest people in the Family knew his address. He was just not available. Gaspar DiGregorio was a very introverted person and, however ambitious he might have been, he simply did not mix well with others. His business interests were located mostly out on Long Island, where he wanted to remain. The actual number-three man in the organization, the consigliere, was John Tartamella—who might have been expected to do the work I wound up doing. But John had suffered a couple of strokes and was incapacitated. He remained as consigliere—my father's instruction was that John was to hold his office for as long as he lived—but his ability to conduct business was so limited that much of what he did fell to me. In this position, I took on my Family's troubles and, because of who I was, added significant new ones to the mix, as well. I was the new kid on the block—younger by decades than any of the older leaders who were around—and my experience, as I say, was limited.

I did not yet have a full appreciation of the way a Family administration worked on a day-to-day basis. I was used to the big picture, to the decision making that kept us connected to power—my father sitting down with Joe Kennedy or, in a place like New York City, sitting down with the leader of Tammany Hall, Carmine DeSapio, who was also a Democratic National Committeeman.

During the mid-fifties and beyond, when I spent summers in the East and then when I shuttled back and forth after Apalachin, I met DeSapio many times—at first, with my father, then with other leaders from our Family. We used to socialize. We'd meet at places like the Italian-American Professional Businessmen's Association on Bushwick Avenue in Brooklyn, at local restaurants like Crisci's or the Enchanted Hour.

But I was not at all used to the everyday inter-Family problems that could crop up, the stresses and strains of the Five Families packed like a carton of volatile chemicals into too small a space. Our Family's interests in the outer boroughs of New York City were never a problem because territory was clearly defined. In Brooklyn, for example, you had only two Families—the Profaci and the Bonanno. The only possible area of dispute was the waterfront—where the Gambinos had some interests. But in Manhattan, all of that was different. There, the Five Families were all vying and striving for advantage. The situation inherently was explosive and unsettled, always calling for conciliation, mediation, and talk, talk, talk. Manhattan was where the action was; it was where the social life of the Families—the interplay, the arguments—took place; it was the nerve center of power.

In my daily rounds, there were constant sit-downs over territory, bookmaking, gambling, hijacking. There were problems in the markets, such as the Garment District, the fish market, the meat market. Out at the airports, you never knew when a little issue could suddenly blow up in your face. It was dizzying to keep up with. I remember one day when one of our group captains, Joe Notaro, came to me all worked up and said we had to get to a leadership sit-down immediately because there was a real threat of violence between members of our Family and some others.

So we got to this meeting place down on the Lower East Side after a high-speed ride through Queens and down the East River Drive. We walked into a roomful of grim-looking people—all of them big shots: Carmine Gribbs from Lucchese, O'Neill Dellacroce from Gambino. I was prepared for the heaviest sit-down of my career. And what was this all about? Pushcarts.

One of our guys was in a street-corner dispute with a guy who was under the protection of one of the other Families. If this was going to be a war, it was going to start over hot dogs. I couldn't believe it. I sat there patiently listening and eventually learning why pushcarts were so important. This little dispute between a pair of umbrellas was really about something far more important and, as far as the Families were concerned, far more lucrative.

Pushcarts in New York City, it turned out, cost a lot of money—up to ten thousand dollars a cart. Most small operators were unable to afford that kind of expenditure. So they turned to others—us—who had money and were willing to go into partnership with them in buying a cart. Some operators had fleets of pushcarts, others just one or two. All of the pushcarts had licensing agreements with suppliers of hot dogs, with other food distributors, with butane and beverage companies. And all partnership agreements, for sure, involved making purchases from companies owned by our people. A lot of money was involved. The city itself charged a nominal fee for licensing pushcarts so they could do business on the streets, but the positioning of those carts became the subject of territorial agreements among the Families. You just did not set up on a street corner. You could try it, but it wasn't a wise idea, as any experienced pushcart operator knew.

I was stunned by the intensity on the faces of the people involved in this sit-down. Even as I was learning, it was all I could do to keep from laughing. But this was serious, very serious. One of our guys had carts on Monroe Street and Essex Street, sharecropped from a captain in our Family; the other guy, from Lucchese's Family, also sharecropping a couple of carts, wanted rights on the same corner. It took an hour, maybe more, to get things straightened out. We left the meeting actually feeling a sense of accomplishment, as though we had brokered a blue-flag truce between two warring nations.

Cigarettes and jukeboxes were big, too. Who would think that any of this mattered? Millions of packs of cigarettes smuggled into the city meant huge additional profits that didn't have to be paid out in city taxes. Jukeboxes? If you controlled jukeboxes in the biggest market in the country, you effectively controlled the recording industry. Years before, Willie Moretti, Frank Costello's right arm, sponsored a neighborhood singer he liked, Frank Sinatra. You want to be a star? You better have your records in an awful lot of jukeboxes—just the way Sinatra did in the early days.

And in every area of city life, from traffic in and out of the airports and rail yards, to trucking routes in and out of the Garment District and the Diamond District, we were there. Garbage pickups, police protection—all of it went through us in one way or another.

I had something of an "office" in the Wentworth Hotel in midtown. Every day except on weekends and holidays, I could be found in the dining room there from around 1:00 to 3:30 in the afternoon. Guys would come to me with all kinds of different problems. I remember once I was sitting there when a couple of young soldiers from one of the crews came in and told me how they had hijacked a truck, as scheduled, out on the New Jersey Turnpike. The way hijacking worked was that there would be an arrangement between the drivers or dispatchers—whom we controlled— and our hijackers. The drivers, who had matching sets of keys made for their trucks, were told to pull into one of the rest stops along the way, leave one set of keys in the truck, and go have a cup of coffee or visit a rest room. When they got back, the truck would be missing, the drivers would be in the clear, and we'd have the merchandise. Well, these kids complained that they went out to the turnpike and then when they took this truck off to the assigned drop, they discovered that their cargo had been tampered with. They thought they had hijacked a load of sneakers. They had—except the truck was carrying only right-footed shoes. Obviously, the sneaker manufacturers had figured out that they could beat their hijacking problems by shipping half pairs of shoes, sending the matching halves on other trucks. It took a little while to match left-footed trucks with right-footed ones, but we did.

The on-site training I was getting as a leader during this time was one thing; the exposure was another. I had no problems from the authorities. We had been part of the system for so long that all we had to do was make sure the proper payoffs were made and no one hassled us. My biggest problem then came from within my own world. Because I was so obviously out front, there was a good deal of resentment toward me. I was younger than other leaders, many of whom thought that I had not earned my way, and that I had been handed my position because I was my father's son. I was conscious of this, certainly, and I am sure that whether or not it was my actual intention, I went out of my way to fit in. It's odd, but in my world people sometimes seem to talk the way gangsters do in movies, without being aware of it. I was never into flashy cars, gaudy dress; my speech reflected the college education I had had. Yet I was aware, during this time, that my clothing was a little flashier, my speech a little more colloquial than normal. I consciously made an effort to become one of the boys. In truth, I felt more comfortable around people closer to my own age, whose energies and ambitions were nearer to mine, than I did with many of the older people, who had already had their careers. But still, there was this edge of having to prove myself.

One of the hot points for me—and, it turned out, for my Family—occurred in the Garment District. The district was a hub of life in New York that could not run without us. Every truck that went in and out of the area, every pipe on wheels carrying a rack of clothing moved only with our approval. We effectively controlled the International Ladies' Garment Workers' Union; we directly controlled Local 102, a truckers' union for the industry.

Years before, the Lucchese, Profaci, and Bonanno Families had made a business agreement that effectively carved up the area. It will be remembered that after the Castellammarese war of 1930, Lucky Luciano sat down with my father and offered him a "piece of Manhattan," and my father had declined, saying he was interested only in Luciano's friendship. That changed only to the extent that, in time, my father's consigliere, John Tartamella, had been given an okay to purchase a one-half interest with the Profaci Family against a one-half interest with the Lucchese Family in a Manhattan trucking association that effectively dominated the commercial life of the district. This tripartite agreement served our Family's needs well. Though the business was surely profitable, it was more valuable as a practical instrument of cooperation. Keeping friendship among the Families meant keeping the system functioning smoothly and efficiently.

There was always a delicate balance in this business because the leaders behind it came from different sides of the table. My father and Joe Profaci, the conservatives, held the balance of voting power over Lucchese, the liberal, although there had never been any contention between the parties in running things.

When Joe Profaci died and John Tartamella from our Family became seriously ill, all of that changed. While the financial side of the business remained strong, the political side suddenly became unstable. For a while, Joe Magliocco's leadership of the Profacis seemed to guarantee that no great changes would be forthcoming. But when he died and Joe Colombo—an ally of Lucchese—assumed command of the Profaci Family, there was a new reality. The Profaci Family's shares in the business were technically owned by Rosalie's brother and cousin, who, so long as their Family leader was an ally of ours, were in no position to do anything on their own. But when Colombo took over, suddenly Rosalie's kin were able to step forward legitimately and say they wanted to sell their shares directly to their boss, thus effectively changing the balance of power against us.

I have no idea if Lucchese put them up to it. In a way, it didn't matter. On behalf of John Tartamella and my Family, I opposed the move, but I could do nothing to stop it. The choice we had was to go along in minority partnership with Lucchese and Colombo, risking whatever enmity they might be harboring toward the Bonanno Family over Magliocco's aborted plan to assassinate them, or to sell out.

In the midst of this, Tartamella had another stroke—this one paralyzing him completely. Because it became impossible for him to enter in any way into business and policy decisions regarding the trucking concern, we decided that the only choice open to us was to sell his shares for him so he might benefit immediately and personally. There was no question about going ahead with this, but at the same time it meant that an important instrument of practical cooperation in New York—cooperation between us and Lucchese—had been removed.

Even more than upsetting a power balance in the Families, Tartamella's final stroke also meant that he could no longer serve as consigliere, even in a nominal capacity. John was a longtime friend and ally, a man who was simple and shrewd, utterly faithful. He was hardworking and widely admired, especially within the Family, where, as consigliere, he was enormously skilled in mediating between the top of the administration and the guys below. It was clear when we went to visit him, first in the hospital and then at home, that he was no longer able to function in any capacity. He was paralyzed and unable to speak, and he required round-the-clock care. It was now necessary to replace him, and this was a momentous step in our organization, as it would be in any Family's.

Largely through popular sagas like *The Godfather,* the role of the consigliere has been grossly misunderstood. What he is not is a legal adviser. Rather, he is a man in the middle, someone specifically asked, in a formal way, to be a buffer between the ordinary street-level people and the administration of a Family. That is a tricky and delicate task. The consigliere is concerned with administration, no doubt about it. But in order for him to be accepted by the troops below, they have to have confidence in his ability to stand up for them.

John was easy to identify with. He was a working guy, like nearly everyone else in a Family. He had two or three other businesses, in addition to the trucking concern, that he had to look after. Contrary to what most people think, the day-to-day life of a mafioso is not spent in illegal activity. Most people in a Family, like people anywhere, work long hours at jobs they often don't like; they are burdened by all of the daily problems of living—paying taxes, dealing with illnesses, taking care of their kids, trying to scrape together enough to provide for a slightly better future than their parents had. The consigliere must be attuned to that life, must have a feel for it beyond any intellectual understanding of the office. Only if he has that feel will he be able to gain the confidence of the troops he is going to represent.

When John fell, I could no longer continue as his unofficial stand-in. We reached a point where it was necessary to name a new consigliere. Given the timing, this could not have come at a more sensitive moment. The assassination of President Kennedy was still fresh in everyone's mind. Though it seemed there would be no repercussions in our world, there was no certainty of that. The wheels of government continued to grind and things seemed to be as they had been before the assassination. The fallout from Joe Valachi's public testimony continued. There were five different grand juries looking into organized crime before the assassination, and there were five grand juries working away afterward.

My father, contacted in Canada, gave instructions for a business meeting of the Family's group leaders. At this meeting, my father spoke by phone personally to each of the captains. Through them, he let it be known that he had selected officially John Morales as his underboss (John had been unofficially acting in that capacity since the retirement of Frank Garofalo in 1957), that he had named two others to positions of captain, that he had replaced still another captain by naming my uncle Frank as group leader, and that John Tartamella would no longer continue as consigliere. What that meant was the floor was to be open for nominations for the position. Because the consigliere was the people's representative, the position was the only one in the entire administration other than leader that was filled by election rather than selection. My name was then placed in nomination.

I definitely had mixed feelings about this. I was pleased and flattered, but I also had reservations because of the commitment involved, because of my youth, inexperience, and distance from the street, and then, finally, because no one else's name had been put forward. If ever there was a way of demonstrating that I had just had something handed to me because I was my father's son, this was it.

I suddenly remembered something from my father's past. When he had been named head of his Family, he had insisted at the time—because of his youth (he was in his twenties then)—that he be elected in a closed vote by the members. He himself nominated someone to run against him, someone who he knew harbored ill will toward him and who, in any secret ballot, would bring out opposition. In that way, he would be able to gauge the depth or shallowness of his support. The vote for him turned out to be almost unanimous.

I asked Angelo Caruso, a family elder, to nominate Gaspar DiGregorio. Gaspar was an older man, my godfather, and an ally of my father's, one of the temporary triumvirate in the Family. In retrospect, I think I understood on a gut level that he was disappointed that he had not been picked first and that, in his own mind, he saw my nomination as something inherently underhanded and unfair. But he said nothing. Instead, he simply declined to have his name placed in nomination, thereby ensuring that I would be elected. But I insisted that Angelo put his name forward. And there matters stood for two weeks, until we all convened again at La Scala restaurant in Manhattan. In the interim, the group captains polled their crews by secret ballot. All members were free to vote their conscience without any penalty of disclosure. I was elected by a near unanimous vote and we followed the announcement of the result by placing a call to my father in Canada to let him know. In the speeches toasting my victory, one of the most eloquent was given by Gaspar.

Ideally, this should have settled the questions of favoritism—at least within our own Family—but it did not. My election, my place in the administration, far from creating the unity we needed in a dark time only made things worse—both within and without. The dynamic at work in our world was larger than any single act of violence or of democracy, though, in the end, it was measurable by nothing more substantial than the egos of individual men.

14

It was protocol to keep other Families informed of major internal changes, such as the elevation of new officers. In my case, common sense was just as powerful a motive. Within a week or so of my election, I had separate lunches with representatives of the Lucchese, Genovese, and Gambino Families. Natale Eboli (aka Tommy Ryan), the temporary head of Genovese's Family with Vito in prison, was there; so was Carmine Gribbs and Stephen Lasalla of the Lucchese Family and Joe Riccabono from the Gambino Family. The few hours we spent together were unremarkable; there was no hint of any discontent or anxiety beneath the surface of smiles, handshakes, toasts, and small talk. I made sure that I relayed all of the administrative decisions that had been made in the last weeks, naming our new group captains, including changes my father had made in the crews in Arizona.

I was asked about my father, his health, his plans, when he might be thinking about returning to New York. I answered as best I could—that he was fine, that he was taking care of business in the Midwest and in Canada, and that, as far as I knew, he was more and more thinking of retirement. My parents had, for some time, been talking about taking a trip around the world, I said. The information seemed to solicit nothing more than nods of acknowledgment that easily mixed with the cigar smoke and laughter in the room. I chose not to see how this information might be interpreted as a signal that my elevation was far more significant than I let on.

Within weeks, however, there was a new and major development. My father briefly returned to town and called a meeting of the administration of the Family. He wanted to go over the changes that had been made and talk about different issues, ranging from the Lucchese-Gambino liberal alliance to his own long-range plans for retirement. When we got together, all of the captains were there except for one: Gaspar DiGregorio. We thought there must have been some mistake. Attendance at meetings was mandatory. There were immediate objections raised. My father waved them off, sure that some kind of mistake had been made. No matter how keen his disappointment at not being elevated, Gaspar still was believed to be a loyal friend and someone who went along with Family decisions.

I was instructed to contact Gaspar. He told me flat out that he was now under the protection of the Commission and that he was not allowed to go to any meeting called by the leadership of our Family.

When I told my father what I had learned, he said this could not be, that I had misunderstood what Gaspar had said. But I had not misunderstood. He then asked that I call Gaspar once more so that he might talk to him directly. It took time, but I finally arranged the call.

I did not hear the conversation they had, but the results were obvious. My father was seething as we went back to a house where six or seven captains were waiting. "Well, Steve has really done it this time," he said. He was referring to Steve Maggadino, the Buffalo boss, who was his cousin. There had been a Commission meeting, he said, and at that meeting Gaspar had been brought in by Steve and told that he was now the leader of the Bonanno Family, that he was not to take orders from me and our leadership, and that he was henceforth under the protection of the Commission.

This was a joke, but not a very funny one. Gaspar, by himself, could only be a puppet of Steve Maggadino's. Gaspar was Steve's brother-in-law (he had married Steve's sister, who had died many years before), he was family, someone who was always around for dinners on Sundays and holidays. Yes, he had wanted to be consigliere in our Family, but he was no conspirator.

We met again in a couple of days and at this meeting a vote was taken by all the group captains to condemn Gaspar for disobedience in failing to follow a direct order—namely, to appear at a meeting. The vote meant that he was sentenced to death. But there were elaborate protocols to follow. There had to be discussion first—and then another vote.

When someone is sentenced to banishment or even to death, it is understood the action taken will be irreversible. If someone is banished, that person—under pain of death—may never again make contact with anyone in our world. And anyone initiating contact with him will similarly be placed under a capital sentence. A death sentence has the weight of law behind it—just as it does when the state decides to execute someone. There are appeals built into both systems to minimize the possibilities of mistakes.

I argued to spare Gaspar. It had nothing to do with being softhearted. As far as I was concerned, his action was traitorous. But there was still a lot that was unknown, beginning with his personal motivations and also including the motivations of many people, such as Steve and the other leaders. Also, I was acting as a consigliere, as a representative of the common soldier—as opposed to the administration. It was my duty to give the common guy every chance. I wanted others, who might have been wondering about how I would fill my position, to see where I would come down in a crisis. Here was an example where everyone in the Family could see that I was prepared to take a genuine risk by standing up for Gaspar. I had to make clear that my position was nevertheless based on putting the Family's interests first.

My argument was that it was important for us as a Family to see where we all stood, that it was absolutely necessary to make sure that everyone understood this was more than a fight between quarreling Castellammarese—Steve Maggadino and my father. There were captains in our Family who were not Castellammarese. They weren't interested in who came from what town in Sicily. They were mainly interested in keeping our house in order without anyone from the outside pushing us around. In making an appeal for a stay, I proposed a committee of non-Castellammarese captains be formed to go and talk to Gaspar and bring him in for a meeting.

The proposal was accepted. Two of the oldest members, Angelo Caruso and Nick Alfanio—widely respected throughout our world—and a third man, Tony Cristi, were selected. If they succeeded in bringing him in, then everything would be forgotten; we would go on as before. But, then, if they failed, protocol required that they formally ask for a death sentence to be imposed. When they returned with word that Gaspar had rejected their invitation, Angelo and Tony—non-Castellammarese—asked that the formal punishment be carried out. I, and the rest of the Castellammarese, then had to go along. We next sent word of our decision to the Commission. Yes, they knew from the start that we would not accept changes in leadership in our Family dictated by them. But now they were being presented with a slightly different kind of scenario. We were following protocol. Gaspar's condemnation came not directly from leadership but through his failure to respond to a formal request made by an official Family committee. This may sound like hairsplitting, but it is not. The committee system in our world is sacrosanct—two men in agreement or two out of three in a situation where a vote may be required decide things as representatives of the whole. So what we were telling the Commission was that the decision to condemn Gaspar—and thus to reject their authority to interfere in our Family—was procedural, according to law, not personal.

My father soon afterward returned to the Midwest and then to Canada. What followed was predictable. All hell broke loose. On the street, everything was calm; below, there was turmoil, jockeying for position, power, authority. Within our Family, we had to ascertain just how many people were really with us and how many were going to follow the Commission's lead and go with Gaspar.

Supposedly, we had thirty days to elect new leadership, so the question of determining loyalty was urgent—even more so than it had been in the Magliocco Family. Aside from the threat of banishment—excommunication—which hung over every soldier's head in our Family, there was also an everyday, practical economic threat. We had people on the government payroll, out at the airports, the docks, in the unions who soon began reporting to us that they were losing their jobs. Clothing manufacturers were not getting their shipments; anyone who did not immediately indicate they were taking the side of the Commission wound up being harassed in one way or another. The Bonanno Family, at that point, had about four hundred members. About two hundred wound up staying firm, while the others didn't necessarily drop away, but, rather, drifted off into a separate faction, waiting and watching. Some of these people eventually wound up following Gaspar and the Commission, but some of them returned to us.

The next visible spasm occurred when, one day, I got a call from Sal Profaci, my brother-in-law, asking me to drop by and visit him at his house. "Uncle" Joe Zerilli, the Commission member and Family leader from Detroit, he said, was in town and wanted to see me. Zerilli's son was married to one of Joe Profaci's daughters, and the Bonannos and Profacis were tied by blood; it was possible this was a Sunday gathering with the relatives. But still I was wary. I asked him who else was going to be there. He said Joe Cerrito (a Family boss from San Jose), Sam DeCavalcante (a boss from New Jersey), and Angelo Bruno (a Commission member from Philadelphia).

The thing about my brother-in-law was that even when he tried to be devious, he was a weak conspirator.

"Did you say Uncle Joe was going to be there or Joe Zerilli?" I asked him. Sal didn't get my meaning.

"I said Uncle Joe Zerilli."

"No, no," I said, "am I going over there to see our uncle, or is this a business meeting with the Representante of Detroit—Joe Zerilli—and the other so-called Commission people?" Sal assured me the get-together was going to be strictly social. I told him then that I would be there. But as soon as I hung up, I immediately contacted Johnny Morales and told him what had just happened and asked him to accompany me to Brooklyn.

Obviously, this was no social gathering. The men were there as couriers from the Commission and their mission was to contact my father and have a sit-down with him.

By going to this meeting, I exposed myself to its protocol. I trusted their instructions would have to be limited, because my father was not in any way involved. My hunch was correct. They wanted to see me only because their first instruction was to get my father to appear before them. Fine. That was no problem for me. I answered them truthfully, that my father was not in town, that I believed he was in the Midwest or Canada on business, and that I would relay their request as rapidly as I could. We set a tentative date for a meeting two days hence, time enough, I assured them, for me, rather than they, to make an attempt to convey the information to my father.

I did locate him that night, in Wisconsin. He said he would return immediately, and he asked me to set up a meeting at a motel we owned near the airport in Newark. When I called Sal Profaci with the news, he sounded as if he had been struck dumb.

"What are you telling me?" I replied.

"Weren't you there yesterday?" I replied.

"Oh, that?" he said. "Well, that's not necessary anymore. Uncle Joe's gone back to Detroit and everyone else is gone, too."

Now, this was interesting. What was going on here anyway? The idea of the meeting was ostensibly from the Commission, hence important. But if that was so, why would the official delegation have so quickly taken off? It was obvious then that the Commission itself was divided, with not all of the members as serious as some others in wanting to restructure our Family.

There was no way to reach my father. He was somewhere between Wisconsin and New York, traveling by car. So, at the assigned hour, 10:00 A.M. the following day, a delegation of people from our Family—Johnny Morales, Joe Bayonne, my uncle Frank, Vito DeFilippo, and I—were all there to greet him at the Suburban Lodge motel in Newark.

When I told him what had happened, he laughed.

"This is a farce," he said, asking me to contact Sam DeCavalcante and to set up a meeting at one of our safe houses in Queens as soon as possible. I contacted Sam and told him my father wanted to see him, and he agreed. DeCavalcante, to us, was no more than a message bearer. His nickname in our Family was *"Porta Bilagge"* (literally meaning "bring baggage," it is Sicilian slang for "the porter"). Sam was a porter, not a power—but we needed him to deliver and carry "baggage" between us and the so-called Commission. To his credit, Sam agreed to go along with us when we rendezvoused with him at a bar in New Jersey and told him my father was waiting (where, we did not say) to meet with him. We had two cars outside. There were three of us—Joe Notaro, Joe Bayonne, and I—who got into one car with him. The two cars headed out.

Sam was clearly nervous as we made our way to the Lincoln Tunnel. He and I sat in the back. We made occasional small talk. At one point, when we emerged from the tunnel and turned uptown rather than in the direction of the Midtown Tunnel, he said, "I thought we were going to Queens."

"Relax," I said, "we're just going to pick up a couple of extra guys." We were, but Sam must have briefly felt as if he was being set up. When another carful of our people slid in behind us near Mr. Richard's Steak House on Forty-sixth Street in Manhattan, Sam wanted to know why we needed three cars to go to one meeting. I could feel the coldness and clamminess in his words. I just shrugged. (It's funny. I realize now, many years later, that people in other Families thought I was a little crazy in those days, going the extra mile to prove myself as someone more than just Joe Bonanno's kid. Sam's office was bugged by the FBI in that period, and when he was picked up shortly after this get-together, he told some associates that I was nuts: "The kid's a bedbug; there's no reasoning with him.")

When we got to the house in Queens, all our captains had assembled in the basement. My father was upstairs. We took Sam downstairs, had him wait while I went upstairs to make sure my father was ready to talk with him. I then went back down and got Sam and escorted him to the living room, where the two men greeted each other in the formal style of the old country, kissing each other on both cheeks. Then they sat, my father in a chair, Sam in a facing sofa. I brought them anisette and espresso. My father carefully explained that the Commission had no business intefering in his Family, that Gaspar DiGregorio was our Family's—not the Commission's—problem. He insisted that the Commission would have to send its delegation of three members if it wanted in any way to communicate with him on an official basis, then concluded by saying that if the Commission really wanted to meet with him, he would wait around for a reasonable amount of time to receive its delegation. Sam had nothing to say, only that he would try to arrange things.

Sam got back to us two days later to say that Zerilli was unavailable (he was at his farm in the north of Michigan) but that perhaps Angelo Bruno would be available. No, my father pointed out, an official committee, as Sam well knew, had to have at least two voting members present, along with a third party, in case tie votes needed to be broken. If that was not possible, then the meeting would have no standing and would be meaningless. We waited for another day or so but heard nothing more.

What was clear to all of us was that this clumsy move reinforced the sense we had that the Commission, as such, no longer existed. The different leaders who had at one time been members of the Commission were hardly in touch these days and less united about matters of policy. Though on the surface it seemed that Steve Maggadino was the most likely person behind all this, he could not have been acting entirely alone. The likelihood is that he was in some devious manner being manipulated by others, most likely Tommy Lucchese and his "squirrel," Carlo Gambino, and possibly Joe Colombo, leader of what was left of the Profaci Family. Their alliance made sense in that, with Steve induced to be a take-charge guy while they remained in the background, the balance of power in our world would be fatally tilted toward liberals and away from my father and what he stood for. These men clearly did not command wide-enough support to make a move like this openly—any more than they did when they tried to oust Joe Magliocco. But their intentions could not be ignored. The key figure in all of this, for us, had to be Cousin Steve Maggadino. What was goading him? Ostensibly, he was one of the conservative mainstays in the power balance against Lucchese, Gambino, and the other liberals. Why was he allowing himself to be drawn in and used by them?

Sometime during this period—I am not sure exactly when—Peter Maggadino, my father's cousin and his oldest friend in the United States, left Buffalo, where he had been a member of his cousin Steve's Family. Cousin Steve had mistreated him for years and Pete had had enough. When he sat down with my father, he told him what he knew.

Cousin Steve had seen my elevation as consigliere as part of a grand design by my father to become a "Boss of Bosses" in our world. As absurd as this idea was, Steve was obsessed by it, Peter said. Lucchese and his allies must have known that and used Steve's jealously for their own end.

Pete disclosed that after I was elected, Gaspar DiGregorio, whom I had wanted to run against me, had actually gone to Buffalo to visit Steve and complain to him about what had happened. Steve also believed that we were the prime movers behind Magliocco's plans to eliminate Lucchese and Gambino. Steve thought my father was trying to move in on territory that was his because of my father's business interests in Montreal and Quebec; Steve concluded my father was an "imperialist," planting flags all around the world. Steve Maggadino was living in another world—he knew how territory had been allotted—but he also had had a bee in his bonnet about my father for many, many years.

Steve's jealousy went back to the early days in Brooklyn. As the older cousin, he had more or less taken it upon himself to be my father's protector. There had been an incident where a local big shot had tried to muscle my father's bootlegging business. My father faced down this neighborhood bully, literally sticking a gun in the man's mouth and threatening to pull the trigger if he ever heard from him again. The big shot took his case to Maranzano himself. My father had to defend himself in a special "court." Steve appointed himself as my father's "attorney." But after Maranzano listened to my father's story, he brushed Steve aside and praised my father for his show of courage. Shortly thereafter, Steve had to watch from the sidelines as my father became Maranzano's top aide.

And then, over the years, my father's career had simply been more impressive than his cousin's. At one point, Steve's son was arrested on an embarrassing morals charge—which Steve, with all his Buffalo power, was unable to fix. My father interceded for him and the case was eventually dropped. It is not hard to imagine that Steve, while grateful for my father's help, was also humiliated by having to ask for it.

Everyone in the family knew Steve had been the prime mover behind the fiasco of Apalachin, and that he had gone about organizing the meeting only at a time when he knew his big-city cousin was out of the country. No one jumped to any conclusions over that. Steve was insecure—what could you do? And because Steve was family and because he wasn't part of the big-city scene, he was able to turn his private jealousies into plots and intrigues without making himself obvious. In political terms, Steve was old-world—in the same way my father was. He was as familiar with tradition and as devoted to it as my father. Both men revered history and both scorned the ease with which newer members seemed to sluff off their roots and traditions.

Yet, at the same time, Sicilian tradition might have better alerted my father to Steve's willingness to conspire against him. It must be emphasized that his ambitions at this point were personal and did not really reflect any sense of an active conspiracy involving Lucchese, Gambino, and other Americanized bosses. Lucchese was just too smart to expose himself in that way, to risk provoking an all-out war in which he might well wind up the loser. But just because Lucchese was that smart, it is easy to imagine how he might, all the while, have been massaging Steve's ego, stroking his vanity, whispering things into his ear about my father's questionable ambitions and inexplicable behavior.

And then, even more to the point, was the question of drugs. Though Steve himself always aligned himself with the Mustache Petes in the ban against drugs, members of his own Family were known to be involved in trafficking. And Steve, it is clear to me, knew it—and profited from it, as well. He had willingly benefited from something he genuinely opposed on principle but knew, on a practical level, he could not stop. At some point— when, I don't know—he had thrown in the towel and decided to go along. Lucchese and the Americanized leaders, at that point, became natural allies. Still, he was blood, my father's cousin.

In the middle of all this, my father was arrested in Montreal by immigration authorities. There are people I know who swear to this day that Steve was behind that, too, but I am not sure of that at all. The arrest just happened; it did not appear to be the result of prior planning. My father, in fact, probably was inadvertently responsible for it himself.

What occurred was that one day, because he had been in and out of the country so often, lawyers told him it would be helpful in his business contacts to have an immigrant's visa. Never intending to take up Canadian citizenship himself, and very much against my mother's advice, he went to an immigration office to fill out the necessary forms. He was then taken into custody—and whisked away without being allowed to make a phone call. For days, his status was unclear—other than that he had been arrested. Canadian authorities obviously knew who they had and, under pressure from U.S. officials, wrangled among themselves about what they wanted to do.

When my mother called to tell me my father had been arrested, I got lawyers on the case immediately; then I went up to Canada so I could get my mother out of there. She was not about to budge until she knew what was going on. When our lawyers had determined that a deportation hearing was being set, that it would take some time, and that, in any case, my father would be allowed no visitors in jail, we convinced her to return to the United States. She moved in with an aunt of mine in Queens, awaiting the outcome of the hearing.

In all, my father was in jail for almost ninety days. In that time, our lawyers and the Canadian authorities worked out a deal. They would allow him to return to the United States voluntarily—thereby enabling him to avoid any record of deportation—if he in turn dropped any legal challenge to his arrest. In fact, he had good reason to make a court challenge. The Canadians said he had lied on an entry visa form where he had been asked to state if he had ever been convicted of a crime. He had answered—

truthfully—in the negative. The Canadians pointed to a violation of a wages and hours statute that had been filed against him in 1941 by the federal government when he was a partner in a garment factory in Brooklyn. But the charge had been against my father's company, not against him personally. His company paid a four-hundred-dollar fine at the time. The U.S. Justice Department, through the Canadians, were grasping at straws.

But there was really no challenge to make here because, obviously, far more was in the works than his status as an immigrant, desirable or otherwise. My father accepted a deal because he knew by leaving Canada as a free person, he could not immediately be taken into custody across the border. When and if he was arrested or given a subpoena, he would then have the ability to stay at arm's length from the authorities by means of bail, preliminary court challenges, and the like.

The plan for his release was as carefully scripted as a military maneuver. Upon his release, he was to leave the country immediately, flying nonstop to Chicago, a city he had chosen because it was a hub that would more easily connect him to other points. His plan was to fly immediately on to Tucson and have my mother meet him there.

The day before he arrived, I flew to Chicago. I wanted to be at the gate to meet him and I also wanted to use the time to confer with Chicago leaders about the changes that had taken place in our Family. The night before my father's arrival, I briefed Paul Ricca and Tony Accardo on what had been going on. Ricca and Accardo were old-time leaders, predating Sam Giancana, who had come up through the ranks. Ricca, in particular, was a tough, enigmatic figure whom I wanted to read as best I could. He was smooth-looking, radiated wealth and breeding in a carefully groomed appearance. But he had a long history of violence going back to 1920, when he was released from jail in Italy after having committed something like a dozen or more murders. He was an old associate of Capone, much smarter than his gaudy boss, who moved into power after Capone was brought down. Ricca had backed us in supporting the Kennedys and had, in fact, been something of an associate of old Joe Kennedy's in Hollywood, where together they had invested in different motion picture companies, strong-arming some unions along the way. I counted on Ricca, particularly, to let me know where he stood with respect to our troubles.

We met at a restaurant in Melrose Park and the three of us spent the better part of an afternoon. Ricca and Accardo both said they had heard about my personal problems.

"You hear these things. They're unfortunate, Bill, but they happen. Too many people talk to too many other people," Ricca said, sipping mineral water and smoking a cigarette in what looked like a gold holder.

"My personal problems are under control; I am more worried about the government and my father," I said.

"What does he have to worry. He didn't do nuthin'," Accardo said.

"Knowing your father, they will have a hard time. I'm sure they will be able to do little more than harass him," Ricca said.

"That's what I expect," I said.

I left the restaurant and headed back to the hotel where I was staying, feeling more, not less, uneasy. I could not put my finger on it, but there was something in the ease with which they talked, expressed opinions, and seemed so willing to befriend me. *Watch their eyes.* Their eyes, all the while, were unsmiling, hard, distant. Suddenly, I thought of the airport gate at O'Hare and a chill sharp as a knife went down my spine. I would be by myself. There would be no protection at the gate. My father would step through the carrier tunnel from the plane into an open, public area.

I was at O'Hare two hours before the plane was scheduled to land. I walked up and down the terminal, in and out of shops and arcades, searching out faces, peering over the tops of magazines I had casually picked up, looking for any person, any movement that seemed suspicious.

Then the arrival announcement of my father's plane was flashed on the message board. I had a piece under my jacket and instinctively I reached for it just to be sure I would be able to withdraw it easily if I had to. I waited by the gate. Waited and waited. And then, as quickly as that, it happened.

Three or four cops suddenly materialized out of nowhere, positioning themselves at the exit from the carrier tunnel. They were joined by three or four plainclothesmen—FBI agents—and as soon as my father and his attorney, Lawrence D'Antonio, stepped off the ramp into the terminal, they swarmed around him. I pushed my way forward, trying to get to his side, but I was shoved back.

"This is for you, Joe!" I heard a voice call out. My hand was on my gun. I wanted to separate bodies, shove people to the floor, but I did not dare do it. Then my father caught my eye and called out to me. The knot of police and agents were still around him. He held up his hand. There was a document of some sort in it.

"Salvatore!" He called out, smiling. He said in Sicilian, *"L'menza figure* [a figurehead] has given me a subpoena!"

It was true. The document in his hand was a subpoena, an order to appear in New York before a grand jury the very next day. And so there was no attempt on his life, but no trip to Arizona, either. Our travel plans changed on the spot. After I embraced my father, I quickly hustled him away from the gate. I booked the first flight I could—an hour later—back to New York, the place my father loved to call "the Volcano," the place where there always seemed to be smoke and rumblings and where, now, the threat of a catastrophic eruption was all too obvious.

My parents, Fay and Joe, and my sister, Catherine, and I, in 1936. (© Farrentino)

Unless otherwise noted, all photos are courtesy of the Bonanno family.

My family on vacation at my grandfather's summer place, on Lake
Ronkonkoma on Long Island, in the early 1930s.

Dad and I at my
grandfather's place.

Even on vacation, Dad had every amenity.

Sparring with Tony Canzoneri, the boxing champion, at his family's resort in the Catskills.

My sister and I on the way to church, 1937.

Dad flanked by Johnny Morales *(left)* and Nick Guastella *(right)* in California, 1941.

Dad with Frank Garofalo on Willie Moretti's boat during one of the Commission meetings.

My father's cousin and close ally, Peter Maggadino, in the Army, 1941.

Whenever my father's associates came to see him in Arizona, we'd always have a big picnic.

At the Moulin Rouge in Hollywood with my dad, my brother-in-law Greg, Tony Mirabile, a business associate of my father's, and my kid brother Joe in his military school uniform.

A family dinner in Arizona after my engagement to Rosalie. Judge Evo DeConcini and his wife sat near my father at the head of the table. (© Ray Manley Photography)

My bachelor party, held at the Latin Quarter, was attended by several of the Profacis, as well as Albert Anastasia, Jr.

Our wedding party. (© Ida Portrait Studios)

Tony Bennett sang at the reception. (© Ida Portrait Studios)

Rosalie and I on our honeymoon, 1956.

Joe Magliocco, who lead the Profaci family, at his Islip, New York, home, where Rosalie and I lived in 1963.

Four generations of Bonanno men—my father, son, grandson, and myself—in 1987.

My daughter Gigi's
wedding, 1988.

Nowadays, my life
revolves around my
twelve grandchildren.

Dad and I celebrating the continuation of the Bonanno family tradition.

15

When my father stepped off the plane in New York, he stepped into a world bristling with rumor, innuendo, and threat. Every day, the newspapers were filled with crime stories, some of them outlandish, some—like a story that ran in the *Daily News* about mob infighting over the question of Joe Bonanno's leadership of his Family—suspiciously accurate.

Federal prosecutors were obviously pleased to have landed a big fish. They asked my father every conceivable question about his Family and about the activities of organized crime in general. He declined to answer all questions, citing the Fifth Amendment. When he was asked to give the names of his children and wife, he still took the Fifth. The exasperated prosecutor hammered away for three days. At one point, my father whipped out a three-by-five card, which he placed on his knee and glanced down at before making his replies. The prosecutor immediately demanded that the card be seized. My father quickly ripped it to shreds. A court officer bounded out of nowhere to retrieve the scraps, which were then carefully pasted back together. What suspense! The prosecutor asked that the writing on the card be read aloud. The officer held the card in front of him and intoned the words of the Fifth Amendment: "No person shall be . . . compelled in any criminal case to be a witness against himself." There were snickers of laughter in the courtroom. The prosecutor was red-faced, and the show continued. My father was finally dismissed but told to keep the U.S. Attorney's Office informed of his whereabouts in case the prosecutor wanted to recall him.

If this all seemed like a harmless piece of opéra bouffe, it really wasn't.

The authorities were serious in their pursuit of the mob. It had been a year since the Kennedy assassination and Robert Kennedy was still the attorney general. If anything, he was more relentless than ever in pushing his anticorruption campaign. It didn't take a rocket scientist to see that prior to the assassination of his brother, Bobby had concentrated his efforts mainly on the Teamsters. I have no way of knowing what kind of intelligence he had about his brother's death, but it was clear from his shift of focus that he was now targeting the individual Families themselves. There were five different grand juries empaneled in New York, for example—one for each Family.

One day, I and a couple of captains from our Family paid a visit to Roy Cohn, the attorney who, over the years, had maintained bridges between our world and the government. At the time, he was representing Lilo Galante, an ex–group leader of ours who had been convicted of drug trafficking and in whose case we maintained an active interest for a variety of reasons.

We met Cohn at his posh offices on the northwest corner of Fifty-seventh Street and Madison Avenue in Manhattan. Everything about the setting of Cohn, Sax and Bacon was meant to convey power and prestige. The walls of Cohn's office were decorated with dozens of celebrity photos— politicians, movie stars, athletes, religious figures, and people from our world. Cohn was an honorary fire chief and his hat was on display. He was the kind of guy who incorporated all that into his everyday life. He was driven around, for example, in a limo that had a fire siren mounted on it (Cohn was an appointed member of the New York City Fire Commission), which was sounded whenever he was whisked through the streets. He was a little guy, with a nose like a potato and eyes that looked as if they had been blackened in a prizefight. He lived alone with his mother and, so the story went, made a good chunk of his money from family-owned stock in Lionel, the company that manufactured toy trains.

We were only marginally interested in how Lilo's case stood. We went to see Cohn because we wanted, as best we could, to get a reading on what the government was up to, how far they were likely to go, how much heat there was beyond the obvious smoke coming from those grand jury probes. We were quite specifically concerned with the impact of Joe Valachi's ongoing and increasingly well-publicized assaults on the mob—and the repercussions they might have on us.

Cohn told us that he thought Valachi was being rewarded by the government financially and in other ways. He had been moved to a "safe" prison, was segregated from other prisoners, housed in quarters usually reserved for big shots, being fed to the public in a very controlled and planned way. It was as though the government were his press agent.

"But where does that leave us?" I asked. "Whom can we count on as a friend?" Cohn mentioned J. Edgar Hoover. But I said that Hoover no longer seemed reliable to me or to anyone else. He waved a hand. "You know how many FBI agents are assigned to 'organized crime'? About half a dozen," he said.

I was as aware as anyone that for years Hoover had followed a hands-off policy toward us, but times had changed, I told Cohn; anyone could see that. Ever since Valachi, Hoover, like everyone else, had had to go along with the tide.

"He hates Bobby," Cohn said matter-of-factly. "You know, he still won't use the term *Mafia,* he has an active, professional stake in believing there's no such thing." Cohn laughed, a dry cackle of a laugh, whose mixture was one part cynicism, one part mirth. "Wanna show you guys something," he said, getting up from his huge desk and strutting into another room, from which he returned in a moment carrying a manila folder.

"Ever see these?" he said, untying the stay and removing a batch of photos. There were seven or eight of them. Most were five-by-seven shots, a couple were eight-by-ten photos. They were all pictures of Hoover in women's clothing. His face was daubed with lipstick and makeup and he wore a wig of ringlets. In several of the photos, he posed alone, smiling, even mugging for the camera. In a few other photos, he was sitting on the lap of an unidentified male, stroking his cheek in one, hugging him in another, holding a morsel of food before his mouth in yet another.

"Louie [meaning Lewis Rosentiel] took most of these," Cohn said, "at a party on a houseboat in the Keys, 1948–1949, I think. There are one or two others taken earlier, maybe in the thirties. Who knows? Hoover knows about these, believe me; he's always been aware of what would happen if they ever got out."

I had heard there were pictures of some kind but had never seen them before. I had believed over the years that Hoover had been compromised because he had been an addictive gambler—a problem that had put him in association with people in our world going back to the twenties. I handed the photos back to Cohn.

"We could get a picture of him crossed-dressed with the Pope and I don't think it would do any of us any good anymore," I said.

Cohn shrugged. "You want him to see the pictures again?"

"Show them to him, but it won't do any good."

The irony or ironies was that 1964 should have been a banner year for us. It was a presidential election year and, from the start, the result was a certainty. Most of the country was scared to death of Barry Goldwater, the Republican candidate. Lyndon B. Johnson was a shoo-in—and he was someone who in better times would have been our man in Washington. LBJ and the Families in Dallas, New Orleans, and the Southwest had been connected for years. The reason he had been the first choice of so many of us in 1960 was because he was a known commodity. He was a friendly man; his door was always open. And if his door wasn't open, then the doors of his aides Billie Sol Estes and Bobby Baker were.

Weeks before the Kennedy assassination, Bobby Baker, LBJ's closest aide, had been forced to resign over charges of fraud, tax evasion, and theft. There was a huge uproar over that. LBJ had gone wild—not because Baker had betrayed him but because somehow he had let himself get caught with his hand in the till. We knew—and this was later backed up by a Washington lobbyist who talked to the press—that LBJ had offered Baker a million bucks to keep his mouth shut and take the rap. Baker did just that, but in no way did that indicate that LBJ had changed his stripes—or could have changed them if he had wanted to. The first time he ever got himself elected to the Senate, he did it by vote fraud. He had been on the take ever since. He took money from Jimmy Hoffa; he took it from corporate moguls—it didn't matter who it was. LBJ biographer Robert Caro wrote that "for years, men came into Lyndon Johnson's office and handed him envelopes stuffed with cash. They didn't stop coming even when the office in which he sat was the Office of the Vice President of the United States." If we had had our house in order, we would have been far more attentive to helping LBJ make sure he never forgot his roots.

But now there was just too much turmoil in our world. Whatever was going on in grand jury rooms, the danger in the streets was infinitely greater, far more unpredictable. As an opponent, the government moved

like any bureaucracy—slow as an elephant, plodding systematically along
in a direction even the half-blind would be able to pick up from a mile
away. Everything it did could be thought about, chewed upon. In the
streets, there was anarchy. The system we had taken so many years to
perfect was in shambles. There was no coordination among leaders to keep
the peace. We had always been a confederation of individual fiefdoms working in willing harmony. Not any more. Our motto for years might have
been Living Separately Together; now it was little more than Survival of
the Shrewdest.

Everything was in flux. We did not know, literally, whether the next
hour, the next day, the next turn of a street corner might mean the opening
shot of a war. We could not know for sure who were real friends and who
were false ones. Allegiances had suddenly become as sullen and unpredictable as the New York weather.

When my father was finally dismissed by the grand jury, he was under
orders to keep himself available for further grand jury appearances. The
government reserved the right to keep my father on a perpetual string, to
jerk it up and down at will, for whatever purpose. He was allowed to move
about freely, to do all the things any citizen, fully protected by the Constitution and the Bill of Rights, was allowed to do, but he was now unofficially handcuffed by the government.

Aside from my father's desire to spend time in Tucson, we all concluded
that for security reasons it would be best for him to stay away for a while
until things were better sorted out—or, rather, until we were better organized.

At that point, we decided to organize for war against various groups that
had separated from the Family leadership and had allegedly had the support
of the Commission. The media tagged these conflicts as the "Banana
Wars." We had no choice. We had a meeting of the administration, went
over what it was we knew—and didn't know—and decided that for our
own safety we had to prepare for a war we hoped we would not have to
fight.

We intended from the start to use only twenty or thirty people to do
the actual fighting. That may seem like a small number, but the best way
to weigh numbers in this case is to think of the way a guerrilla war is
fought. Great numbers of fighters are not required. What is required is

planning and a very elaborate support system so the fighters can always swim with the fish, fly in the midst of the flock.

In a Family of, say, four hundred, there will be only so many who are able to use firearms and other deadly weapons skillfully and reliably. Also, as is often the case in low-level guerrilla warfare, it is not economically feasible for too many people to leave their jobs and homes to fight. The fighters' families have to be supported while they are gone. An arsenal and a quartermaster depot have to be established.

We set out to make sure we had enough weaponry to carry on a protracted struggle. Each member, each fighter, of course, had his own weapon. My weapon of choice was a six-cylinder Smith & Wesson .38-caliber pistol. This was an unusual weapon because most .38s have five-cylinder barrels. But other weapons were needed, weapons that could be stored, distributed to other fighters if need be.

Over a period of time, we had weapons smuggled into the city. Hidden in crates of Canadian liquor, they were shipped in through Nova Scotia. Our people at the airports alerted us to shipments made by legitimate arms dealers to private groups or to government agencies. A crate stolen here or there gave us a variety of weapons: AK 14s with fifteen-cartridge clips, .45-caliber Thompson machine guns, shotguns—a particularly favorite weapon—that could be sawed off and hidden under the sleeve of a coat when walking down a street in broad daylight.

We had weapons' depots all over town: a dry-cleaning store on the Lower East Side, where the crates could be stashed behind walls of newly cleaned garments; bars in Brooklyn and Queens; a bakery shop in Queens where guns were carefully wrapped and buried among the sacks of flour.

We had a private gunnery range where our fighters could come together to practice and talk strategy. Hank Perrone, a close friend of mine in the Family, had a house out on Long Island, set back from the road, well protected. Day after day, over several weeks, he moved bags of dirt into his basement, lining the walls to soundproof them and provide for a target area.

We came in groups of twos and threes to Hank's house—never too many at a time—to spend an evening practicing. These were social occasions, too, but they were deadly serious. Sometimes what was deadly and what was merely good-natured fun could get inextricably mixed.

One night, Hank showed us a prize he had picked up from a friend that day: two sawed-off shotguns. They needed to be tested before they were approved for use. In order to prevent tracing from gun and ammunition stores, we often loaded powder into the casings ourselves. First, the guns had to be beveled properly, because if they were not, the powder charge, instead of discharging from the front of the barrel, could kick back, blowing up in your face. And then the charges themselves had to be accurate—not too little but not too much. Too much powder could mean an explosion. So on this particular night, Hank handed me one of the shotguns.

"Try it, Bill; it's a great gun," he said.

"Fuck you. You try it," I said. We both laughed. We argued like a couple of kids for a few minutes; then we resolved the problem by putting the gun in a vise, tying a copper wire to the trigger, and backing out of the room. I held the wire—and pulled. *BOOM!* It was perfect.

Then there had to be backup throughout the ranks. Doctors, garage mechanics, drivers, priests, storekeepers, and landlords all became necessary support people. We had to find safe houses and apartments. We had to assemble a fleet of cars, all with phony registrations, each to be used for different purposes. There were "crash" cars, cars that could be wasted in deliberate accidents to stop or slow traffic on streets where fighting or pursuit might occur; there were cars assigned for primary and backup actions, cars that might be used solely for the purpose of misleading eyewitnesses and police. We had to set up an elaborate communications system involving dozens of phone booths all over town, using a coding system that each soldier was required to memorize. All of that took time and patience. We took weeks locating places in different parts of town so that the four or five squads of fighters we had would be able to move freely—and unpredictably—around the city. It was important to make sure that the fighters never got trapped by their own daily routines.

We had to find just the right kinds of living quarters, too. Apartments were better than houses because they were easier to protect. An apartment building, by its nature, made stealth and secrecy of approach more difficult. We always selected apartments at the farthest end of a hallway, rather than near an elevator or staircase, so that we would have time to spot anyone coming toward the door. We always kept dogs in our apartments—not big watchdogs that might have made neighbors feel uncomfortable, but little ones, fluffy white poodles and floppy cocker spaniels, likely to make neighbors smile when you walk them but which would always bark whenever someone was in the hallway.

At the same time we were organizing to fight, we continued to live at peace. It was eerie. So long as a shot had not been fired—and we were not going to be the ones to start anything—life went on as before. While we had our squads, apartments, cars, stashes of weapons, and support crews all in place, we tried as best we could to appear in the world as though nothing was wrong.

I continued to go in and out of the city every day, conducting Family business as before. This in itself was a kind of test, a risky one, to see just what level of hostility we were facing from the opposition—the opposition being members of other Families and those who had been supposedly supported by the Commission. In our world when an edict of banishment has been given, that person might as well be dead, even if a death sentence has not been included. No other member is allowed even to exchange words with this person. If I, Johnny Morales, and my father were to be "removed" by the Commission, then, ostensibly, no one other than our own people would have anything to do with us. That turned out not to be the case.

Out on the street, I was as exposed as I could be. I went to all the familiar street corners, stores, social clubs. I was in my "office" at the Wentworth every day (never at the same time). I came and went from East Meadow almost like any other junior executive on his way to Madison Avenue, with this exception: I really didn't know if I would return home alive at the end of the day.

People met me, talked to me, did business with me as before. I ran into group captains from other Families, sometimes even bosses like Gerry Catena (standing in for Vito Genovese) and Carmine Gribbs, and they had no problem openly associating with me. In fact, at one point, we all teamed up to do a little business together.

At that time, there happened to be a chambermaids strike at the Waldorf-Astoria Hotel. The chambermaids were hired and fired at a whim; they were terribly paid, badly treated—and they wanted to unionize. They approached the Teamsters, who approached us, and we all got behind them.

We had a meeting in midtown one day, leaders from three of the Five Families, and we decided to send a representative over to the Waldorf to see if we could get some favorable action on behalf of the chambermaids. Joe Notaro, from our Family, contacted the business agent of a New York Teamsters local, advised him of our support of the chambermaids, and urged him to make an appointment with Waldorf officials. This was done.

The business agent had dinner with us after his meeting and told us what had happened.

"I said to them, 'You don't let us organize the chambermaids, that's okay. But beginning next week, you don't get a single delivery of food or linens. No garbage gets picked up. Nothing moves in; nothing moves out.' Then they told me, look, they never thought chambermaids were Teamsters, but if they thought they were, that was okay with them!" We all laughed.

I couldn't begin to figure out what we were up against then.

It might have been expected that ordinary soldiers, the "little people," would want to keep their distance, but I had no problems there, either. I remember that my daughter Gigi was born around the time all this began. One day, I happened to mention that I had three sons but that having a daughter now meant that I had to go out and get clothes for her. One of the people standing around was a guy we all called "Crazy Louie"—someone from another Family. He suddenly volunteered. "Hey, let me take care of it." A couple of days later, when I got home, Rosalie was beside herself. She told me to go downstairs and look in the basement.

What I saw there was a lifetime's supply of girl's clothing, ranging from baby things to teenager's stuff—enough to outfit a good-sized store. Rosalie explained that when the doorbell rang that morning, she had answered it and there were these people with a huge truck. They asked her if she was Mrs. Bill Bonanno. The question scared her a little, but she nodded to them.

"Then they took the next two hours moving all of that into the house," she said.

My Family and others remained close with the people who owned and operated Progresso, the food company. They might have been warned to keep their distance from us. Obviously, they had not been. One day, Progresso sent a van to the front door. It was the same thing: in honor of our new baby, a lifetime's supply of Tuscany peppers, spaghetti, minestrone, olive oil, the works.

What was I to make of all this? It was hard to believe that a decision of any kind had been made by the Commission, yet it was clear that Gaspar DiGregorio was acting on orders from that body—in whatever way it was then constituted. All of us in leadership concluded there was as much confusion as determination, as much ambivalence as purpose coming at us. But we were wrong. Because no one took action against us, because we were banished but, clearly, not banished, we were simply unable to see, to interpret anything clearly. All the while, the wheels were turning

My father was recalled by the grand jury in October 1964. What they wanted from him was anyone's guess, but one day he came east and moved in with Rosalie and me and the children. This immediately created a security problem.

My father tried to keep his movements in and around the city to a minimum. I tried to keep mine separate from his so would-be assassins would be unable to kill two birds with one stone. Our house was a guarded fortress. And this, I soon saw, was a mistake—physically and psychologically.

My father was restless and irritable. Rosalie was increasingly withdrawn and uncommunicative and I was increasingly irritated with the whole setup. I was also aware that irritation and personal considerations at this point could be much too distracting. I decided then that it would be wisest for me to move into one of our safe apartments with my uncle Frank. From there, I could keep a handle on security arrangements. I shuttled back and forth, had dinner with my family regularly, saw and played with my kids— but I also kept at a distance, in hiding, able to act as I needed to.

My father, no doubt, was a difficult guest. He had his own people around him and his own willingness to express strong opinions. I remember that the day before my father was scheduled to appear in court, we had an argument of sorts on the phone. He told me he was leaving the house that afternoon, by himself, to travel into the city so he could have dinner with his lawyer, William Maloney. He intended to stay over at Maloney's apartment that night.

"Why are you doing that?" I asked.

"Because I gotta be in court in the morning," he said.

"I don't want you to go anywhere unless you have people with you," I said.

"I go where I want when I want," he said. The snap of authority in his voice made it clear that I could say nothing more.

I remember this episode only because of what followed. My father went out to dinner with Maloney that night. It was raining, and after dinner the two men were driven back to Maloney's Park Avenue apartment building in a cab. When they got there, the cab stopped, and Maloney stepped out of the car first and began walking quickly toward the canopy of his building. Then my father got out of the car. Before he was able to step from the gutter to the curb, two men came out of the shadows, unseen, and suddenly seized him by the arms. My father let out a cry. Maloney wheeled around. A shot was fired, whining off the pavement, kicking up a shower of sparks, and driving the attorney backward, toward the building. In a matter of seconds, my father was hustled to a waiting car, a door was opened, and he was shoved into the backseat. The two men who had jumped him got into the car, front and back, doors were slammed, and the car roared off down Thirty-sixth, around a corner, and out of sight.

I was in the safe apartment at that moment, lazily watching television. Uncle Frank was reading a book or a magazine, stroking a small dog we kept in the apartment.

We went to bed early that night, and the next morning I heard Frank get up at dawn to walk the dog. He was gone for a while as I stumbled around and made coffee. I was still in a fog when Frank returned, literally bursting through the door. He had a stack of newspapers with him, which he threw down on the kitchen table.

"Wouldja fucking look at this!" he cried.

Because I was groggy, it took me a couple of seconds before I saw the first headline. It hit me full force, like a wave of ice water: MOB KIDNAPS JOE BANANAS—CALL HIM DEAD.

16

Maloney's account of what had happened was all over the papers. I got on the phone to him immediately. I wanted to know every little detail he could remember so that I could see if there might be some clue worth picking out and pursuing. Even more, I wanted to check his state of mind. I weighed everything he said, waiting for him to contradict himself. Obviously, I didn't trust him. I thought it was entirely possible that he himself might have been a participant in the kidnapping. I kept pressing him for details: What did the men look like? Where were they positioned when he saw them? Was my father struggling? If so, how could they, as Maloney reported, have held him and shot so carefully at his feet? The lawyer's answers were all coherent and full of distress. He appeared to be genuinely upset.

The phone in our apartment soon began ringing off the hook as different captains began calling us to go to predesignated pay phones. I don't know how much time I spent answering these calls, then making others, but I learned nothing new. I ordered all our front-line squads to break off contact with their families and friends immediately and await further instructions.

Over the next days, I met with different captains in our organization. Each of them had been under orders to scour their territories for any clue, any stray word they could come up with from the different soldiers, bookies, vendors, shopkeepers, hangers-on out there on the street. One of our captains, Joe Notaro, supplied the first real lead.

Joe came forward, saying that he might in some way have been responsible for my father's kidnapping. He mentioned that on the day of the kidnapping he had been in a car with another captain and that they were talking about my father's plans for that evening. Notaro said that his driver, a gofer in the organization, had undoubtedly heard every word that had been spoken—and that this driver, "Little Nicky Glasses," was now missing also. The reason Notaro felt he was responsible was because he had just found out—from the street—that Little Nicky was now under the protection of Gaspar DiGregorio.

That was news all right. Now the question was, How much had there been between DiGregorio and the leaders of the other Families?

A few days following the kidnapping, a gofer in the Gambino Family named Arnie Bigelow, who had the street name "Smiles," let slip that he had heard my father was alive and well. One of uncle Frank's men brought Bigelow in and we spent a little time with him. We blindfolded him, put him in the back of one of our cars, and took him to Hank Perrone's house. After a couple of hours, it was clear he knew nothing. False start. Just a rumor, one more lousy rumor in a rising windstorm of rumors.

We took Bigelow back to Manhattan—alive—and dumped him out on a sidewalk in front of Ripley's Believe It Or Not on Forty-second Street. He was strongly advised not to play fast and loose with the truth in the future.

I thought constantly of Rosalie in this situation. From the time we heard the news, I had not spoken with her. I had word passed to her that I was okay—but no more. I was sure she would be able to manage. I wanted to spend time with her, but I could not take the chance. Even though there was an unwritten law in our world that the spouses and children of members were never to be harmed in a time of conflict, I did not want her implicated in this situation. A phone call, a visit from a soldier, a piece of mail—anything that might have established a link between us—would have exposed her unnecessarily. If it had not been before, our house was now under twenty-four-hour surveillance for sure. The press had besieged the place. Every day, I read stories in the papers about the kidnapping and its aftermath. There were stories about Rosalie. In one report, she responded to the incessant demand for interviews by speaking with reporters from an open window in the house. The story said she looked as though she had been crying.

And it was likely that the authorities and members of other Families were staked out side by side, basement to basement, parked car by parked car, waiting and watching to pick up something. There was also a good chance that the police, executing a search warrant, might enter the house at any time—and there find guns, debugging devices, personal and business correspondence.

We were mainly confined to living through interminable days in our safe apartments. We passed the time reading the papers, watching TV, receiving reports from our people in the field. We learned nothing, did nothing. I was left with my fears—and my knowledge of history. I kept thinking about the last time a Don disappeared. Don Vincenzu Mangano, my father's old friend, leader of his Family from the time of Maranzano, a man who had bounced me on his knee and had told me stories in Sicilian, gone in a dispute with Albert Anastasia in 1950. For days, no one knew anything. There had been the same kind of panic then, the same kind of confusion. Then one day, a body was found on a street in Brooklyn. It was Mangano's brother, left in the gutter like a dead dog. There was symbolism in this act, obscure but meaningful symbolism. To be murdered and dumped in the street was to die without respect or honor. But Mangano was shown respect by being kidnapped and killed without a trace of his body ever turning up.

I could only take so much of this. After awhile, I simply had to get away. I decided that a change of scenery was in order in lieu of going crazy. I literally took my men for a ride. "We're gettin' out of here," I told my uncle Frank.

Ten of us piled into three cars and drove upstate, planning to rendezvous at a motel outside Albany. Once there, we decided to go on, to keep driving and driving. We drove through parts of Massachusetts, New Hampshire, Vermont. Each night, we settled down in motel rooms and talked and watched TV. To relieve the somber mood we were living with, we would often tune into shows like *The Untouchables* and *Perry Mason*— shows that so ludicrously distorted our world, we actually found that we could laugh to relieve the tension.

On one of the episodes of *The Untouchables,* mobsters burst into a roadside speakeasy and began spraying the place with machine-gun fire. Shelves full of booze exploded; bodies fell left and right faster than stalks of corn at harvest time. There were close-ups of the mobsters, their lurid features jumping up and down in the light from their firing guns. Then the scene cut to a young boy and girl dying in each other's arms. She was already gone; he was saying they would see each other again in heaven. Romeo and Juliet—and one hundred or so other patrons—wiped out by these mad-dog killers. It was so ludicrous, it was funny—for a moment or two.

But no matter what we did, I could not shake the feelings of uncertainty and foreboding that kept clutching at my throat, twisting my insides. I was tense and restless all the time. And so were the other men. We all wanted to do something, to make something happen, but we were as helpless as passengers on a life raft adrift in the middle of an ocean.

Then suddenly one evening, I remembered something. A long time ago, my father and I had devised a plan that if ever we found ourselves cut off from each other, in danger or having to lie low, we would contact each other by placing a phone call at a set time to a predesignated phone booth not far from my home on Long Island. I remembered this with the force of a physical blow—I could not believe I had overlooked it. The plan had been to place the call on Thursdays at exactly 8:00 P.M. So far, I had missed three Thursdays, including the day after the kidnapping. It was Wednesday. I told the men we were going back to New York immediately.

When I went out to the phone booth the next night, I wanted to be sure that I was not obvious, so I waited nearby in a car with uncle Frank, then got out and walked up to the booth at precisely the time the call would have been placed. I waited for what seemed like an eternity but was less than five minutes. The phone did not ring. My planning was futile, as was everything else. Adding to the sinking feeling I had was that my home was so close; my wife and children were within minutes of a reunion I longed for but could not yet bring about. It was back to the apartments.

I went to the phone booth week after week. November turned into December, autumn into winter. This part of my life had become so regular that I was almost like Pavlov's dog when Thursdays came. I seemed to reach a peak of excitement and anticipation on Thursdays, only to be let down once more when at the end of the day the phone remained silent.

Then came Thursday, December, 17, 1964.

I remember the date, the look and feel of the day, as though it were yesterday. It was cold enough for your fingers to snap off, for your face to freeze into brick. We got to the phone booth that night, as usual, about five minutes before eight o'clock. I rolled the window of the car down and remember that I resisted the urge to turn the heat blower higher because I did not want the noise of it to drown out the ring of the phone if it should ring, a ring I had never heard. Then it was eight o'clock—and once more there was silence.

And then suddenly, just like that, the phone rang. I exploded out of the car; I could feel the force of my body shaking the phone booth as I closed myself into it. I picked up the receiver and held it to my ear. To my dismay, the voice was not my father's, not even a man's. A woman's voice intoned words, slowly, carefully, asking me if this was the number of the phone I was holding. It was. The next thing I heard was the sound of coins being placed in a phone box on the other end and then a voice—a man's voice, but not my father's.

"Hello, Bill?"

"Yes?" I said. "Who is this?"

"Never mind, just listen carefully. Your father is all right. Do nothing. You'll probably see him in a couple of days."

"How do I know he's okay?" I asked.

"How do I have this number?" the voice replied.

"But wait a minute!"

"Just don't make waves; everything's okay. Just sit tight and don't do anything."

Before I had a chance to say anything else, the line went dead. I hit the cradle of the phone, once, twice, half a dozen times—I don't remember. I shouted into the receiver, but there was only dead air. I finally hung up, slumping against the wall of the phone booth. I could feel my heart pounding under my overcoat. It was only when I felt I had control over my own body that I opened the door of the phone booth and walked back to the car.

I told Frank what had just happened. He made me slow down, play the conversation back to him as best I could, word for word. All I could think of was that my father might really be alive after all, and that I might be seeing him again in just a few days.

I have never been a drinking man, but I asked Frank to accompany me to a bar where we could just sit for a while and let go. But my uncle was more clear-eyed than I. No, he cautioned, the words of the message were clear: *Don't make waves. Sit tight.* Frank started telling me something about the *Odyssey,* a book I hadn't read since grade school. At first, I couldn't understand why he was rambling that way and I was annoyed. But he persisted—until I connected the names, Telemachus, Odysseus, father and son locked in a mythic journey of separation and reunion. When Odysseus had been away for so long and then returned to his home, which had been overrun by enemies, Telemachus was not free simply to welcome him with open arms. Absence had allowed enemies into their house. There still was the very basic problem of enemies on one's own turf.

"But the call, Frank, the call. Somebody called us on that line; only my father knew that number. What do you make of that?"

"I don't," Frank said, "because I don't know any more than you do. I don't know anything—yet."

But I could not keep from acting, I could not simply sit tight. The first thing I wanted to do was make sure that others in our organization knew what had happened. I especially wanted my father's attorney, Bill Maloney, to know. If my father was returning, there were sure to be immediate legal problems. He had been kidnapped just before he had been scheduled to make a grand jury appearance. Regardless of what we knew, the law believed he was a fugitive. There was a warrant out for his arrest now. I had to smooth the way for his return—and I also now needed to make amends of a sort to Bill Maloney.

I had treated him like a leper. I had continued to believe he was implicated in my father's kidnapping. Whenever he passed word that he was trying to reach me, I had ignored him. Different mutual friends with whom we were in touch would tell me that Maloney really wanted to talk with me, but my answer was always the same: that unless he had something to tell me about my father's disappearance, I would be in touch with him only when I felt the time was right. I knew I had made Maloney feel like dirt— and now I wanted to make sure he was still on board.

I called him early the next morning. I stayed on the phone with him only long enough to give him the number of the pay phone I was calling from and told him to leave his office, go to a pay phone himself, and call me back. I was pleasant and friendly with him—but brief, because I wanted to take no chances on being overheard. He was overjoyed to hear from me because he had been worried about my disappearance, too, he said. I politely cut him off, telling him only what I had been told on the phone, that my father was alive and that I would probably be seeing him in a couple of days—that was it. I told Maloney then that I would be back in touch as soon as my father made contact with me.

How I wish I had listened to Uncle Frank. If ever there was an instance when I learned that I was still young and wet behind the ears, this was it. Just *Sit tight, and don't do anything.* Yes, those were the words. Frank understood them and I did not. After I spoke to Maloney, I called in other captains in the Family and told them what had happened.

Frank and I spent the weekend in the apartment; we played cards, watched TV, walked the dog, read the papers, waited, waited, waited. I remember doing the Sunday *Times Magazine* crossword puzzle—and giving up because I was just too restless. When would the next contact be made? How would my father contact us when he did reappear? Would he be turned out on a street somewhere? I couldn't imagine him walking up to the front door of our home in East Meadow—with all the world still watching—and ringing the bell. Where would he go, and what would he do?

I turned into a cook. It was all I could do to keep my hands and my brain occupied. Chop mushrooms, dice garlic, slice tomatoes, cut an eggplant, salt the slices, let them bleed till they could be floured. Frank slept. As always, the television was on. I kept thinking obsessively about that first phone call. I read all the newspapers I could lay my hands on, did the crossword puzzles, watched TV, cooked, cleaned house. Frank slept. I think he was blessed with a nervous system that enabled him to deal with edge-of-the-cliff situations far better than I. That was one of the main reasons I trusted him so much in tough situations.

I don't remember exactly now what it was I was watching on the tube—it may have been a football game, though I wasn't much of an eastern football fan—but in any case, I was in the kitchen cooking up a sauce for dinner that evening when I heard an announcer suddenly say, "We interrupt this program to bring you a special news bulletin."

I instinctively turned down the flame on the stove, wiped my hands on an apron I was wearing, and walked back into the living room, anticipating some momentous foreign-policy development.

"Hey, Frank wake up. Here comes World War Three," I said to my uncle, who opened his eyes and pulled himself to a sitting position on the sofa.

"What's up?" he asked blearily. We both turned our eyes toward the TV.

When the words *Special Bulletin* blinked out and an image appeared, it wasn't the face of the President we were looking at but, incredibly, a still photograph of my father. With that, an announcer's voice explained that Mafia boss Joseph Bonanno, missing and thought to have been murdered in gang warfare, had been found alive and well and, according to his attorney, William Maloney, was going to appear before a federal grand jury in lower Manhattan Monday morning at 9:00 A.M.

Suddenly, my uncle Frank was standing next to me. I could not believe what I was hearing! We both listened as the announcer said that Maloney had released a statement earlier in the day disclosing news of his client's whereabouts and plans to appear in court. Then there was a cutaway to an impromptu news conference held in front of Maloney's apartment building—the site of my father's kidnapping. When Maloney's face and voice came on the screen, I screamed, instinctively, as though I had been hit or had just seen someone I love get hit.

"OH SHIT!" I shouted. "What the fuck does he think he's doing!"

My rage at him—and myself for having compromised my father's safety so foolishly—became so great that I picked up a heavy glass ashtray and fired it at the television set. The screen exploded, sending a shower of splintered glass all over the living room floor. Frank and I both stood there, momentarily amazed as the interior of the TV set literally disintegrated before our eyes.

"That fuck is a dead man!" I said.

"Find out what he knows," Frank said, "find out what he knows."

It did not dawn on me that Maloney might actually be in possession of further information, more than we had. Eventually, I calmed down: then, with Frank at my side, we walked outside, down the street to a pay phone, where I put in a call to Maloney's home.

Maloney sounded pleased to hear from me. I cut to it immediately.

"Has my father been in touch with you?"

"No," Maloney said. "Has he contacted you?"

I paused, feeling my stomach muscles twist.

"You went on television and told the world my father is going to appear in court tomorrow morning at nine A.M.? Who authorized you to make such a statement?"

"Bill, you told me that your father—"

I cut Maloney off immediately. "Look, you put my father's life in jeopardy by what you did, you understand? I hold you responsible for that."

"Bill, I didn't do anything—"

"And except for the fact that I hold myself responsible for confiding in you in the first place, you'd be off the case, permanently, you understand?"

Maloney cleared his throat, clearly upset.

"Bill, I swear to you, from our conversation, I believed your father was coming in—today or tomorrow. I wanted to preempt the law, let them know your father was voluntarily coming in. . . ."

"Listen," I said, my fury on a taut leash, nearly breaking, "you do not speak for my father or for my family unless you are contacted and specifically told to do so, you understand that?"

"Bill, I swear—"

"You understand?"

"I understand," Maloney said.

"Good," I said, slamming the receiver back into its cradle.

It was cold out and I was shaking. Frank was waiting nearby. I explained what had just happened. We walked on in silence, around the block, once, twice, maybe three times before heading back upstairs. I was too upset to continue cooking, even to eat, for that matter. Frank tried to calm me down. He told me that whatever Maloney thought he was doing, in the end it wouldn't affect my father's safety.

"If your father was alive Thursday night and you were told he was coming back, at some point he will."

"They told us to do nothing, remember? Weren't you the one who pointed that out to me?"

Silence. There really was nothing to say. The days following were the longest in my life. I heard nothing from my father or his captors. Thursday was Christmas Eve. Frank and our other leaders had made careful plans to spend time with their families in locations where they would be unobserved. I lied to Frank when I told him that I, too, was going to spend time with my family. I told him I was planning to meet Rosalie and the kids at one of her relative's homes—but there was no way I could do this. Having blundered as I had already, I was not going to complicate anyone's security further. I knew that Rosalie's movements would be as carefully monitored as anyone's in our world. I did not even make an attempt to let her know that we would be unable to get together.

Instead, I got into my car and headed out to that phone booth again so that I would be there at eight o'clock, though I well knew what to expect. When the moment came and the phone remained silent, I sat for a couple of moments and then, having no real idea of what I was doing, headed the car toward Manhattan. I got there perhaps a half an hour to forty-five minutes later. There was little traffic. I was aware as I drove through the streets of all the Christmas lights in apartments and of the people gathered inside around their trees, maybe preparing to go out to midnight Mass. I parked my car somewhere near Times Square, got out, and just began walking. I thought of my father, my wife, my children. I wondered what each of them was doing at that precise moment, what they were feeling, what they were planning for that night and the next day. Christmas in our home was always the high point of the year. It did not matter what was going on; everyone got together at my father's house or at my aunt Marion's. We'd get together for days, exchanging gifts, sharing meals and stories. There was no backing out. You had to be there; you had to take part. Whether you were eight or eighty, the hum of conversation, the songs, bright lights, and delicious smells from the kitchen were part of a life all of us shared.

I stopped before different shop windows, all decorated with lights and tinsel. I remember passing a bookstore and pausing to look at different titles displayed in the window. There was a book, whose title I forget, with a picture of President Kennedy on the cover. I studied his face for a moment or two, thinking about all that had happened in the last year. I thought of his family and the picture of his little son saluting during the funeral. Whatever else I thought about JFK, I thought about him now as a father and a son, as a man who had felt called upon to answer to his father's dream of power. I wondered if he would have appreciated the deft way his successors had managed to limit the investigation into his murder. That was the game of power, the same one he had been into till the moment of his death.

I don't know how long I walked the streets. At one point, I saw a cop on horseback and almost simultaneously I remembered I was carrying a gun. The gun was like an extra limb, strapped to a holster under my arm.

I no longer thought about it, but now I wished I had remembered to leave it in the car just in case, unlikely as it would have been, I was stopped and questioned.

I passed the Astor Hotel—and I was tempted to go inside and walk around, perhaps even to go and look at the ballroom where the reception and dance for Rosalie and me had been given following our wedding. But I kept walking. It was still before midnight. I walked up to a Western Union office a few blocks away. I went inside and arranged to send Rosalie a bouquet of flowers—along with holiday greetings. Then I walked back to my car, got in, and began driving—again with no real destination in mind.

I drove around the island of Manhattan, past the piers and wharves where so many of our people worked. The lights on the Jersey side of the Hudson looked like they came from another country. Somewhere out in the dark harbor there were ships on their way to unknown destinations—even though it was Christmas Eve.

When I drove around lower Manhattan and up the East Side, I decided to head back to Queens. I don't know what time it was exactly when I got to my neighborhood, but when I parked the car and got out, I could see lights blazing in window after window. When I reached the door of my apartment, I heard the television—the new one we had just purchased—and for a moment, I was unsure if Frank was home. When we went out, we always left the TV on to discourage would-be intruders. The apartment was empty.

I sat around watching the tube for hours. Finally, sometime near dawn, I had had enough and I went to bed. When I got up a few hours later, it was Christmas Day—and I simply could not bear it. I wanted to move the day off the calendar, out of the year, beyond the limits of the city and my mind. I decided then and there it was time for another trip.

I went out to a pay phone and called two of my soldiers and asked them to accompany me on a trip across country. I gave them the option of declining, because it was Christmas, but I also knew that these particular men were loyal and could always be counted on—for anything, anytime. Less than an hour later, we set out for Arizona—my home, my father's home.

17

I called ahead before we reached Tucson to let our people—like Charlie Battaglia, who had been running things in my absence—know that we were going to be in town and that arrangements should be made for us. I was told there had been no messages. Even so, I could think of no better place to be between Christmas and New Year's. I believed, in my heart, that my father would turn up here.

Once I was home, I tried as best I could to occupy myself. I took long drives out into the countryside, up into the mountains. I spent leisurely evenings with friends and then returned to the motel, a place called Spanish Trails, where the three of us were staying.

A day or so prior to New Year's Eve, a few days before piling back in the car and heading east again, I was walking near the motel on a solitary road, enjoying the mild winter sun and the dry desert landscape around me, when—I am not sure why—I suddenly had the feeling I was under observation. I stopped and quickly wheeled around. There was nothing. I walked to the motel and told my friends what had happened. They didn't think anything of it. But I always followed hunches of this kind. I went outside again and, quite deliberately, walked around in front of the motel so that if anyone was looking for me, they would see me, out in the open. I know that was dangerous, but I had my friends out there with me, at a strategic distance, also watching. We saw nothing.

I decided after this that I had been mistaken and turned my thoughts toward New Year's Eve. I needed a haircut, a trim, so I decided to try out a barbershop located at the front of the motel. I had one of my drivers accompany me to the shop. He sat off to the side, leafing through magazines.

While I was sitting in the chair, the barber casually asked me about the commotion going on out front. I didn't know what he was talking about. I looked up in the mirror in front of me and saw a number of police cars and other unmarked cars pulling into the driveway.

Oh shit, I thought, I've had it. At the same time, because it was impossible to be sure and because there was always hope in uncertainty, I made no move to do anything. The barber forgot about my haircut. He was fascinated by the goings-on in the driveway. He began chattering about it.

"Hey, hey, lookit that, will you? Lookit how many of 'em there are." When he finally walked back to the chair where I was sitting, he said, "I wonder who they're looking for."

I answered, "I think they're looking for me."

The barber laughed. He began again to snip at my hair. Then the front door opened and several FBI agents walked in, headed by an FBI agent I knew named Kermit Johnson, who had been on my case for some time. I said very pleasantly, "Hiya, Kermit, howya doin'?"

"Good, Bill, how are you?" he replied. He walked up to me and said very discreetly, "Hey, Bill, you don't have a gun on you, do you?"

"Come on, Kermit, you know me—I'm not that type."

At this point, I thought the barber was going to have a heart attack. He stared at me and said, "Who are you anyway, mister?"

I answered him. "Just a poor guy trying to make a living."

I turned straight to the agent. "Look," I said, "are you gonna let me finish my haircut, or you gonna take me in looking like a fool?"

The agent told the barber, "Go ahead, finish up. It's okay." The poor barber nodded, but his hands were trembling so hard that it felt as if the scissors were bouncing off my head when he went back to work.

When the haircut was finished, I was placed in a patrol car and driven downtown to the old county jail. I wasn't charged with a crime of any kind—no one had accused me of anything—but I was placed under arrest as a material witness for the New York grand jury investigation of my father's kidnapping. Because this was a federal grand jury, I was not beyond its jurisdiction; the law permitted my arrest and return to the location of the grand jury. I was placed under $25,000 bail, but now I was on a leash—held by the government. I was given a subpoena and a date, January 5, when I had to appear in New York. What I did with my time was fine—so long as I showed up when and where the law said.

I had no time to drive back. I flew to New York, booked my flight into Newark because I thought it would be the least likely place to draw a crowd, and discovered that with the government monitoring my every move there was no way I could hide from anyone or anything. There were photographers and reporters swarming all around me when I got off the plane. I had to fight my way through them with the attorney I had contacted, Al Krieger, who had agreed to meet my plane and drive me back to the city, directly to his office.

I had been subpoenaed for one purpose—to find out my father's whereabouts. Bill Maloney's press conference—and my own stupidity—really did have consequences. And I was on the receiving end of them.

At Krieger's office on lower Broadway, we planned a strategy for my appearance. We agreed the smartest thing for me to do—the only option I really had—was to use my constitutional privilege against self-incrimination. But, Krieger explained to me, the government had gotten smarter in their ways around and through the Fifth Amendment. Their new tactic—which hadn't yet cleared the many court challenges that were already in the pipeline—was to grant different forms of immunity to different witnesses. One form was called "transactional immunity," whereby a specific transaction—covering one limited activity, like the kidnapping of my father—was protected, therefore allowing the witness to reveal, in a very limited way, information that might otherwise be incriminating. Conditional immunity was similar but wider in scope.

When I went before the grand jury, I gave them my name and nothing else. To each succeeding question, I pleaded the Fifth. At one point, I was asked, "Are you going to take the Fifth to every question we ask you?"

I replied, "I refuse to answer on grounds of the Fifth Amendment." The prosecutor wasn't miffed so much as he was baffled by my answer.

"What's the harm in answering that?" he demanded.

"I take the Fifth to that!"

My reasoning, and the reasoning of so many others—including my father—who took this tack, was simple. If you answer any one question, no matter how innocuous, you open a door. Once one door is open, there are all the others beyond it. You cannot then expect to control what happens. If the prosecutor asks you, for example, whether or not you have children and you decide to answer yes or no, they then are entitled to ask you any other questions that might pertain, no matter how far-fetched. Children? Did my children, for example, know anything about their grandfather's kidnapping? If I lied, I would be subject to prosecution for perjury. If I answered truthfully that they did not, I was then bound to say what I knew—and if I was in any way evasive, then I could be held in contempt.

But by my consistently refusing to answer questions, the government was finally forced to go before the judge and ask for permission to grant immunity. This was a time killer. In order for the grant to be okayed, Washington had to be consulted and then, when the matter was reviewed and the order approved, there had to be a hearing.

The government finally got its grant of conditional immunity and the ball was back in my court. With my lawyers, I still decided to answer no questions about my father but to give as much ground as I could in other areas. I told the government prosecutor, Gerald Walpin, that I might consider answering any questions that were about me exclusively but that I could make no promises beyond that.

Naturally, I was led down a primrose path that led directly to questions concerning my father's whereabouts, so again I took the Fifth. At that point, I was dismissed and told to come back the following day, since the government had at last decided to take action against me. Almost two months had been taken up by these futile proceedings and it was clear that there was going to be no more time granted for delays, evasions, and privileges. The court was asked to hold me in contempt.

Krieger and I had prepared for this. It was no big deal. We anticipated that the judge would ask me a series of questions, I would refuse to answer them, and I would then be held in contempt of court—a criminal violation—and placed under arrest. At that point, my attorney would ask for bail, pending a court hearing on the contempt charge, which, because it involved a crime, required a trial and, hence, weeks, if not months, of further delay. But suddenly, there was a new wrinkle.

At the point where the judge was going to hold me in criminal contempt, the government asked that I be charged with civil contempt. Going this route allowed the prosecutor to circumvent the whole issue of bail. Because there were no criminal charges involved, the judge ordered me to jail without any right of hearing or bond. That was it.

Krieger was genuinely taken aback. He got to his feet to protest, wanting to know what it was in my testimony that warranted this kind of finding, which was usually reserved for very different kinds of cases, but the judge waved him off—and waved me on to the pen.

Before I knew what was happening, federal marshals surrounded me, then escorted me from the room and downstairs to a holding cell, where I was a booked and ordered to empty my pockets and take off my tie and belt. I was fingerprinted and then shackled—both feet and hands—and then led to a bus waiting outside the building. A short while later, we pulled up in front of the West Street jail in Manhattan and we were led inside, where, for the next six or seven hours, we went through all the tedious formalities of admission. There were all kinds of forms to fill out. We were taken upstairs to an infirmary, where our medical histories were taken; then, finally, we were given sheets and blankets and were supposed to be marched off to our cells. All of the other prisoners who were with me were led away, but I was asked to remain behind.

I was taken to an office where I had my wristband checked—I assume to make sure I was who they thought I was—and then a guard took me downstairs to another part of the building. I was placed in a cell so narrow, there was barely enough room for one small cot. There was a broken, seatless toilet and a small sink—neither of which worked. The place stank. As soon I was in this cell, the door slammed behind me. There was a light on—embedded in the ceiling—which remained on twenty-four hours a day. I did not know what time it was. Within hours—or was it days?—I lost all sense of day or night. I had no sense that anyone was nearby—guards or other prisoners. I might have had a fatal heart attack and lain there for hours before anyone found me. What was I going to do? How was I going to get through this?

Through all those years when I was slowly moving toward what seemed like a predestined place in a world where my obligations would always come before my feelings, I had never feared jail. The notion of having to do time was an assumed risk, an occupational hazard, and I, like so many others in my world, assumed it lightly.

But now, in this dreary, stinking place where the lights never dimmed, I was suddenly shaken and disoriented. I worried about myself, yes. But my father was still missing and it was now impossible for me to be present, on duty, to deal with the problem. His loss grew inside me, eating me alive like a cancer. The couple of days had turned into weeks, weeks had turned into months—my hopes and then my fears had multiplied and spread throughout my consciousness. And now I was in prison, in a position to do nothing for him or my Family. For me, because I could help myself, *survival*—just getting along—became my watchword, my hold on sanity.

I was in the West Street jail for almost three months. It was on a dreary old, pile of bricks out on the Hudson River, in its last days. It was a federal facility, but it was a rat hole nevertheless. It had been home to many famous prisoners—people ranging from Louis Lepke of Murder Incorporated to the poet Robert Lowell, who was jailed there for being a conscientious objector.

I, of course, wasn't into the history of the place then—only into gearing myself up for whatever came my way. I was determined not to go crazy, and it was hard. Because of the constant light, it was difficult to sleep. I had no human contact save for the opening and closing of a slot in my door when a guard shoved a tray of food in for me and said, "Hey, Bonanno, here's breakfast," or whatever. I tried to mark off the days by these meals. Breakfast—juice, a roll, and coffee—meant morning; meat and potatoes or a heavy stew meant evening. I made it a point of trying to talk to the voice with the hand that shoved the tray. I'd ask questions about how the guy's day was going, how the weather was outside. I always tried to be cheerful, though, in reality, I was anything but. I could not eat. Or rather, would not eat, because I feared that the food might somehow be poisoned. I did not yet know how the system worked in this jail, though I was aware that there were many people from our world who were in the general population and many of those people came from Families that might be lining up against us.

I was terribly lonely, enough so that I was aware of it as a problem. Because I had no one to talk to, no radio to listen to, no reading material allowed, I had only my own thoughts to keep me company. So I would just lie there all day. I had no clothing save for a prison-issued robe, which I kept on at all times. I lay there thinking about my family, about the fact that my father might have been dead now for some time. How had he been killed, who had done it, and what were his last moments like? I could not think about him. I thought about food and wondered how long I could go until I would be forced to eat. I did not know what was involved in starving to death. I remember thinking that when I got out, I would have to look that up so that I would better be able to deal with situations like this.

One day, one night—who knows which?—I heard a noise in my cell. It wasn't much of a noise, but it might as well have been a bomb going off. I sat bolt upright and saw a mouse in a corner of the cell. He moved a few paces along the wall and stopped and we looked at each other. I felt like laughing. And then I thought of something. I ripped a piece off the belt on my robe, attached some food to it, and gently shoved it across the floor. The mouse scurried into a corner but then when he saw me remaining where I was, motionless, he cautiously made his way forward. He sniffed at the morsel and then took a tiny bite, followed by another, and then, leaning back on his haunches, using his forepaws to grasp the wad of gravy-soaked meat, he began devouring it with thousands of little nervous bites.

The mouse and I developed a significant relationship. I learned from him that my food was not poisoned and so was finally able to eat. He (or she—I never could tell) also let me know, just by his mere presence, that there were no rats around. Rats and mice never share the same space. After awhile, he began to trust me—to the point where he actually would come up to the bed and let me touch him. We became friends. I started talking to him, gave him a name, Topo, and began telling him what was on my mind.

It was strange: I could talk to this mouse in ways I never would allow myself to be overheard talking to a human being. I'd tell him, "Fine mess I've gotten myself into, Topo. I wish I were small like you so I could fit under one of those cracks and see some daylight. Have you been outside today? Is it cold? Is it raining? Did you get wet? Come over here, little fella, and let me touch you."

The mouse really did become a friend, my first in prison. If I wanted to, I could have picked him up and put him in my pocket, but I never did because I didn't want to frighten him or take the chance of injuring him. So one day, when the door to my cell suddenly opened and a guard told me to grab my gear and go with him, Topo went out of my life as suddenly as he had entered it. How in the world could I have explained to the guard, to anyone, that I wished there was some way I could take a mouse along with me. I wound up missing him.

I was moved into a tank with ten other inmates—not the same cell, but a large cell subdivided into five smaller units, each one with a double bunk. For a long while, I had a cell to myself. During the days, the doors would be open and you could go out, sit around and talk, play cards, even go up on the roof for a while. Still, there were plenty of dangers to contend with.

Because there were many people I knew (or, rather, who knew me) from the street, I continued to remain wary. But just as I had learned my food was okay, so it was with the general population. The war I was involved in was a very strange one indeed. In jail, a pronouncement of banishment should have been especially risky because there was no place to hide. That was what had made Valachi so crazy and what led him to lash out and murder another inmate, who he was sure was coming after him. But no one made a move toward me.

Callousness and indifference, the everyday companions of prison routine, were also real and present dangers. There was a Puerto Rican guy who committed suicide just a few cells away from mine one day. His cell mate could easily have saved him, but he never lifted a finger because he couldn't have cared less.

The Puerto Rican fellow told his cell mate, who was reading or playing solitaire or something at the time, that he was going to kill himself. He shrugged and the Puerto Rican prisoner proceeded to move a little stool over to the center of the cell, right under a light fixture, where he attached a belt and then looped it around his neck. Then just before he kicked away the stool, he called over to his cell mate and asked him not to cut him down after he hung himself. The guy told him, "Look, if you're going to do it, do it—don't just talk about it." That was it. The roommate continued to play cards while his buddy dangled.

For me, however, just getting out of solitary was enough. All the while I was in segregation, I had been unable to wash myself, even brush my teeth. Now, it was as if luxury had descended on me. I had a toothbrush. I could bathe. When I looked up, I could see light streaming through the windows—or fading as night fell.

Such as it was, I had human companionship.

I can't say I ever enjoyed myself, but I did soon come to realize that life went on in prison as elsewhere, with its own rhythm of laws and regulations. There were opportunities as well as dangers.

One of the unexpected opportunities that came my way was that I learned to play chess, a game I knew nothing about before but which became something of a passion. One of the guys I became friendly with was a Russian named Petrashansky. I liked Petrashansky because he was smart, very outgoing, and cheerful. He was in the film business and was in on a murder rap, waiting to be shipped out, he said. He had taken out someone with a javelin on location for a U.S. film company in Mexico—hence the federal charge. In any case, he was a terrific chess player, and because we had become friendly, he very patiently taught me all he could about the game—from naming the pieces to intricate strategies of offense and defense.

The visits I had from my family also turned out to provide an opportunity, in a completely different way.

When I was arrested in Arizona and forced to testify before the grand jury, I was able to see Rosalie and the children again. I don't think she understood why I had been in hiding and then why I had been arrested and was being forced to testify, and what the consequences might be if I failed to cooperate. When I went to jail, it was important to me that she and the children would feel no shame or fear in coming to visit me. I could not control what they felt, of course, but I was given the opportunity to show them what I felt about my own incarceration. And I made it a point to show them that I was the same person in jail as I was out, that I had nothing to bow my head over, that I was not defeated, demoralized, or shamed because I happened to be behind bars. This was a struggle because my fears—and my despair—were then so deep.

But whenever I saw them sitting on the other side of the glass, holding a phone so they could speak to me, I welcomed them with little jokes and good-natured kidding in order to let them see for themselves that I was fine and that they had nothing to worry about.

If there was a payoff of any kind, it came one afternoon when Rosalie and the children, following a visit to me, stopped off to see my aunt Marion. I was told my aunt asked the children where they had been. They told her they had been to see me. "Oh," she said—the way adults do in talking to small children—"and where was that?" My son Joe replied, "In a telephone booth. I saw my daddy in a telephone booth." Everyone laughed.

I don't know how long I could have held out. The cancer of fear was always growing. I kept in constant touch with my associates outside. Some visited me regularly, brought me news from the street, dressed up in funny, impenetrable language about food, grandchildren, vacation plans, insurance payments, and the like. I knew from these visits that things remained quiet, that our people and those from other Families continued to see each other and do business on a daily basis—a fact that only deepened my sense of what might have really happened to my father.

If everyone was getting along, I thought, then Lucchese and Gambino, in all likelihood, were not directly involved in the kidnapping. If they were, if they had eliminated my father, then surely they would have moved by now in a more forceful way on my Family instead of allowing the leadership split between our faction and Gaspar's to fester.

But the more I tried to piece together some plausible scenario for what might actually have happened on that rainy night the previous October— which now, in February, seemed to belong to another century—the more heartsick I became. I did not think I would be able to make it much longer.

Then one day in late May, my uncle Frank made one of his regular visits to see me. He sat across the way in the visitors' pen, behind a thick partition of Plexiglas, looking as if he had just had a good meal. He was cheerful, almost jaunty.

"I saw Rosalie and the kids before I came over. They say hello," he said.

"They're okay?"

"Yeah, they're fine, fine. Have a funny story to tell you about Joey and Chuckie," uncle Frank said, referring to my two sons.

"What's that?" I asked.

"I'm at dinner with them last night. I say to them, 'Which one wants a dollar?' Chuckie waves his hand like a wild man; Joey doesn't make a move. I give the dollar to Joey. Then I say again, 'Which one wants a dollar?' Same thing. Chuckie shoots his hand up; I give the buck to Joey. Third time around, Chuckie catches on. Keeps his hands in his lap. I give 'im a dollar."

My heart was in my throat. Uncle Frank had just signaled me that my father was safe and sound. The story he told had nothing to do with Uncle

Frank and my sons. The dollar-waving catechism had been performed by my father the Christmas before last, the last time our family was intact on that holiday—and the story had since become a legend in our household. My father was back. Frank smiled and lowered his eyes when he saw the shock of recognition on my face.

"I wish I woulda been there to see it," I said to him.

"Me, too," he said. "Youdda gotten a real boot out of it."

18

Johnny Morales sent a message telling me that he thought it was time for me to purge myself of contempt, to get out of jail and back out on the street. I took this as a direct command from my father, so I summoned Al Krieger and told him in as contrite a manner as possible that I had had enough and that I would do whatever it took to free myself. Krieger was a little taken aback. Obviously, I did not—and would not—tell him my real reason for wanting out. I would have to tell the court that I was willing to come in and talk, he said.

"Tell them I am," I said.

"They'll really go after you once you say anything," he warned.

"I can handle myself," I said.

So Krieger then began mapping a strategy—one that he hoped would allow me to give the government what they had originally wanted—whatever information I had about my father's kidnapping—without allowing them to go further.

"You know, they'll try to use it as a Pandora's box," he said.

"Let 'em."

"Okay. We'll see. It's worth a try."

It took a couple of additional weeks of wrangling, but I finally appeared in federal court one day in June. I was taken in chains from West Street to the federal courthouse, unchained, and then marched into court.

As my lawyer and I had anticipated, the prosecution immediately asked me what I knew about my father's disappearance. I told them about the phone call I had received from a third party back in December.

"What was the sum and substance of the conversation?" the feds asked. I said it was just as I told had them; the details were exactly as I remember them, nothing more, nothing less. The prosecutor pushed on. Where had the call been made from? Who was the person who had called? Where was my father? What subsequent information had I received? To all these questions, I said simply that I knew nothing, that I had volunteered all the information I had.

After several futile attempts to exact more, the prosecutor asked the judge to continue my contempt citation. The judge, however, reminded the prosecution that I had been put away because I had failed to answer the questions about my father that had been asked—and that having now received an answer from me, he was in no position to hold me. The judge ruled that I had purged myself of contempt and then he turned to our table and ordered me released forthwith, which is legal jargon for "now."

There were howls of protests from the other side, but to no avail. The government prosecutors were stuck—just as Al Krieger had thought they might be—and it was amusing to now see them in danger of being cited by the judge themselves as they continued to object to the judge's ruling. But I walked out of the court that day a free man, and that night in East Meadow, there was a huge impromptu welcome-home party before I went into hiding again.

My aunts looked at me and shook their heads because I had grown so thin; one of them even induced another relative, my uncle Jim, a tailor, to begin work immediately taking in some of my clothes. I could not convince this uncle of mine to wait for another day. He sat in a corner of the living room—before and after dinner—his head tilted in concentration, threads and needles in his mouth, hurrying to finish a pair of trousers that I might be able to wear that very night.

But my getting-out party was just a stopover. That same evening, the first chance I had, I pulled Johnny Morales aside and asked him about my father. Contact had been made, he said, a couple of months before by phone. There had been several additional calls.

"He's coming back; he said he'd contact us in his own way, in his own time, and that till then we need to make sure we protect ourselves," Johnny said. That was all he knew.

"I spoke to him last time when he heard you were going back into court.

He was pleased and said we wouldn't hear from him again until you were out. Then, he said, he would come back and we would see him."

The news was as tantalizing as it was gratifying. I believed Johnny, but the fact that my father was alive and still in hiding meant that, once free, I still had the Bonanno Family and all its interests to take care of. There was just no choice but to go back to the apartments.

First, I had to make sure we were still prepared to fight. The war, although never declared, had never been called off, either. At the same time, we were still a powerful and functioning Family. Just as before, I traveled into the city as much as I could, making myself as visible as I dared, enough to let everyone know that the Bonanno Family was still present and accounted for.

Then, after several weeks, I made business trips outside the city, checking on long-standing commercial interests we had in Wisconsin, Montreal, Arizona, California. We had gambling interests in Atlantic City, in Vegas. At this point, just showing up, making sure others saw that our Family had leadership and direction and was not about to back off, was, in itself, a way of countering any suspicion that we were weak and divided.

Oddly enough, as beset as we were, we even managed to take care of some international business during these weeks. One day, Joe Notaro met with someone who identified himself as a representative of the government of Haiti. Joe didn't know who this representative was, but he assured me that he was legitimate.

Haiti, like Cuba, as well as other islands in the West Indies, had always been a lucrative place for the Families. And unlike Cuba, it had been lucrative for the Bonannos. During the era of cooperation among the Families, the government, and the Duvalier dictatorship, Haiti was a haven for gunrunning, gambling, money laundering, and, believe it or not, coffee. Just as Batista had fattened up on profits from all these enterprises, so had Papa Doc and his heirs. The Duvaliers got rich, the Families could operate without being hassled, and the U.S. government got a pair of reliable partners in waging overt and covert war against communism.

Because of the turmoil in our world and because there was now a different policy toward organized crime coming out of Washington, we—and others—had neglected business opportunities in this area. So, one day, this delegation of Haitians showed up in New York wanting to meet with us.

"Bill, we got a problem," Joe told me on the phone. "I met this guy and he wants to meet with us. I told him I'd have to get back to him. What are we gonna do with a bunch of niggers in New York?"

"What do you mean? We'll meet 'em."

"Yeah, but where? You gonna sit with 'em in the Waldorf? They're staying at the fucking Waldorf-Astoria for Chrissakes!"

"We'll call up La Scala," I said. "They'll close up the place for us, don't worry."

And that's what happened. I phoned one of the owners, Arturo, and told him what the situation was and that we needed privacy. He said to come in after lunch the next day and everything would be taken care of.

When we met, the Haitians announced to us that Duvalier was very unhappy with the current neglect of the casinos and other profitable businesses for him that had gone through the Families in the past. He was appealing, he said, for the Bonannos to come in and get things working again.

It was hard for me to tell just what was involved. The meeting at La Scala was supposed to be secret, but it was a little too public for me. There were big long limos outside the place, with bodyguards standing out on the street to make sure no one but us entered the restaurant. The invitation we received—reopen the casinos, take care of the slot machine businesses that had once flourished in and outside Port-au-Prince—seemed real enough, but what went with it was an invitation for us to go down and visit Duvalier to finalize everything. I had no way of knowing what to expect. For all I knew, this was an invitation to go and get my head chopped off in a place where the body could be disposed of easily. But I decided to go ahead. If my Family's interests could be furthered at a time when our influence was in question and our resources had been stretched thin, I was going to do it.

I traveled to Haiti with Vito DeFilippo and Joe Notaro, people I could turn to for advice if anything came up, although in no way would they be able to provide security if anything went wrong. I felt completely unprotected in making this trip, even though I was sure this visit was as official as the one made by Duvalier's representatives to New York.

When I entered the Presidential Palace, my aides and I were surrounded by men from Duvalier's personal police force, the Ton-Ton Macoute. They escorted us upstairs to his office, a huge flag-draped room, where guards with submachine guns and machetes were stationed every two or three feet from one another. Oh fuck, I told myself, I'm not getting out of here. Duvalier got up to greet us. He had a big smile on his face. I smiled, too—but not because I was glad to see him. I realized that since his guards were positioned in a circle, if they decided to open up on us, they would likely wipe themselves out along with us and Papa Doc. Go ahead, you bastards, I told myself, do it; it would almost be worth it—if I could live to see it.

Duvalier gestured for us to be seated, and for the next ten minutes or so he discussed general policy with us as if we were all heads of state—or at least ministers of commerce. Duvalier complained that once-profitable businesses were lagging and needed attention and that we were the ones he was counting on to revive things. Revenues had decreased dramatically in recent years, meaning his take from the variety of legal businesses such as gambling and beef. He promised we would have a free hand in whatever we needed. We would be the sole operators of the casinos and we'd have control of the slots in and out of Port-Au-Prince; he would do everything in his power to make sure all the international connections and payoffs were made to reestablish the coffee trade so that we would be the beneficiaries. The Haitians, of course, did not grow coffee. The Venezuelans did. For years, we—and others—had run a black-market coffee business through Haiti. Venezuelan beans were moved clandestinely to Haiti, repackaged there, and, with the active connivance of U.S. officials, shipped stateside at lower rates, duty-free. Duvalier's stake in all this kindness most assuredly was increased revenue. As we were facing hard times of our own due to internal conflicts, he was facing the same on a national scale at home. He was getting old; revolution, always a threat, was simmering in the countryside. The price of vigilance was that his own personal treasury had been steadily declining.

I knew what doing more business with him would mean. For as long as we had been on the island, we had had to make our payoffs to him. That went without saying. But Duvalier, like Noriega in Panama and any of the other pretty dictators who were protected by the United States and who did business with us, never could get enough. For as long as he was in power, he would pass the word that he needed to put a relative or a friend or an associate on the payroll. No one ever saw one of these new employees turn up at a casino or other business, but the payments would be made just the same. Duvalier's greed knew no bounds, but there was nothing anyone could do—that is, other than close shop and get out.

So I arranged with Papa Doc to have a couple of our people come in and get things moving again, to take charge of the casinos, the slots, the coffee exports, making sure that he understood that times were different now, that the government was harder to deal with, more unpredictable. We both agreed, though, that with Lyndon Johnson as President, there was a good chance things might improve. The Vietnam War was a big question mark, though. Johnson's decision to escalate the conflict had already created problems at home that no one had foreseen. Duvalier hoped Johnson had committed enough force to end the conflict quickly, but he was unsure whether he had. I was unsure, given the kind of protests under way in the States, that he would be able to. But there we left it. Our delegation returned home safe and sound, having negotiated new opportunities for us.

Meanwhile, back in the States, the combination of government pressure and internal strife increased. The newspapers were daily running stories of arrests, prosecutions, exposés on organized crime. My father's disappearance continued to be the key in all of this. What was going on in the underworld, and why had my father been targeted by his own? the tabloids kept asking. One newspaper referred to the situation in New York as "the Banana Split" and then the rest of the media, unable to resist, began producing variations of the same.

We got word from the West, the East—and from abroad—that the government was intensifying its search for my father. Roy Cohn had met with a couple of our people to tell them that he had recently seen J. Edgar Hoover, who had said there was no turning back the different investigations that were under way. We had contacts in Sicily and even in Interpol tell us that the heat was definitely on in Europe. Even my old German girlfriend, Helga, contacted me to say that she had been questioned by Interpol. All the while, the pressure was more keenly felt by us because we knew not only that my father was alive and hiding out somewhere but that, one day, impossible to say when, he would be on the street with us.

About a week after I got back from Haiti, Johnny Morales came over to my apartment one evening and said he wanted to take a walk with me. I took the dog and we went outside, heading toward a park a few blocks away.

"I heard from your father today," he told me when we were alone on the sidewalk. I said nothing.

"I got a call from him and he said to meet him at this grocery store in Brooklyn tomorrow afternoon."

"You know the store?" I asked.

"Yeah, I know the store and the owner."

I wanted to ask why the hell he would want to meet in a grocery store, but the one thing I knew about my father was never to try to figure out his meaning or his intentions. The only question I had was whether Johnny had actually spoken to my father directly.

"Believe me, it was him," Johnny said.

So the next afternoon, Johnny picked me up in Queens and we drove across the Brooklyn-Queens Expressway to Brooklyn, into Greenpoint and the old Italian neighborhoods my father had spent so much time in during his youth. We parked our car a couple of blocks away and walked to this small supermarket located on a busy intersection. According to Johnny, my father had said he would meet us there at two o'clock. We were there a few minutes early. We said hello to the owner, took a shopping cart, and walked slowly up and down one aisle and then another. Two o'clock came and went—no sign of my father.

We went back to the front. Johnny and the owner spent time talking as customers streamed in and out of the store. I tried as best I could to appear at ease, but I know my head was on a turnstile. I kept craning my neck this way and that, looking for him, seeing nothing, feeling more and more nervous with each sweeping glance. One customer, an old man, bearded and bedraggled, walked slowly up the aisle and seemed to make a point of deliberately jostling us as he passed. I knew my nerves were gone, because I wanted to take a swipe at this person, even though he was nothing more than a neighborhood derelict. The derelict seemed to sense that. He walked on a few steps, stopped, turned around, and apologized.

"So sorry," he said. "Didn't see you, wasn't paying attention."

"It's okay, old man," I said. The derelict smiled and shuffled forward. I tried to turn away, but, in an almost obnoxious manner, he positioned himself so that I could not avoid him. He forced me to look down into his face, into eyes that were steel blue but then, suddenly, very familiar. Before my mind was in gear, before the shock of recognition fully hit me, his hand came up and touched my cheek.

"Salvatore," he whispered. "You were looking, but your eyes were closed."

19

My father looked like the actor he once had been as a young man, when he was a boy studying in New York, hoping to get a break in silent films. But he wasn't acting, any more than Odysseus was when he returned home, in disguise, to move silently for a time in and among the enemies who had taken over his house. We traveled to a safe house, my aunt Mary's, where we were able to spend a couple of leisurely hours together. We ate and drank—and talked. First, he cleared up the mystery of his kidnapping, going all the way back to the moment when he was whisked away at gunpoint.

"They shoved me down on the floor of the car," he said. "I had no sense of where we were going or what was going to happen. I accepted the fact that I was going to die; I had no trouble with that because I had long ago understood that the only real power any of us ever has is over our own emotions—nothing else.

"We drove for hours, so that when the car finally came to a stop and I got out, my joints were so stiff, I could barely move. I realized we had been driving all night because now it was light out. We were in the country somewhere, a farm. I was shown inside an old farmhouse, was told to make myself comfortable—and to wait. There was someone with me at all times, someone I did not recognize. I asked him where we were. He said nothing. It was like I wasn't in the room. He sat in a chair with his arms folded.

"Sometime later, many hours later—it was probably midafternoon—I heard a car pull up outside. I could hear voices, doors opening and closing, and then a moment later in walked my cousin Steve Magaddino. Can you believe that! There he was, looking oh so pleased with himself.

"You know how two old Castellammarese can talk to each other. Steve said he was so glad to see me, but what ever had brought me out to such a godforsaken place? Was there some special business I wanted to discuss with him? Just visiting, I told him; I thought I'd like more than a little visit with my cousin. My goal in that moment was very simple: to make sure he saw nothing of the fury and contempt I felt.

"We talked all through the afternoon, into the night, then the next day—and for the next six weeks. It was always a tug-of-war and there was never a winner.

"For the longest while, I did not think I would leave that farmhouse alive, but the more we talked, the more I understood that I was going to live. There was no reason for this endless palaver otherwise.

"For my part, I was interested in finding out, any way I could, if he had taken a renegade action in seizing me or if, as I suspected, others were involved with him. But I could not tell. Steve was as much a master of disguise as I. As far as I was able to determine, Steve was on his own.

" 'You take up too much space in the air,' he told me—an expression I knew from my childhood to mean that I was arrogant. So far as I could tell, he was complaining to me that I was trying to control the whole show—and that he didn't like it.

"The closest he came to admitting that he might have support from others was when I asked him why he was alone among the Fathers in saying that about me.

" 'Alone? They all think that about you, *Cousine*. Maybe they don't say it to your face, but they think it.' I said, 'Who? Tell me who says I am anything more than the Father of my own Family, who besides you?' Steve walked around the room, waving his hands, shouting like a character in an old melodrama. 'You've always been like this, even with Maranzano. Why do you try to be such a big shot? Why don't you listen to reason like other people? Why don't you turn up for meetings when they are called by other Fathers?'

"Aha. What meetings, *Cousine*, what meetings, called by which of the Fathers? And why didn't you return telephone calls and make yourself available to mediate as a member of the Commission if you were so concerned?" And so it went, as crazy as commedia dell'arte.

"There were no connecting points in our conversations. We took time out for meals. We ate and drank, smoked cigars together—and continued to talk. I was not so carefully guarded that I could not have walked away if I chose, but I did not choose to. One day, after six weeks of talk, I was told I could go. We had obviously reached the point where the only choice he had left was to kill me or let me go. He let me go."

My father, in the end, really wanted to believe that jealousy was what drove Magaddino—but how could he be sure? How could someone so steeped in tradition as Steve was allow personal feelings to so dishonor him? My father had no answer.

Looking back now, with the perspective of all these years, I think I understand why Steve couldn't find it in him to kill my father. As much as Steve was driven by jealousy, a malignant fire that had burned in him for decades, he was also bound by honor, a tradition, a blood tie that he could not easily break. To do so, to have harmed my father, would have made Steve an outcast, marked as surely as Cain was for *his* betrayal.

Perhaps Steve could have been pushed that far had Lucchese and Gambino fully backed him. But they also, at that point, were too weak to commit fully to a course of action. As much as they wanted to see my Family destroyed, to erase its conservative tradition, which stood in the way of expansion into drug trafficking, and to carve up the Bonanno Family's businesses between them, they were unsure of the support they had among all the Families for a direct assault on us.

It was a classic catch-22. Lucchese and Gambino wanted Steve and Gaspar DiGregorio to eliminate my father as part of an inter-Family struggle. Steve and Gaspar, to avoid such a dark stain on their names, wanted Lucchese and Gambino to destroy my father from outside the Family. As a result, all these men were momentarily frozen. So far as I could tell at the time, the situation remained, as before, troubling, confusing, and still very, very dangerous.

When he was released, my father said, his cousin told him that he would be given transportation—by the same men who had kidnapped him—to whatever destination he chose.

"So, I had them take me west," my father said with a gleam in his eye. These men were under orders, you see."

His little private joke turned into a 2,500-mile trip, designed to throw off anyone who might want to pick up his trail. His intention was to go to his home in Arizona, he said, because it would have been the last place where anyone would have looked for him, the place where he could begin to regroup and begin planning for all that was still unresolved.

But first he had to get clear of his drivers. He told them he wanted to drive to El Paso, Texas, a city he had passed through before on a number of occasions. It took them three days to get there. After they had arrived and were driving around, my father suddenly instructed the driver to stop at a certain street corner and let him off. He gave the drivers the impression that he knew exactly what he was doing and that he had a plan.

"I was like Mr. Hyde then," he said, "Ducking in and out of alleys, going around corners, in and out of public places. When I felt like I had finally gotten rid of the drivers, I called a friend in Tucson to come and pick me up. He did, and he drove me back to Tucson."

Once in Tucson, he waited a whole day, until it was dark out, before returning to his house and moving into a secret apartment he had designed for just such emergencies as this. He lived there for weeks, in touch only with my sister's father-in-law, a very close aide who was the regular caretaker of the house in my parents' absence and whose comings and goings would arouse no suspicion. My father received food, newspapers, information from the outside world. He eventually arranged for word to be passed that he was all right and that there was no longer any need for me to remain silent before government investigators.

The big question now was what to do with respect to the government and the other Families. Johnny Morales, Uncle Frank, and I all argued with him to remain hidden.

"For one thing, the minute any kind of word gets out that you are alive and well, the government will come after you twice as hard, believing the kidnapping was a hoax all along," Frank said.

"And we don't know who is with Steve," I said. "We have to find out that first. You really have to stay out of sight until they show their colors. We're at war."

My father initially was reluctant to go along. First, we had to convince him that it was foolish for a general to remain on the front lines and then that we had worked out the means for him to move from safe house to safe house, remaining hidden.

"But I don't want you to be targets, either. I don't want people going after you because they want me," he said.

We explained to him how fully we had already prepared for armed conflict and that we had taken all necessary precautions to protect ourselves.

"You know what I picked up on the street?" Johnny said. "One of Lucchese's people was saying your cousin Steve told the Commission if they didn't get you in a couple of weeks and you succeeded in going into hiding, they would never find you and it would be a long war. They're scared not knowing where you are."

My father slowly came around. He did not like the idea of removing himself from the action but saw that he really had no choice. It was our mutual decision he should not remain in New York City, that it was just too dangerous. There were plenty of safe houses and farms upstate where he could remain hidden and in touch at the same time—and, ultimately, he almost savored the prospect of hiding out under his cousin Steve's nose.

"Maybe I'll pay him a visit, walk up to him on the street and say, 'Regards from Lucchese and Gambino' as I pass him by!"

"Sooner or later, everything will become clear and you won't have to hide," Uncle Frank said.

"I don't mind making people crazy for a while," my father said.

In November of that year, 1965, there was a big social event in our world—the marriage of Gaspar DiGregorio's daughter. Gaspar, the Commission's choice to replace my father as head of our Family, had once been married to Steve Maggadino's sister, who had died. Gaspar had remarried and had a daughter by his second wife. Her wedding took on added political significance here because those obscure old family connections tied right into the war. In this case, wedding invitations—who did and didn't get them, who showed and who didn't—involved questions of security and intelligence much more than social correctness.

It turned out that members from our side of the split in the Bonanno Family were invited. Although leaders like my father, Johnny Morales, and I were not, many others were. Did it mean that the other side was using the occasion of a wedding to lure away people loyal to us or that some of these people who we assumed were with us had actually gone over to the other side?

On the other hand, what did the absence of other New York leaders, like Tommy Lucchese and Carlo Gambino, mean? We were pretty sure that our group captains who went—people like Joe Bayonne—were solidly with us, just as we were sure that people like Tommy and Carlo were not suddenly expressing stronger ties of friendship to us by staying away.

What seemed dimly possible was that the wedding, in political terms, might actually be a tentative expression of a willingness to resolve the war before it got any further. In this context, it was only natural that we would finally pick up rumors that the other side was looking to make peace. It was clear from the start that Gaspar himself was not a person who ever had the stomach for a violent conflict.

We knew that all through this period he was having health problems and that, increasingly, he had been keeping to his house, turning over much of the administrative responsibilities that had been thrust on him to another captain, Paul Sciacca.

Uncle Frank was the one who first came to me with the word that the other side was actually looking to talk. Neither Frank nor I was born yesterday, and our initial reaction to this proposal was to disregard it. In fact, we redoubled all our security precautions, fearing that a betrayal was in the works. Whenever I went into the city, I never took the same route twice in a row. At nights, Uncle Frank and I sat with road maps, devising new routes to follow. We had at least thirty different routes into and out of the city. There were at least that many restaurants or more to choose from whenever we wanted a meal.

But as Christmas passed and a frigid New Year was ushered in, the peace overtures kept coming. Captains from the other side told us over and over again that Gaspar was tired of all this, that none of his people wanted war, that it was time to come in from the cold for all our sakes. Uncle Frank came back one day from the city and told me that the other side was not only willing to meet but that they would do so on our turf, in a house and neighborhood designated by us—to place the control of security in our hands if that was what was required. Frank had been contacted by John Tartamella's son, Sorreno—so we knew he was relaying information he had been instructed to pass along. He stressed that Gaspar and Paul Sciacca both wanted to meet with me, that they wanted to do what they could to resolve the split.

This seemed worth a chance. But what still was not clear was just how this change of heart had come about. We knew for sure that no one had tried to send a message to my father. There had been no contact from Steve or from any of the other members of the Commission. Yet a big decision apparently had been made. How could Gaspar and Paul Sciacca be acting on their own? We had been handed an olive branch: an offer of peace, to be negotiated at a site designated by us, protected by our guns. Treachery was usually coated with honey. But in this case, the hive belonged to us.

We went back and forth over the wisdom of accepting this proposal. My uncle Frank was the one most reluctant to go ahead. It just did not feel right, he said. He recalled the story of the Trojan horse and urged us to remember that that scheme, too, was hatched out of a long and dreary stalemate by men who had grown more desperate, rather than more willing, to make peace.

It was at this meeting when I realized how much of the leadership of our Family had silently passed into my hands. A question arose as to whether we should or should not contact my father over the offer. I argued against that because I did not see the need. We were the ones who had built the army, prepared for the war. The whole issue of peace, I knew, revolved around who I was and what role I played in the Bonanno Family. In practical terms, we were the ones who had to resolve the issue.

In addition to my uncle Frank (who, though older, was closer in temperament to me than anyone), I was surrounded by men nearer in age to my own generation than to my father's. I had personally recruited some of these men, bringing them up through the ranks to be at my side. Carl Simari and Hank Perrone were a couple of street guys from the toughest neighborhoods of Brooklyn. They could have easily drifted into dead-ended careers of violence and petty crime, but they were both deeply loyal men who had shown over and over again a willingness to do anything that was asked of them, without any expectation of reward. They were not born in Sicily and they knew little of Sicilian tradition, but they were drawn to the values of our world as surely as if they had lived there forever. I trusted them with my life and I wanted to get their opinion before I made any decision.

Carl believed we would be all right because we would be in control of the neighborhood. Hank, on the other hand, tended to side with Uncle

Frank because he believed that treachery begot treachery. The other side had already shown their true stripes when they set themselves against their own Family.

Others in the room spoke. But in the end, when it was my turn, there was nothing more to consider—only a decision to render. I told them we were going ahead. It was my decision and mine alone. I could not say for sure whether the other side was sincere or not, but I believed we had everything to gain and nothing to lose. I pointed out that the climate was right for a settlement even if the outlines were not yet clear. In the last fifteen months to two years—from the time of the Kennedy assassination through my father's kidnapping—the earth had shifted under our feet; things were no longer secure for any of us. The leaders who might have wished to see my father and me and the conservatives allied with us pushed out were themselves, because of economic strain and government inquiries, less able to exert power and influence than ever before. There was no chance in the world that Steve could influence anyone in New York. And, as for Gaspar and Paul Sciacca and the people they had with them, we, not they, would have the upper hand if it should ever come to a military showdown, and they knew it.

I wanted peace, but I wanted it on our terms, so that our own lives might be secure and coherent afterward. My father was upstate somewhere, on a farm. My mother, for the last fifteen months, had been living in a basement apartment at a relative's house in New Jersey. Rosalie and my children lived under the daily glare of publicity, beset by reporters, curiosity seekers, undercover agents, and enemies from our world.

It was my responsibility to make this decision—not anyone else's—and I took it.

We sent back word to Gaspar and Paul Sciacca that we would meet with them at a house that belonged to one of my Bonventre uncles. It was on Troutman Street, in the Ridgewood section of Brooklyn, in an Italian working-class neighborhood. The whole area, controlled by the Bonanno Family, was familiar territory. We had friends and supporters up and down the street, not only among residents but also among shopkeepers, restaurant people, even the cops who walked the neighborhood beats.

We scheduled the meeting for a Friday night toward the end of January 1966. The time of the meeting—eleven o'clock—was just a little later than

I would have liked, but there had been a death in my family earlier in the week and I had had to attend a wake out on Long Island. Also, it was my oldest son's birthday. In any case, the late hour was a choice I made—not the other side.

There were three of us who drove in from Long Island to meet up with a larger number of our people who were already there for the meeting. I drove with my uncle Frank and Carl Simari and we parked a few blocks from Troutman Street, the meeting site, and walked along the streets, two on one side, and one trailing a little behind on the other side of the street so we would be able at all times to provide cover for one another.

The neighborhood was quiet. It didn't matter really that it was Friday night; for Italian working-class people, it was still early to bed, early to rise. The days were all the same, part of an old, old rhythm that was matched to work and religion. We passed places that I had known from my childhood—an old park where I had once played, a butcher shop that had once been owned by my godfather, Gaspar DiGregorio, a movie theater, a café called the Super Sport. We turned up Knickerbocker Avenue and then onto Troutman Street, still walking slowly, looking around every few steps to make sure no one was following us, eyeballing us, waiting for us. We deliberately passed by the Bonventre house before turning around and finally walking up to it.

The others from our side had arrived a little earlier. We were glad to get into the warmth after that slow stroll in the bitter cold. We stamped off the numbness in our toes, warmed our hands over radiators, sat around with hot coffee, and waited. When the time for the meeting came and passed, we weren't especially concerned, though in our world timeliness is definitely part of the formality of things. We expected the other side to be there punctually and were annoyed—but only mildly—that they weren't. But when ten minutes became a half an hour and a half hour became an hour and more, we knew something was wrong, but we had no way of knowing what it was. Finally, sometime well after midnight, the phone rang upstairs. We were all seated down in the basement meeting room, which had no windows anyone could shoot through, when my uncle Bonventre came to the head of the stairs and hollered down for me to take the call.

It was Sorreno Tartamella, one of the captains on Gaspar's side and the person who had set up the meeting in the first place. He was calling to apologize for their side not being there, but, he said, Gaspar had suddenly taken ill and could not attend. The others, who were unfamiliar with that section of Brooklyn, were out in some godforsaken part of Queens, hopelessly lost. Could we reschedule. Sorreno asked, maybe for the early part of the coming week, whenever was convenient for us? Just as before, they'd leave the time, the place, everything to us.

As angry as I was, his story seemed convincing. These things did happen, I realized, and what was there I could say anyway? Yeah, I said, we'd be back in touch; we'd try to do it Monday, Tuesday, as soon as possible. I hung up and went back downstairs.

I repeated the conversation I had just had as carefully as I could. I felt uneasy. I needed to know what others thought before I made any additional decisions. Uncle Frank said that he didn't like what had happened at all, that the explanation didn't make sense. Sure, Gaspar might have become ill, but he was just one person in the delegation. Paul Sciacca was another, and he knew this part of Brooklyn as well as any of us. The idea that they had gotten lost was not believable, not when so much was at stake. If they hadn't been out here before, they had street maps like everyone else. Joe Notaro also was suspicious, said he smelled a rat. Carl said he thought the explanation was strange but that it wasn't necessarily false. He mentioned how unlikely it would be for their side to try something in this situation. They would be risking too much, he said. The others had little or no opinion but were upset that we had been stood up—for whatever reason.

I agreed with Carl that it was unlikely that we were being set up. More likely, this was gamesmanship, a way of keeping us guessing and off-stride, so that we would be more anxious, more willing to compromise when we finally did get together.

In any case, we decided to sit around for a while. Even though it was late, we thought it would be wise simply to stay put. That way, if anyone was watching the house, they might get the idea we were all going to stay for the night. An hour passed, almost two. The men playing cards and watching TV were starting to doze off in their chairs. I got up from the table where I was sitting and said we didn't have to wait forever, that we could leave. When no one made a move to go, I laughed. Everyone looked so serious.

"Hey, it's not Bataan," I said, "and besides, we gotta get some sleep."

We went back and forth about the security we would use in leaving the house. It was late at night, after all; the street out front was going to be deserted, and dark. We would leave in twos, I said. Carl and I would go first; we would check things out for everyone else. I told Uncle Frank and Joe Notaro to cover us from the vestibule as we went down the front stairs into the street and then for two more men to cover them as they left. We had plenty of firepower if it came to that, and we had position in the street.

We moved quietly up through the house, through the hallway to the vestibule. Carl and I went to the front door and then out onto the steps leading down to the sidewalk. As was my habit, I looked both ways going out the door. I looked across the street, then up and down at the rows of empty cars on either side. As far as I could see, the neighborhood was eerily quiet; the rows of tenement houses stretched block after block, not a person or car moving anywhere. Save for the sudden changing of traffic signals at the corner, it was like looking at a giant still photograph of a scene frozen in time, a petrified neighborhood in a city from another age.

Carl asked to go down the front steps ahead of me, but I told him no, that it was my decision to leave, so I would go first. I welcomed his bravery, but I needed him behind me, watching. Frank and Joe moved into position behind us as we went.

Now, wherever we went during this period, we always had our hands directly on our weapons. We never walked out of a building—no matter where—without doing that. The fraction of a second it took to get a piece out and in firing position could be the difference between life and death.

When I got to the bottom of the steps, all was quiet. Carl was behind me, midway down the steps. I turned right and walked about three steps toward the intersection and then Carl quickly came up next to me. I kept my hand on my gun; Carl already had his out. Uncle Frank and Joe now had come out to the top of the stoop and were looking up and down the street; the others were behind them.

I don't know how he managed to pick it up, but Carl, out of the corner of his eye, saw something move in one of the vestibules along the street. Later on, he told me it wasn't even a movement; it was the barest glint of light, a gun barrel, perhaps, suddenly catching the pale wash of a streetlamp as it was being raised into firing position. In the same instant that the flash of light caught his eye, he impulsively shoved me down to the pavement and simultaneously wheeled and began firing at the doorway. Glass and wood splintered across the way and then the whole street literally exploded around us. Machine-gun fire, shotgun blasts, and pistol shots went off everywhere.

We were caught dead center in the middle of a battlefield, with nowhere to go.

20

Carl Simari saved my life. When he shoved me to the ground, I hit the frigid pavement, came up behind a car, then fired back in the general direction from where the shots had come. Carl was shooting, too—and so were my uncle Frank and Joe Notaro from, who were on the top of the steps of the row house. I think their being in a backup position and so quickly opening up threw the killers off. There were men all over the street, ducking behind cars, firing as they moved from position to position. But they never had the chance to get themselves set to get off shots that were well aimed.

Carl and I moved like a military team, each one covering for the other as we reloaded and ran, dodging in and out of the protection of the parked cars. I was firing a six-shot, fast-reload .38 revolver; Carl was using a .45 with an automatic clip. About thirty yards from the intersection and safety, there was a terrific and sustained burst of gunfire. Someone had us in sight and had opened up with a machine gun. I literally could feel the vibration of the bullets as they passed inches from my head and slammed into the wall of a building behind me, kicking off a shower of sparks and debris. Both Carl and I fired back in the direction of a shuttered fruit stand where we had seen the muzzle flashes. Then we continued sprinting.

When we got to the corner and turned it, we saw a car parked along the curb, maybe fifteen, twenty yards down the street. There were two men sitting in the car. They might have been innocent bystanders, but there was no way to stop and politely inquire. We riddled the car as we approached it, blowing out the glass as we sent volleys of shots into the passenger compartment. I don't believe the men were hit, because they seemed to dive for cover the moment we came into view. In any case, we kept running.

We got to a main intersection and, for the first time, stopped. I told Carl to go one way, I would go the other, and we would meet up at a specific point. I could hear sirens in the distance. We were standing at the intersection of Jefferson Street and Knickerbocker Avenue, a main thoroughfare in Brooklyn. It was easier now to blend in. Carl began walking in one direction, and I headed in the other.

In no time at all, cop cars were whizzing past me, their roof lights snapping round and round, wobbly sirens hurting my eardrums. Still, I just kept walking, trying to remain calm. I could feel the thudding of my heart under my winter coat. A lifetime of discipline and self-control took over, but I literally did not know if it would carry me to the next corner.

However, I kept walking slowly. People were now running past me, streaming the other way. Carl and I eventually met up about ten blocks later and continued on together. We were far enough way from the scene now not to have to worry about being seen together. Cop cars sped past us without ever slowing down.

We got to a phone booth at a corner near a neighborhood tavern and I called Hank Perrone and told him to come and pick us up immediately. I named a nearby diner and didn't say more. I didn't have to. Hank could tell from the sound of my voice there had been trouble.

We walked on to the diner. I had calmed down enough now to realize I was still carrying my piece—and so was Carl. I mentioned that to him, and we both laughed. The first thing you are trained to do when you are involved in any kind of shooting is to get rid of your weapon. Years ago, Johnny Morales told me a story about a knucklehead soldier in East Harlem who was stopped after a neighborhood hit. He still had his piece on him, concealed in his pants. A cop had stopped him—a cop he knew—and he was being questioned by him when the damned thing dropped into his pants leg from his belt and slid down and out the cuff of his trousers. The gun clattered on the pavement and both he and the cop stared at it.

"What the hell is that?" the cop asked.

"I dunno," the soldier said, trying to look newborn.

"Look," the cop said, "put the damn thing away, willya, Willie!"

The soldier thought about it for a minute and then said, "Nahh, I think it'll be better if you catch me with it than if I let them catch me without it." The cop declined the offer and told him to move on. The guy was incredibly lucky. If we had been stopped and frisked, that would have been that.

When Carl and I got to the diner on Flushing Avenue, we waited for Hank to pick us up. He got there a short while later and drove us over to my aunt Marion's, about twenty blocks away on Dekalb and Cypress. It was now around three or four in the morning. My uncle Jimmy let us in. He obviously read the looks on our faces and was aware of the hour. He asked in Sicilian if I was all right, and what had happened. I told him I was okay—and not to ask anything more.

At this point, I still did not know if the others had gotten away, if they were dead, or if they were in custody. I told my uncle Jimmy to take the guns from us and put them downstairs in a safe place. He immediately complied. He had done this many times before.

Then we just waited. We sat around listening to newscasts on the radio, hoping to hear something. Nothing. Four-thirty became five o'clock in the morning. I began pacing the floor. I stood at the living room window, peering out between slats in the venetian blinds, looking for unusual activity on the street. Finally, shortly before six o'clock, I saw two men coming up the street, then up the steps of the house. It was only as they approached the front door that I recognized Uncle Frank and Joe Notaro.

We embraced, exulting for a few seconds simply in having survived. Frank told me the others were all okay. Two of our men had taken off for the Bronx; the others had all managed to get clear even as the dozens of cop cars had flooded the neighborhood.

Uncle Frank said the first thing that happened after he saw the cars was that he and several others went back down into the basement of the house, into a wine cellar, and hid there for almost four hours. The police, he said, had gone door-to-door up and down Troutman Street, rousing people from bed, asking them questions. My uncle Bonventre told them that the police had said over two hundred rounds had been fired but that they had been unable to locate anyone who had seen or heard a thing. We found out later that one of the shooters directly up the street, in the building that Carl had fired at first, escaped by crashing through the living room window of one of the residents, running through the apartment, and then crashing out a rear window into the backyard.

Somewhere around dawn, we decided to clear out. We went out to Long Island, to my aunt Mary's house. It was around seven when we got there. I told her we'd like to use her basement for a while, so we went downstairs while we tried to make sense of what had just happened. My aunt said she'd make breakfast for us.

Uncle Frank reminded me that he had not liked the idea of our agreeing to meet the other side, but I cut him short, saying we had no time for recriminations now. What was done was done and we all had to live with the consequences. It wasn't hard to analyze the mistakes that had been made, for they were obvious. I had no problem acknowledging that it was my responsibility for allowing us to be set up that way. Now the question was, What would we, or could we, do about it? We would fight fire with fire. There was no choice. If Gaspar's side had set up a phony sit-down as a pretext to wipe us out, we could not again consent to talks until the guns were put away. We were prepared for war—and now we would go ahead. Still, we had to be absolutely sure who was behind it. Was Gaspar acting on his own? Was it just Steve behind him? Was there wider coordination with other leaders—Lucchese and Gambino? And, most important, who actually had been out there with guns in their hands?

Aunt Mary fed us a huge breakfast of eggs, bacon, fruit, rolls, and coffee. Her husband went out to get the morning papers, but there was still no word. In fact, for three days we heard nothing. It was strange. Finally, a tiny throwaway story in *The New York Times* announced that Brooklyn District Attorney Eugene Gold was launching an investigation into a shoot-out that had occurred on Troutman Street in the Ridgwood section a few nights earlier.

After that, there were subpoenas rather than news stories.

The question for us then became, Why the media blackout? On the surface, it seemed that it might have been a way for the cops to keep things cool. Perhaps they hoped to keep the gunplay down by keeping the coverage down. But that made no sense. On the contrary, strong media coverage would actually have been a restraining force in itself, because it would have been harder to act under the glare of publicity. Perhaps it was meant to offer people from our world the anonymity needed to come forward and testify before Gold's grand jury and the others looking into our affairs. There was just no way of knowing.

I made two decisions then. The first was to tell the media about the shoot-out myself, then see what would happen. I wanted to make sure every Family in the city—indeed, Families all around the country—knew what was going on and would have the chance to act accordingly. I also hoped the publicity itself might somehow generate information concerning some of the basic questions we had. I got in touch with a reporter I knew and told him as much of the story as I could. He responded as I had hoped, eager to break an "exclusive." A day or so later, my version of the story appeared in the papers, coupled with interviews with different people up and down the street, as well as with cops and investigators.

The other decision I made was to visit my father. Carl and I drove up to see him at an upstate farm where he was staying, about 160 miles from the city. He had been briefly informed about the incident just after it happened, but this was the first chance we had to tell him about it face-to-face. He was glad we had survived, but he clearly was not happy with the details of the story. He let me hear about my poor judgment—how I never should have consented to a meeting in the first place and that I had not really been prepared enough for what had happened. He also stressed what I already knew. The time for talking was past; we had no choice but to hit back and hit hard.

Sometime after this, because we still had no sure information, I sent a message to Sam DeCavalcante in New Jersey, because he had continued to act as a kind of go-between for the so-called Commission. I had Sam inform them that as a result of the ambush there was going to be all-out war. Up to then, we had assumed this was a faction fight, but henceforward, I told him, we were going to regard all those in the other Families who weren't with us as being against us.

I hoped there would be a quick response from the Commission. However, I was not prepared for the response I got—or for the quarter it came from. A couple of days later, Dick Anderson, an FBI agent, turned up at my house on Long Island and asked to see me. I was not there, of course, but I had worked out a system with Rosalie so she could contact me whenever she felt it was necessary. The message I got was to call Anderson as soon as I could, that the matter was urgent.

I got hold of Uncle Frank, Joe Notaro, and Vito DeFilippo and asked them what they thought I should do. They seemed to think that I should go ahead and find out what the agent wanted. At that point, we were all pretty sure that the FBI didn't have anything on us. So we arranged for a meeting—on our terms.

I called Agent Anderson and told him I would meet him immediately at a storefront on Second Avenue in Manhattan, and I had my security people positioned in the pork store and at the vegetable stand nearby, watching. He was there within ten minutes, escorted by one other agent (that was standard; the FBI always interviewed with teams of two). The agents were then led to DeRoberti's, an Italian pastry shop several blocks away, and we sat down in a rear booth and had our chat. By design, it was a public place. Anytime any of us met with the FBI, it was always out in the open, where we could be seen.

Anderson began by telling me that he had heard that there had been a little shoot-out a few nights before on Troutman Street and wanted to know what I knew about it. I was disappointed. He was on a fishing expedition, nothing more. I shrugged and said I knew nothing, that, just like him, I got my information from the newspapers.

Then he said, "I understand you've declared open warfare, and that you've decided that anyone who isn't with you is against you."

I froze. He was using almost the exact words I had passed on to Sam DeCavalcante. I tried to hide the rush of panic I felt, forcing myself to appear as nonchalant as possible. I could not begin to figure out what Anderson was up to—other than sowing discord. My mind was whirling. The only way this man would have been able to feed my own words back to me was if someone in my group who had gone out to see Sam was an informer—or if there had been a bug. I had no way of knowing then that it was the latter and that every conversation that had taken place in DeCavalcante's office for the past eighteen months had been recorded.

Why did he want to speak to me, What could I tell him that would be interesting? I asked. He was just hoping I'd have information for him, that was all. When he left, I was swimming in these waves of new doubt and anxiety. If Sam's office had been bugged or if he himself was talking, that was one thing; but if the problem came from our side, if there was an informer among us, who was he? I went over in my mind all the different people who had known about the message I had sent and the response I had received. People closest to me might be involved, Uncle Frank, Joe Notaro, Carl, Hank, Johnny Morales, people whose loyalty I counted on for my life.

Because Sam was our link to the Commission, we had to stay in touch with him, but it was obvious any further contact had to be severely limited. It took awhile, but we eventually were able to determine the problem was a bug. Nevertheless, extreme caution was in order. For me and the others, moving around town now involved more than following safe routes. We often disguised ourselves to make sure we would not be observed on the street—even by our own people. Following my father's lead, I turned to the art of disguise. I had several of them. Sometimes I was a Hassidic rabbi, sometimes a Catholic priest, sometimes a Greenwich Village character. I used to walk with a limp—because it is entirely possible to tell a person by their gait. The particular rhythm of someone's walk is more distinctive than fingerprints. No one, in that time, ever saw me walking like myself.

Once, I arranged to meet Rosalie and the kids on a street on the Upper West Side of Manhattan. I had on a false beard, horned-rimmed glasses, and a hat with a big feather in it. When I shuffled up to them, my oldest son looked blank-faced and frightened. I couldn't help laughing. And my laugh gave me away. Chuckie's face broke out in a big grin and then I swept him up into my arms.

There were other times I met Rosalie because I wanted her—and then our self-protective routines became almost ludicrous. My men would go to her and tell her I was waiting for her—somewhere. She knew she was to follow them. She would get into a car with them, lie down on the floor, allow herself to be blindfolded, and then later led into a building whose exterior she never saw, to a room whose windows were shuttered, where I was waiting. That way, we could spend a couple of hours in bed together— and then afterward I was the one who blindfolded her. My men came and led her back to East Meadow.

The first real intelligence break we got came through the grand jury. Grand juries are usually prosecutorial instruments designed to solicit information for the government. But this sword of justice is always two-edged; witnesses can pick up information, as well.

When I got to the grand jury room, I had no intention of saying anything. My lawyer waited outside the courtroom. With each question I was asked, I excused myself, stepped outside the door of the courtroom, consulted my attorney, and returned with another version of the Fifth.

Each day I went to the courthouse, I saw men from the other side sitting on benches, waiting to testify. These were people who had once been with us, people with whom it was easy to get into conversations. I got the sense from them just how uncomfortable Gaspar was about the present state of affairs. He did not, in any of these descriptions, sound like a man eager for battle.

On the other hand, neither did it sound like he was looking to relent. One of the guys whom I had made a point of singling out and talking with at some length was killed a short while later—and not by our people.

Then one day, the government presented a display of weapons in the grand jury room. The weapons, ranging from pistols to shotguns and machine guns, had all been picked up off Troutman Street following the shoot-out. I was asked to identify them. I walked over to the table, looked carefully at each gun, and then walked back to the witness box.

They were just guns, I said, I had nothing to tell them. The government had told me plenty. One of the weapons was a .38 pistol with a peculiar rust spot on the front of the barrel. The gun belonged to a soldier named Phil Rastelli, a veteran triggerman and someone we knew was close to Gaspar. When we had all been together, we used to joke with Phil about this gun. Now we had enough knowledge to make a move.

While I had enormous latitude in decision-making, I was not the Family leader; my father was. But with our determination to fight, and now having narrowed our focus through this latest piece of intelligence, he concluded that the time had come for him to return and take charge of the Family. He needed to be in the middle of the action rather than on the margins.

To bring this about, he said, he would have to come out of hiding. This would be tricky, we all realized, not only because of the threat he faced on the streets but, even more immediately, because he was considered a fugitive by the government. Following his kidnapping, a warrant had been issued for his arrest. So far as the government knew, his kidnapping was just another ploy to avoid testifying. The warrant had been outstanding for almost a year and a half. This had to be cleared up first.

Beginning in February, he told me to hold off and to arrange for his surrender. I reluctantly but dutifully agreed. I then became my father's go-between in protracted negotiations with the government. One day, unshaven and dressed rather informally, I went to Al Krieger's office and asked to see him. When his secretary asked to say who it was, I told her to tell him it was an old friend. I would not say more. A few moments later, Krieger walked out of his office and I stood up and said hello. I could see his body let go with relief. He ushered me into his office, where I then asked him if he wanted a new client.

He was confused because he assumed I was already his client. No, no, it wasn't me, I assured him. Perhaps it was fear of microphones, perhaps by now it was just habit, but I went this way and that, explaining that this new client was someone who was wanted by the authorities and had been thinking for some time about surrendering. Krieger at first didn't know if I was talking about someone who needed help with a traffic ticket or a murder rap, but finally, after many turns on the dance floor, he caught on. We never mentioned my father's name, but he understood.

"He doesn't want to go to jail, I presume?"

"That's exactly right."

"We have to find out about the warrant, if he's bailable, a few other things. I need to make some calls. Why don't you come back tomorrow?"

I agreed to return as Krieger had suggested, and when I did, he told me that he had spoken to the FBI and they had told him that they were unable to say anything to him about Joseph Bonanno, that they would have to get back to him on any matters regarding his case.

A little bell went off in my mind. I told Krieger to make another attempt with the FBI, to call a certain agent named Dick Anderson—speak with no one else. "Ask him one question, I said: 'What would it take to obtain the surrender of Joseph Bonanno to the FBI?' "

Anderson hit the bait instantly. He got back to Krieger the next day, saying that he would be willing—personally—to meet with him and go over the possible conditions for my father's surrender.

This was toward the end of February 1966. All through March, into April, and then into May, we met and negotiated. We must have come up with seven or eight different deals we thought would work, but all of them became unglued at the last minute.

The FBI first wanted assurances about the place where they would arrest him. It was important to them, apparently, that the arrest look like an arrest rather than part of a packaged arrangement. Then the question of bail had to be decided—they agreed to an amount, then backed down, then okayed it again, then said it was out of their hands entirely, then switched again. When everything seemed settled, there remained the question of just what charges would be brought, what kind of sentence would ultimately be handed down. It all came down to my father's willingness to accept a three-year sentence for obstruction of justice that would then be reduced to two years of probation, which meant in actual jail time serving nine months and twenty days—with all other charges being dropped. At the time of surrender, bail would be set at $100,000.

When I took this final proposal to my father, he turned it down cold. If I had been arguing for myself, making my own deals, I would have known better what to do—or at least felt myself more comfortable when I agreed with my father that a "final offer" was never really final. As an adviser, I felt compelled to point out that the choice at this point was a clear one—stay in hiding or come in and accept the deal. My father shrugged his shoulders. I knew the meaning of that gesture as clearly as I knew the meaning of a brick wall. No way around the position he had taken.

I went back to the FBI and negotiated with them some more. Inch by inch, day by day, their position began to change. But meanwhile, the reality in our world was that we were at war and my father was unable to postpone that reality. He finally told me one day to make the best deal I could for him.

It was early May now. I worked out a second "final" arrangement with Dick Anderson, which would permit my father to walk into the FBI office on Sixty-ninth Street in Manhattan and surrender voluntarily. The government agreed to lower bail to fifty thousand dollars—a very manageable figure—and to give him six months on the street before proceeding against him—provided he then would do his part by entering a plea bargain to a single count of obstruction, thereby eliminating the uncertainty and expense of a trial.

I made all of the preliminary arrangements and then I went upstate to get my father. When I told him what I had worked out, he said there was no way he was going to plead out to anything. He was not guilty of anything, so why should he have to plead?

I could not believe this. What did he propose to do?

"Tomorrow morning," he said, "I'm going to walk into the federal court-house, I'm going to tell them, 'You've been looking for me; here I am. Ask me what you want!' "

No matter how crazy this seemed, I knew my father was deadly serious. If he was crazy at all, he was crazy as a fox. I felt a surge of resistance; I wanted to argue with him, but there was no way I could. I was someone I knew my father leaned on for support, for advice. I had given all my support and the best advice I had. I could not go further than that. His word was the final one. I could not tell him that my way was the better way, though if it had been left to me, I would have followed my own course—and been foolish for doing so. The relationship I had developed with my father over the years had become a very complicated one indeed, because it was so deeply professional as well as personal. He was my leader, but he had been missing for so long, I had become one, too. He knew that and I knew that. He treated me with the respect of someone who had become a leader, I honored him as the head of my Family, which he was. And this respect, however complicated, was absolute. He expected if from me. And I expected always to offer it to him. I then acted to carry out his wishes.

The first thing I did was to inform Al Krieger what was going on. He looked incredulous. Bail would go through the roof; they would throw the book at him, he said. He didn't understand whom he was dealing with. Nevertheless, we went ahead. "Tomorrow morning" actually turned into a couple of weeks. We went to a bonding company and secured a bail bond for $500,000—not enough, Krieger said, in a time when high bail could easily hit seven figures. We needed more.

I then got on a plane and went to the West Coast to see my sister and brother-in-law. I explained what was going on and asked them to help us secure an additional $500,000 bond by putting up their house as collateral. They agreed.

Following that, my father and I went over and over just how the logistics of the surrender would work. The key point, I told him, was to stay out of the clutches of the FBI because they would in all likelihood react to the sabotaging of their deal by trying to gain custody of him and thereafter keep him out of view, making it as hard as possible to communicate with lawyers, friends, and the media. I argued he should surrender instead to the U.S. Marshal's Service, the security arm of the courts, and let them deal with the situation. Yes, my father said, that sounded right. He told me to make the arrangements.

And so I did.

The way it was to work was that my father would just show up at the federal courthouse at Foley Square in Manhattan, go to courtroom 318, which handled the arraignment calendar, and announce to the judge that he was Joseph Bonanno—then wait. Because he would be sitting in a federal courtroom, he would then have to be taken into custody by the court's cops—the U.S. Marshal's Service, rather than the FBI.

We had been in and out of this building many times over the years. We knew it well. We planned our movements to the second. At exactly 9:00 A.M. on the day of his surrender, my father was to be dropped off on a street corner in a town on Long Island, where he was to be picked up immediately by Pete Notaro and my uncle Frank, who then were to drive him into the city.

We would have two people waiting at the Pearl Street entrance to the court building to shield my father as he arrived at exactly 10:00 A.M. and ducked inside. Another person was stationed at the elevator bank, holding open the door of a waiting elevator car so there would be no delay in the lobby of the building.

At exactly 10:30, Carl Simari and I—according to the plan—were to drive across the Fifty-ninth Street Bridge from Queens to Manhattan. Our destination: Al Krieger's office on lower Broadway. We reasoned that by the time we got there, news of my father's surrender would have been flashed on one of the all-news stations. Because we had been the targets of intense government surveillance and harassment, we wanted to make sure we gave no appearance of having any prior knowledge of the surrender. We would have turned up at Krieger's office because we had heard something on the radio, not because we had special information.

When my father actually entered the Foley Street courthouse that day, he was wearing the same suit, shirt, tie, shoes, and socks he had been wearing the day he disappeared more than two years before. The media, when they caught on, reported this with a flourish. To them, this was a kind of perfect Mafia touch. But this was done not because my father was eccentric but because he reasoned his garments would be carefully analyzed by the authorities for laundry marks and dry-cleaning tags in an effort to trace where he had been. The truth was that he had not worn those garments since the day of his kidnapping.

At the courthouse, my father went directly to room 318, where the federal judge, Marvin E. Frankel, was presiding over a day's worth of penny-ante cases. Al Krieger went to the office of Robert Morgenthau, the U.S. prosecutor, one floor above. As Krieger was announcing to Morgenthau why he was there to see him, my father walked straight down the center aisle of Judge Frankel's courtroom and stopped a few feet from the bench. The judge was startled as my father apologized for interrupting. The judge stared at him but said nothing.

"Your Honor," my father said, "I am Joseph Bonanno. I understand the government would like to talk to me."

That was all. Then there was bedlam.

21

As soon as my father announced who he was, everyone in the spectators section began whispering among themselves. A couple of people slid over to where my father was sitting and asked for his autograph. A couple of federal marshals also moved into position behind him and placed him under arrest.

They took him downstairs and booked him—fingerprinted him, recorded his name on various arrest forms—and then returned him to the court. Meanwhile, Al Krieger had gone to the fourth-floor offices of Robert Morgenthau, who couldn't believe why Krieger was there. Morgenthau was a tall, slim, very self-contained person who normally hid his emotions behind a facade of cerebral detachment. But apparently his mechanisms of self-control jammed. He literally leapt out of his chair, Krieger said, running down the hallway, not even waiting for an elevator. He took the stairs down to the next landing, where Judge Frankel's court was located, and strode into the room just far enough to identify my father. When he realized who it was, he turned and sprinted back upstairs to get his suit jacket. This was melodrama veering sharply toward farce.

When Morgenthau reappeared a moment or so later, he—like my father—strode directly up to the bench, asking that proceedings be set on my father's case. Judge Frankel, who had been contemplating a long and tedious day of petty legal quarrels, seemed to enjoy the prospect of an exciting few hours in the spotlight.

Morgenthau asked that bail be set for my father at $500,000 bond (the exact amount we had originally secured from the bonding company, a fact we all took note of). Krieger countered that the figure was too high, especially as the charge against my father—obstruction of justice—still had to be litigated. The lawyers on both sides snarled and snapped and split hairs over what charges should or should not be filed. Did the fact that he had been kidnapped mean anything? Anyone could stage their own kidnapping, after all—and then there were the nineteen months following the kidnapping. Sure, but in the time Joseph Bonanno was missing, the grand jury that had subpoenaed him had dispersed. Were subpoenas meant to carry over to succeeding grand juries? There was a very subtle distinction to be made here—so said Al Krieger, so denied Robert Morgenthau. And what about the man's criminal record? There was another canister of laughing gas for everyone.

What criminal record? Al Krieger wanted to know. My father's rap sheet showed only one entry—that violation of a wages and hours statute involving a business he was involved with in 1941, for which the company had paid a fine of a few hundred dollars. Well, he had been deported from Canada as an undesirable person, the government said. No, no, he had never been deported, Krieger shot back. Deportation orders had been withdrawn by the Canadian government itself. Joseph Bonanno had, by arrangement, voluntarily left the country.

Eventually, Judge Frankel wearied of the proceeding and set bail at $150,000, ordering my father to stay within the jurisdiction of the court— that is, the Southern District of New York—with travel permission extended to the Eastern District (for him to be able to visit my home) on Long Island and to the Tucson area, my father's home. My father walked out of Judge Frankel's court, flanked by aides and his lawyers, followed by the huge mob of reporters and photographers that had gathered by then, and was whisked away to Al Krieger's office, where I was waiting for him.

There were reporters gathered at Krieger's office, too. They witnessed the two of us embracing, exchanging pleasantries. I felt responsible for misleading one of the newsmen, a friend, by telling him my emotion came from my not having seen my father for almost two years and assuming all the while he had been killed. Couldn't he imagine the feelings of a son in that situation? His story of our emotional get-together appeared in the paper the next day.

My joy in seeing my father was quite genuine, however, because it meant he had evaded jail for the time being. I did not relish the thought of him, at age sixty-one, learning what I had discovered just a short while ago for myself. For now my father was free, back out on the street, where he wanted to be. That had been the objective all along.

The infectious spirit of the occasion carried over. We contacted La Scala and had them set tables for us in their private dining room, the Second Act. We called around to some friends and associates to help us celebrate and then headed uptown in three different automobiles. When we got near the restaurant, my father suddenly wanted to get a haircut for the occasion. Of course, we had to stop the caravan. Two or three men stood guard outside a hotel barbershop on Forty-eighth Street while my father renewed old acquaintances and had his trim.

When we got to the restaurant, there were embraces, tears, kisses all around. It was odd. I felt like a participant and a stranger at the same time. I was increasingly aware that so many of the people involved in this impromptu festival, from the barber, to Arturo and Roberto, the owners of La Scala, to the different captains like my uncle Frank and Joe Notaro, were older men who really were sharing memories and experiences of better and easier times. But it was the present that was on my mind, a present where we were hemmed in by danger, ringed with fire, uncertainty on all sides.

My father presided at the head of a long table that had been specially prepared for us. He offered numerous toasts to different people. The toasts were invariably in Sicilian; the stories he told, many of them, hearkened back to the old days, the days when troubles could be surmounted, order maintained. At one point, his eyes glistening, he raised a glass and told the room that we were living proof to him of the goodness and strength of the Bonanno family. When he talked about the day he had just been through, however, he was sharp and funny. He described his day in court—and in the holding pen downstairs, where, he said, FBI agents had gone crazy tearing through his belongings.

"They took my hat in their hands, and they turned it inside out and pulled down the band like this," he said, pantomiming the way agent Dick Anderson had hunched over the sweatband and the silk interior lining of the hat. "They found nothing!" he added, his voice dropping an octave to emphasize the point. Laughter and applause filled the room.

The drinks flowed freely with the speech making; the food was served up plate after plate. But it wasn't like the old days; it never could have been—and never would be.

We were living in the present, not the past, and we were in the middle of a war. Many of the men sitting in the room were old warriors. They wore their years, which they could not escape. They were fighters but they had all the ailments of middle and old age. Despite having good trigger fingers, they suffered from high blood pressure, failing eyesight, disorders of heart and lungs. They were men who still could defend themselves against the enemies of the street but not those within their own bodies.

In the middle of yet another round of drinks and stories, this other enemy struck. Joe Notaro, so important to our organization, suddenly became ill. He cried out and tried to push himself away from the table. His face was contorted, but he could not raise himself to his feet. As though a triggerman from the other side had found him, his whole body seemed to jerk forward and his face came smack down onto the plate of food in front of him. We rushed to his side, but it was too late. He had had a massive and fatal heart attack; according to a physician who was at his side within minutes, he was probably dead before his face hit the table.

He was only fifty-six, but he had had a history of heart trouble and had been under enormous pressure since my father's disappearance. After the kidnapping, he was one of those who bore the brunt of government investigators. I don't know how many times he was hauled before grand juries. Whatever personal threat he felt, there had been the added one of what the government might do to his son, Joseph, a young lawyer who—it often had been suggested—could easily have been disbarred for the work he did on our behalf. In fact, Joe Notaro was carrying a subpoena with him in his suit jacket when he died.

For me, Notaro was one of two people whom I depended on in running things. Where it was possible to imagine other long-standing members weakening in their loyalty under pressure, that would never have been the case with him. He, like my uncle Frank, was someone I could trust with my life. And, in practical terms, I did just that. He and my uncle Frank were the only two men in the Family who always knew where I was. People contacted me through them. My security and my ability to make myself available depended on them. Now one of them was gone.

We buried Joe Notaro on a beautiful late-spring day. Many people from our world attended, and there were also scores of government agents hovering around the funeral home, on the streets outside, snapping pictures of everyone who came and went, recording the license plate of each car that pulled up.

Once the funeral was over, some of us went back to my home in East Meadow, where it had been decided my father was again going to reside temporarily. There was some danger in this, but it turned out to be less risky than housing him at a new location, where it would have been harder to guarantee his safety. The way my home was situated made it easy to provide protection, and there was little likelihood that anyone would try to penetrate the kind of security we threw up. Initially, my father did not like this arrangement, but he soon saw the logic of it.

As difficult as it was for Rosalie, my plan to secure the house was to have several of our people living there with us at all times, virtually turning the place into an armed camp. Another factor in our favor was the unwritten understanding in our world—never violated in three-quarters of a century in the United States—that members of a personal family were never to be harmed in any dispute involving the *borgata* (strictly speaking, the Family). I put stock in that—especially with soldiers standing guard everywhere.

I know this was terribly hard on Rosalie. I saw how completely she seemed to withdraw around everyone, including me. She deferred to my father in ways that made me feel she was as frightened of him as she was respectful. She had known him for years—he was her father-in-law, after all—yet she still referred to him as Mr. Bonanno or Mr. B. As for the others, it was as though they were not there. She rarely spoke to any of the men, though day after day, she prepared meals, cleared the table, did the dishes, cleaned the house, and looked after the children.

We now could turn our attention to the business of going from the defensive position we had been put in to the offensive position we wanted to be in. The first matter was intelligence. We had to be sure of many things—the movements and habits of our opponents. And, even more, just who our opponents were. It was one thing to say that anyone who wasn't with us was against us; it was entirely another to have actual knowledge.

Pete Maggadino, who had defected from cousin Steve's Family, was a real help to us. He was an invaluable source of information about Steve's thinking. He wasn't sure, but he believed Steve had less support from other leaders than we imagined. Also, through Pete, we discovered that Steve had singled me out as the person who stood in the way of peace in our world. I was, in his eyes, the real target to be eliminated.

If that was so, did others think that, too? Pete could not provide the answers. We decided among ourselves to test the waters by sending word to the Commission, asking that they receive a message to be delivered by a delegation from our Family. Following form, we picked three men, including two of my father's oldest associates, Angelo Caruso and Nick Alfano, to represent our position.

Our delegation carried a specific, carefully worded message that my father was in good health, that he sent his best wishes and deepest affection to everyone, and that he was still the Father of his Family and that the only problem he now faced was between himself and his cousin, Don Stefano. He and his cousin, he said, would undoubtedly resolve any differences they had between them.

The message was loaded with strategy before anyone said anything. The language, subtle and disguised, meant to convey sentiments of friendship while at the same time creating a situation in which it might be possible to see if Steve Maggadino had real support among other Commission members.

Our couriers reported that no one seemed willing to go out on a limb for Steve. Present at that Commission meeting were Steve, Carlo Gambino—who was then acting as chairman—Tommy Eboli, who was standing in for Vito Genovese, Joe Colombo (now head of the Profaci Family), Joe Zerilli of Detroit, and Carmine Gribbs, standing in for Tommy Lucchese. It may have been Lucchese's absence that weakened the resolve of the Commission. Recently, he had been diagnosed with an inoperable brain tumor. For all intents and purposes, he was no longer a factor in our world.

With Lucchese unable to lend support, Carl Gambino seemed to have no resolve of his own. He welcomed my father's bid for peace. Colombo was another one who seemed to want out. Steve had been courting him and using him for some time, but when he was asked to give his opinion about the message, he declined, saying he was too inexperienced to have an opinion. Angelo Caruso—and later Joe Zerilli—told us that Joe Colombo, when pressed by Steve, told him outright that he did not want to get involved.

The picture we got of Steve was of a man so discomfitted by the proceedings that he seemed to be chewing on something he didn't like as people spoke. He made remarks—barely audible, we were told—about how the Bonannos continued to cause problems, but no one seconded a thing he said. In fact, one acting Commission member, Tommy Eboli, seemed to turn on Steve. He told him, with our delegation in the room, "If the shoe fits, wear it."

In the end, the Commission passed a resolution declaring their peaceful intentions toward my father and our Family. However, none of us was taken in by that. It was one thing to have leaders of other Families standing off at a distance; it was another to assume they were unwilling to see the administration of our Family overturned. What was clear was only that Steve was now the sole driving force behind the split in our clan and that he wanted me out of the way so that new leadership—controlled, no doubt, by him—could move in.

So far, Steve had not committed his own Family to the struggle, nor was it thinkable that he would. He was a boss from Buffalo. If he sent men into New York City, he would stir up far more than he ever could settle. If he wanted to control the Bonanno Family, he would have to do it through his surrogates, especially Gaspar DiGregorio.

The atmosphere around my house grew heavier with this sense of waiting for the inevitable. The strain affected all of us, but no one more than Rosalie, and communication between us became more and more strained because my attention was focused on my larger Family.

The days and nights grew wearisome and interminable. The men sat around with little to do other than watch television, eat, and play cards. My father and his cousin Peter Magaddino, almost as though they were an insulated, separate unit, talked about the old days, about what our world had come to. It was hard at times to listen, because I had heard it all before.

They talked about tradition a lot. What we were unable to sustain here, they kept saying, was a set of values. Those values—loyalty, responsibility, bravery, generosity, devotion to the group over selfish interests—were the real wellsprings of our power, not the displays of wealth or muscle that so many newer, Americanized members were given to. Yes, we were Americans, my father would say in his heavily accented English; we could not escape that. But we would not survive if selfishness and greed came before tradition.

It was strange sitting there between Pete and my father. I understood every word of Sicilian, I felt like I was part of every dream and memory of theirs; but I also knew that I was part of the very country and set of values that had undermined the dreams and memories they were talking about. As in any war, there was a process of disintegration going on all the while—and it had little to do with what was taking place on the battlefield.

While we had a surer sense that we were not up against four of the Five Families but only the faction that Steve had pried loose from our Family, there were still formidable problems to deal with on the street. Many of our people were continuing to defect to the other side, not because they liked Gaspar, Paul Sciacca, or Steve, but because their jobs were at stake. Some captains who had defected happened to control places like the docks, the airports, different unions. Many of the people who went over were ordinary working people, old-timers whose values were probably far more in accord with those of my father than those of the captains who were leaning on them. The bleeding in our organization was real and ongoing, and because of it, we could not move until we were absolutely sure of who was with us.

It happened that as our numbers diminished, we, ironically, grew stronger. Where we once had been a Family of about four hundred, we were down to two hundred or fewer. But the people who stayed with us were really tough, loyal, and reliable. We knew what we had to do and how to do it.

First, our fighters became invisible, really invisible. It is one thing to "go to the mattress," to hole up in safe apartments; it is another to break off all contact with the outside world, to avoid all familiar places, to shun friends, family, social occasions, movies, to come and go before anyone knows you're there or sees you depart.

By late spring, we left a few calling cards. Gaspar's top triggerman at Troutman Street, Frank Mari, was followed home one night by unidentified men and wounded in a shoot-out. There were others not so lucky. On our side, invisibility and planning kept our fighters out of harm's way. We could not control what happened to noncombatants, and so we took losses, too. But now it was known to the other side, to all the Families—and to the police—that we were not going without a fight, that our intention was to meet force with force.

There were two major events that summer. The first was another round with the grand jury, which was still looking into the Troutman Street affair and its continuing aftermath. I was not cooperative and was eventually cited for contempt, but I was freed on bail while my lawyers and the court wrangled over when, where, and for how long I would have to do time. My case was continued till the fall, and the extra weeks on the street were welcome.

The second major event of the summer was that while all my workings with the grand jury were taking place, Uncle Frank became ill. He had battled cancer in the past, but now suddenly his condition worsened, complicated by emphysema. He was in and out of hospitals, which posed an additional problem, because we had to be sure he had security at all times. But I knew he was going this time. He deteriorated so rapidly that the physical change from day to day was noticeable.

During these weeks, in addition to having to run a war without Uncle Frank's council and the vital communications support he provided, I also had to keep up with the administration of our Family. My father could not travel; we had interests outside the state—in Wisconsin, the far west, Canada, the Caribbean. There was no one else who really could attend to those out-of-state matters. I traveled as the need arose, but now with the sense that anytime I left for two or three days, I was taking a chance that I would not see Uncle Frank when I got back.

I had to make a trip to Canada in August, and when I visited with him before I left, I told him I would be gone for a couple of days. He nodded. He was too weak to say much. His face was covered with an oxygen mask; his eyes opened and closed as though he was fighting off sleep, though in reality it was because he was so weak. As it turned out, he died while I was in Canada. I said a prayer for him when I saw him laid out in the funeral home; I was sorry for his family and wished there was some comfort I could provide. For myself, though, Frank was closer to me than anyone outside my immediate family. I would no longer have him as a friend, counselor, and adviser. I was bitter, too, when I looked around during the funeral and saw all those people who had come to pay their last respects who had gone over to the other side, people who might have been planning to shoot Uncle Frank, for all I know, but who were now crossing themselves and wiping away tears.

I did not cry, did not feel then—or afterward—any sense of grief that matched the love I felt for him, Perhaps that was just an occupational reflex, but I don't think so. I have this strange place in myself, one I shared with my uncle, that death is just a fact of life, too common to cry over. Frank would have felt the same way if he had been standing next to my coffin. What I was sorry about was that I had not been there at his side to comfort him when he died.

22

With the passing of Uncle Frank, something of my own spirit seemed to pass with him. I was just as committed to fighting and winning as ever, but it was harder now to overlook the fact that things were falling apart.

Strangely, the government and the mob could still find time to cooperate openly during this same period when war was raging in the streets and grand juries were flourishing. All through 1966, there had been ongoing racial disturbances in south Brooklyn between blacks and whites. There were gang fights, muggings, assaults, neighborhood meetings that were forever threatening to spill over into full-blown riots. City officials quietly contacted known Mafia figures, including Albert and Larry Gallo, and asked them to do something, anything to help ease tensions. Albert organized meetings in the white neighborhoods—predominantly Italian—and told young people there to knock it off. There were other contacts made by other members of the Families, including members of the warring factions of our Family. The result was that tensions eased. To be sure, because the Mafia effort was so public, there were howls of editorial protest. How could New York City compromise itself by employing mafiosi to do its bidding? If the editorial writers knew their history, they would have easily been able to answer their own questions. Instead, Mayor Lindsay supplied the answer. When speaking of stopping violence and disorder, he said, "You can't always deal with people who are leaders in the Boy Scout movement."

But if there was advantage to be had from this, we were no longer able to take it. War, not peace and cooperation, was the order of the day in our world. By the fall of 1967, Mafia leaders from around the country were so disturbed by what was happening with New York's Families, they made a pilgrimage to New York to see what they could do to restore order. With no functioning Commission, their conclave, urged on by people like Gambino and Colombo, quickly turned into a farce.

The leaders came together at a restaurant in Queens called La Stella. Among those attending were Carlos Marcello from New Orleans, Santo Trafficante from Florida, people from the Midwest, West, and South, along with Gambino, Colombo, and a number of second-rank people from the Genovese and Lucchese Families with whom we had no experience. Our Family was invited, but we wisely chose to stay away.

Knowledge of this impending clambake soon got into the hands of police and prosecutors. Before hors d'oeuvres were served, the meeting, dubbed "Little Apalachin" by the media, was over. The Dons swaggering into the restaurant might as well have checked their coats at the local police station before they sat down to eat. The waiters and busboys were probably cops.

The evening news had pictures of the men being led out of the restaurant to waiting police vans. According to reports, when the raid was announced inside the restaurant, many of the people from our world, far from being surprised, just continued to eat until the slow process of arrest was finished. For years, prior to "Big Apalachin," whenever large numbers of our people got together, raids such as this would have been impossible.

During that fall, I had other business to attend to. I was summoned back to court and finally given my sentence on the contempt charge that had been brought against me that summer: thirty days. I was not pleased to go off to jail; in fact, I was a little apprehensive because others—on both sides of the Troutman Street shoot-out—were going off at the same time. When we all got to the facility—on Thirty-seventh Street in Manhattan— we discovered that the entire third floor of the jail had been reserved for us alone. We were side by side, in open rooms, free to talk or kill one another for the next thirty days.

The surprise for me was that where there might have been hostility and violence, there was none. There was instead, on both sides, a kind of world-weary truce; implicit in our behavior toward one another was the shared sense that the war we were involved in was impossible.

Just as the death of my uncle Frank had sapped my spirit, so did this brief and surprising time in jail undermine my will to fight. All of us knew we would be back at it. Any one of us might have taken advantage of a turned back or an overlooked tray of food, but it was as though the effort and the risk that would have gone with the killing was too great. We all decided to just sit back and relax.

Actually, if jail could be enjoyable, it was at this loosely run state facility. The guards and all of us maintained friendly and cooperative relations. Because the jail was in the middle of the Garment District, we were actually in our own territory, able to do some things for the guards. For example, the guards complained about the noisy clatter of nighttime garbage collections on the street outside. I told them I'd see what I could do about it. The guards thought I was kidding. But when Hank Perrone came to visit me the next day, I told him to fix things. Beginning that evening and thereafter, garbage collections in the area became as quiet as church collections.

The guards, in turn, winked at all kinds of regulations. Hank brought me a huge hero sandwich one day and, on other occasions, bottles of wine, which I shared with everyone—including the guards.

I spent Thanksgiving in jail that winter, coming out into a reality I did not want to face. It was the darkest time of the year in more ways than one. The war was by no means finished, and I had my responsibilities, regardless of how I felt.

But the first problem that hit me was at home. Whatever I was feeling, Rosalie had her own demons to contend with—and I probably was one of them. She had grown more weary of the war in her way than I had. For her, the war meant the occupation of our home, the men, the meetings, the rooms full of cigar smoke and trash. She was constantly fearful of what she said and how she acted around my father, because even though she respected him, she neither understood him nor believed he understood or even cared for her. It was as if she had to be on tiptoes with every step she took, and she was constantly stubbing her toes.

She was also worried about money. We had money, of course, but our resources were getting thin because so much was going into maintaining the Family on a war basis, which meant not only having to support our fighters but their families, as well. Money was needed to maintain cars, pay for rents, supplies, weapons, ammunition, travel. With the bodies in the house and the heavy weight of my father's presence, it all added up to more than Rosalie could bear.

Because Rosalie and I did not talk about such things—I would not have been willing to listen even if she had told me what she was thinking—she simply and silently planned a rebellion of her own.

We said little when we saw each other at our designated meetings or when we occasionally spoke by phone. I told her very little about what I was doing, only that I was well and that she was not to worry about expenses or anything else.

But that was easier said than done. One day, there were erroneous stories in the papers about my being arrested in Canada along with several Montreal members of our Family (the illegal possession of a firearm and consorting with mafiosi was the way it was reported) and then deported. Another time, there was a huge commotion in the house when a suit of mine, fully pressed and on a hanger, was located in the back of one of our automobiles out in front of the house. No one knew how the suit had gotten there. In our world, it was easy to assume that this was a sign, like a dead fish wrapped in newspaper. Rosalie was sure I had been murdered, I believe some of my men thought so, too—including my father. When I contacted the house that evening, I could feel the weight of relief on the phone, but in talking to Rosalie, I did not pay attention to the deeper sense of fatigue and anger that was also there.

One evening, Rosalie went to the movies with a friend. This in itself was a gesture of defiance because it meant that she did not want to be confined, guarded, or watched by the Bonanno army. Before she left the house, my father asked her if she intended to drive her own car. No, she told him, she would go in her friend's car because she wouldn't have to worry about there being enough gas in the tank.

If she had read a book on how to insult a Sicilian man, she could not have done better. To tell the patriarch of a family—in front of others— that he hadn't been able to provide well enough for there to be gas in his daughter-in-law's car was akin to telling him that he was not a man. My father was waiting for her when she came home, and he denounced her for having humiliated him.

Rosalie said later that she was literally struck dumb by my father's anger. And seeing her freeze in that way prompted my father to assure her that he cared for her, understood the difficult position she was in, and that he hoped she would simply have the patience to wait through what was a difficult time for everyone.

All through that late winter and spring, the tension kept building. My father, in this period, became jumpy, vigilant, too careful. He was constantly poking through the house to make sure everything was in order. He inspected all mail and packages that came to us. He began going through drawers and closets, checking everything. And in doing this, he one day let Rosalie know that a watch of mine that had always been in a top drawer in our bedroom was missing. Aside from feeling that her room and her privacy had been invaded, she believed my father had accused her of stealing, which indeed was the case.

All through these months, she had begun squirreling away money—not for a rainy day or to make sure she would be able to fill a gas tank if she needed to, but because, in her unhappiness, the idea of independence had been growing and growing in her mind. She had hocked my watch to add to a little freedom fund she had been building.

Meanwhile, she devised subtle strategies to try to make the house as uncomfortable as possible for my father and the other men. She became a den mother to a Cub Scout pack in which my eight-year-old son, Chuck, was enrolled, and she began having the Scout pack over to our house for meetings during the afternoons, hoping the noise and commotion might get on my father's nerves enough to make him and his men want to move out.

Instead, my dad was cheered by the sound and sight of children running through the house. He made a point of inspecting the children's uniforms, telling them about the virtues of bravery, loyalty, and obedience. The children, in turn, became enamored of him, as though he was a kind of supreme commander. They lined up to salute him, and to listen to his stories.

It was more than Rosalie could stand.

I'm not sure what single thing finally drove her over the edge, but one day in July she and the children just left. No note, no message, no phone call—nothing. She piled the kids into the car, as though she was going out for a couple of hours, and she was gone.

When I was told that she and the children had left the house and had been gone for several hours, I was not worried at first. Her family lived nearby; perhaps she had gone to visit them. But when she did not return after an entire day, I was upset—and then angry. I was pretty sure I knew what was involved. If there had been an accident of some kind, I would have heard about it; it was not possible that anyone coming after me would have gone after my wife and children. That left only one possibility: She had left me.

I was as upset as I was angry, but I could afford none of that in the middle of a situation where I was responsible for my larger Family's survival. Worrying about what Rosalie was going through was a luxury I simply could not allow myself. I knew I would hear from her or from someone soon enough—and I did.

I got word from Rosalie's mother that she had heard from her and that she was all right. She did not know where she was, only that she was all right. For the time being, that was enough for me.

But a whole month passed before Rosalie called one of the numbers where she knew she could leave a message for me. By then, I did not want to speak to her. I had Hank Perrone talk to her instead. My feeling was that Rosalie had compromised me personally in the way she had left and, even more, had compromised the Family in the sense that wherever she had been and whatever she had been doing, there was now the chance, especially given the knowledge our enemies had of our marital problems, that they might have gotten to her during these last weeks.

Days after she moved out of the house, I had had the locks changed. When she now called, so many weeks later, and said that she was unable to get into the house and that one of the children was sick and she was out of money, I agreed to talk to her.

I made careful arrangements for her and the children to register at a motel. I met her there, gave her some money so she could get our son Joe's asthma taken care of, and then I left. A week or so later, after I was sure none of us was being set up, I brought Rosalie home again. We were together finally, but the strain all of us had been living under for so long had left its mark.

People like me, who believe in our tradition and the way of life that it entails, should probably not get married in the first place, because it is a classic act of bigamy. We are already married when we go to the altar. The normal allegiances and loyalties that occur in a marriage are distorted and forever divided. Looking back on my life then, given what my wife, my family, and I were all going through, I can neither excuse myself nor apologize for anything that happened. I would have done far better, and so would Rosalie, if we had never married—but that is a statement as useless and as devoid of responsibility as denying one's history.

It is strange. There were others, I know, who took the oath in my time who were able to sidestep the kind of division I am talking about. But that is only because there was never any question about where their loyalties lay to begin with. Their loyalties were always, first, to their personal lives, not to this other, more abstract, more punishing reality of loyalty to a larger Family. I have no real explanation for the depth and power this distorting commitment has had in my life other than to observe—and never disown— the damages it has inflicted on people I love and on myself.

The Vietnam War was in high gear. There were protests in the streets and on college campuses; the TV news every night was filled with pictures of the bloodshed over there and the chaos here. It was the climax of our war, too, and though it seems a little grandiose to say, I have always linked those two wars in my mind because both were about the misuse of power and the resulting disintegration of the personal and collective values that went along with it.

By the end of 1967, Tommy Lucchese was dead of brain cancer, Vito Genovese was dying in prison, Carlo Gambino had suffered a heart attack, Steve Maggadino's heart was giving out, Gaspar DiGregorio, because of his health problems, was out of the picture, and Paul Sciacca, the handpicked successor, was hanging on by a thread.

But the war went on.

In October, two of our men, Vincent Cassese and Vincent Garofalo were shot, but both survived. We hit back—hard.

Our squads had their assignments along with the autonomy as to where, how, and when they were going to move. The story that got maximum coverage in New York shortly thereafter was a triple murder in a restaurant on the Queens-Brooklyn border.

The target was one person, but when the two shooters entered the restaurant, they saw that their intended victim had been joined by two other men. Contrary to what the papers said, the shooting was surgically precise. As the two gunmen entered the restaurant, one of the three diners recognized the first gunman and stood up. At that point, he was shot—he had made it easy. Then, simultaneously, the second shooter began spraying the place, high along the walls, forcing patrons to duck down under their tables so that they could not see what was taking place. Then the first shooter took care of the remaining two men, who were just starting to scramble to their feet. The shooters quickly slipped out of the restaurant to a waiting car and drove away. Behind that car, parked out on a one-way street behind the restaurant, was another, blocking off the street so that no other cars could enter the area and possibly interfere with the getaway.

This was a classic maneuver. The two gunmen each had very different assignments, the one going for the hit, the other for the distraction. The two cars also were following a familiar pattern. Obviously, a getaway car was essential, but so was the covering car. The getaway car was strictly a military vehicle; since it had a phony registration and the engine numbers had been filed off, there would be no way of tracing it to an original owner or lot. The driver of that car was one of the squad members. But the other car and driver were absolutely clean. Here is an example of where a lawyer, a schoolteacher, an upstanding citizen—who also happened to be a member—was part of the support team behind the fighting people. If he was stopped, if his car was searched, nothing would turn up on any police blotter anywhere.

The principal target had been Smitty D'Angelo, the trusted captain I had once sent to Florida following the Kennedy assassination who had gone over to the DiGregorio faction. His brother Jimmy and another long-standing friend, Frank Telleri, were the two other men.

The triple murder in Queens, though it was not immediately apparent, was one of the final battles of the so-called Banana War. Though none of us knew it then, the peace that was soon to follow was only a prelude to another and far more deadly war—one that involved the United States government, with all its resources, against what was left of the Family of Joseph Bonanno.

23

All we could think of was continuing the war. The new enemy and the new era came upon us subtly, almost invisibly.

In the early months of 1968, I planned to go to Arizona to do some needed fund-raising so we could continue fighting. Two years of almost constant warfare had drained our resources as much as it had our numbers and our spirits.

We had a plan. My father had returned to Tucson to spend time at home because there still had been no action in his case (the feds kept him on a string for years but never brought charges against him regarding his disappearance). I was due to make a trip to Arizona, as well—for an appearance having to do with a civil income tax matter. That was a perfect cover for fund-raising.

But I had to leave for Arizona much earlier than anticipated because my father suffered another heart attack. I needed to scramble my plans so I could immediately go west, but haste led to my making a serious error of judgment. I had anticipated using monthly payments from my captains to finance my trip. These funds were not yet available. No problem, said my aide Hank Perrone. He told me a mutual friend, Don Torrillo, a person we both knew and who had been helpful to us over the years, was willing to turn over one of his credit cards for me to use as I wished. I liked the idea because I wanted to make sure there would be no paper trail attached to me as I moved around—something I would normally have covered by using cash. Torrillo was a young guy who had been a gofer, a Jack Ruby type, in Hank's crew, though never a part of our Family. Torrillo was a real estate investor who had already done a service for me by taking on the mortgage to my house in East Meadow so I would not have to deal with banks, finance companies, and federal investigators. I frankly didn't think twice about using the card Hank furnished me with as I took off for Arizona.

My father was not nearly as sick as first thought. He recovered quickly and soon returned to New York. But I remained in Tucson for the tax case, which dragged on—and which was important in terms of my larger objectives. The government claimed I owed something like sixty thousand dollars in back taxes. They had recently confiscated large chunks of property I owned—property that I had intended to sell in order to raise money.

I was confident that the case would ultimately go in my favor because our businesses in the West were always run scrupulously. I trusted that my attorneys would eventually prevail and so, for the time being, I tried to relax even as I went about the business of attempting to fatten up our war chest.

Sometime during the second or third week in Tucson, I went into a men's clothing store and made some purchases. I handed over the credit card to the sales person and waited for him to process it. Instead, the clerk turned the card over to his superior, who phoned the credit card company. I was then confronted and asked several personal questions—mother's maiden name and so forth—which, not being Don Torrillo, I could not answer. The card was confiscated. I became furious, explaining that I was using the card with permission of the owner and that he would confirm that if contacted. But the store manager was unwilling to do anything.

I phoned New York on the spot and told Hank what had happened. He assured me that he would get in touch with Torrillo immediately and that he would get back to me, that there was absolutely nothing to worry about.

I didn't have time to hang around the store because I had an appointment with my tax man. But a couple of hours later, after my appointment, I got a call from an uncle of mine who was staying at my father's Tucson home. He told me to call Carl Simari in New York immediately, that the matter was extremely urgent.

I called my home in East Meadow, where Carl was staying, and he said that he would call me right back at a prearranged number. A few minutes later, he was on the phone, telling me that he had terrible news: Hank had just been killed. I couldn't believe it. He was leaving a warehouse in Brooklyn where he had an office and he was shot on the street. Two gunmen jumped from an automobile and fired eight shots. The street had been blocked off by an abandoned dummy car and the gunmen sped away in the opposite direction.

For some reason, I looked at my watch. It was exactly 5:31. Hank had been alive just hours ago; his look, his voice, even his manner of speech were in my head. I felt like I had been hit by lightning and survived. I wanted to get on the next plane back to New York.

But very shortly thereafter, I got a call from Peter Maggadino, who told me that my father wanted me to stay in Tucson for a while, that it would be perilous for me were I to attempt to return home. The word out on the street was that Hank had been taken out probably by Frank Mari, one of Gaspar DiGregorio's gunmen, and I was probably next on the hit list.

I felt rage, frustration, and icy determination to do whatever had to be done to make sure that those who were responsible for this would pay. But because I was so distraught, I forgot completely about the little practical matter of the credit card problem Hank had been working on when he was shot.

The next day, the FBI visited my father's house, where I was staying. I hadn't slept all night and the rage and fatigue I felt were fueled by the sight of the two clean-cut, mannequinlike agents standing at my door. They were there to question me about Hank's shooting, obviously, but when I refused to talk with them, one of the agents, David Hale, uncharacteristically began taunting me about being so far from home when a buddy of mine had gotten it. I told him to perform a contortionist's act on himself. Hale then whipped out a document and placed it in my hand.

"For you, big shot," he said. It was a subpoena ordering me to appear before yet another grand jury investigating Troutman Street, the Banana War—and this latest killing.

"We can take you in right now or you can go voluntarily," Hale said, a grin on his face. I wanted to punch him, but instead I took the subpoena, then returned to New York, where I wanted to be anyway.

I had revenge in my heart. Whatever war-weariness I had felt was now gone. I wanted the people who had killed Hank. I wanted the cover of the apartments, the streets, the disguises even as I walked through the waiting jungle of court proceedings.

At the Brooklyn courthouse, where I had to answer the subpoena I had been given, there were other men from both factions in the Family also waiting to testify. Many of these people were the same ones who only a while ago had been jail mates of mine on Thirty-seventh Street. I quickly found out just how taut the atmosphere really was. That first day, I said something to one of these men, Michael Consolo, an elderly man who had been a friend for years before he went over to the other side. It was his kiss of death, not mine. He was found shot to death on a street near his home that night.

But I also discovered that people in my own Family, people I had always counted on, were no longer reliable friends. I saw Johnny Morales in the hallway of the courthouse and I went up to him. His eyes shifted left and right, never resting on me. Later, my father told me Johnny had split off and formed yet another splinter group within the Family.

I had nothing to say to the grand jury because I did not know anything—other than that my world was falling apart.

"I don't know who killed my friend any more than you do," I told the prosecutor. To each question he asked—about Hank or about Troutman Street or about the war—I gave the same answer. I knew nothing. I could not be cited for contempt because I was responding. I was doing what I had to do to remain on the street.

Our fighting units were still intact. I don't know who got Frank Mari—I never asked—but one night he disappeared. Maybe he decided to take one of those permanent vacations, or maybe he figured he just wanted to live by himself somewhere. Who could tell? I was informed by one of our captains, Angelo Caruso, that it looked like Mari had just vanished. That was good-enough news for a small private party.

My father was very much involved with day-to-day decisions. This was his Family and he was firmly in charge. He moved in and out of the house at East Meadow, traveling in three-car convoys over routes that were always different, arriving at safe houses for meetings only after it was certain no one had followed him.

We were going to make peace, he said; that was the goal. The *borgata* was going to be brought together and then the war would be over.

"We will physically remove ourselves from this place once this is done; we will be gone, but we will be here," he told me elliptically one night. "We are going to make sure of these other Families once and for all. We don't yet know their involvements, so we will make sure that peace will come only when it is certain they will stay out of our affairs."

I did not know what he was talking about. I asked him and he waved me off. To be present and not present was an old concept, he said; it was one you understood or did not understand. My father seemed almost beyond reach, as though he was talking to himself—with me in the room. "Nothing exists anymore; there is only this anarchy in the streets, and if that is the rule, we know how to deal with it," he said. "We will make peace on their terms as well as ours, but it will be a real peace, which they will honor."

One night in early April 1968, a soldier in one of our crews, still loyal to us, was returning to his home in Coney Island. He was shot as he got out of his car. A companion escaped injury and thought he recognized one of the shooters—a gunman from the Columbo Family, the old Profaci group. This was reported to us—and within days, there was another shooting. A group captain in the Columbo Family, Charley LoCicero, was found shot to death. Shortly after that, Carlo Gambino contacted my father and told him that he could arrange peace on whatever terms my father wanted.

"We will take him at his word until it is proven otherwise," my father said. He then called a meeting of all the captains in the Family, a meeting at which, he told me, he was going to announce his retirement and name a new administration. It was clear that I was being "retired" by him, as well. I knew that he did not intend to name me in the new leadership— and I knew why. I knew just as surely as he did that there was a bullet out there with my name on it. And he also knew, without my having to say anything, that my sense of revenge had by no means been satisfied. There had been just too many casualities, too many betrayals.

"When we leave here," I told my father, "I want you to let me come back and do what needs to be done to leave this Family intact."

My father looked away. He knew my heart and he knew the depth of my loyalty to him.

"I intend for this Family to achieve peace" was all he said.

I listened to my father for many days before he made his "surprise" announcement to the Family. Because I was an adviser and a counselor, I raised all kinds of questions about whether or not leaving and turning over the Family to others would really end our problems. He did not know. He intended to live peacefully and quietly in Arizona with my mother, tending a garden, visiting with his many grandchildren.

In my own mind, of course, I knew why he was making this move. The fundamental problem was that there were no leaders, no tradition left. "The Volcano," as he called New York City, was no longer the center of power in any real sense. The world was changing around us; the old relationships that had guaranteed our place at the table were gone. My father's decision to move west was a recognition of reality: that our time was over and that there was no purpose in a bloodbath where even winning meant losing.

My father's decision to leave was spelled out at a long and difficult meeting we held out on Long Island in April 1968. There were no protests—one did not challenge the word of a Father. But the atmosphere in the room was heavy. Many of the captains who spoke, pledging their life-long loyalty to my father, wherever he was, whatever he did, were deeply moved. When my father told them what he had told me—that we were physically removing ourselves from New York but would always remain behind—one of the captains, Angelo Caruso, said, almost choking on his words, "Excuse me, Don Pepino, but how can we leave and remain here at the same time?" My father's eyes suddenly lit with energy. He pounded his chest with a closed fist several times.

"Here!" he said. "We remain here."

My father then named a negotiating committee, which included me, Joe Bayonne, and Vito DeFilippo, to enter into talks with Gambino and the other Family leaders.

These negotiations were conducted over a period of days. The talks we had with Gambino, Stephen Lasalla, Joe Columbo, and Carmine Gribbs were tense and filled with an unspoken paranoia on both sides. We went to these meetings without security—and unarmed. There was always in my mind the sense that at any moment the facade of amity in the room could crack like an eggshell, that between the end of one sentence and the beginning of another, blood might flow. I could see lights and shadows of doubt and suspicion on the faces of the men with whom I spoke. The other leaders harbored, as surely as I did, the sense that there were bullets with their names on them already housed in cartridge chambers, waiting only for the right moment, the irresistible opportunity.

We worked out in formal detail what my father had already agreed on with Gambino. The war was over; there would be no grudges, no acts of retaliation from any quarter. We agreed that upon this formal statement of unity, my father would officially announce his intention to retire and would name a new administration for the Family, and that this new administration—not anyone from the outside—would then have the authority to make whatever further changes in the Family seemed appropriate.

Ultimately, my father named three captains—Joe Bayonne, Vito De-Filippo, and Angelo Caruso—as the leaders of the new administration. "We have achieved unity," he said. "Now we can go." Gambino had been a boss in his own right and a member of the Commission since 1960. By mere attrition, he was now the New York head, with Gaspar DiGregorio and Steve Maggadino more or less out of the picture because of their ages. I was personally looking forward to leaving the whole East Coast imbroglio and getting back to my turf in Arizona.

My first responsibility was to make sure that my father's leave-taking would be secure. Between twenty-five and thirty men from different crews agreed to go back to Arizona with him and my mother.

I also had to look out for my own family. I did not want them to stay behind now, because I still harbored in my mind the sense that the war was not over. My plans, still unclear, included the real possibility of very quickly returning to New York and taking care of some still-unsettled scores.

I went to Rosalie one evening and told her to get ready, that we were going to be leaving immediately. I remember the moment vividly because it was the day before Martin Luther King, Jr., was shot, and my announcement to her seemed part of the chaos of the day itself. She was shocked and confused.

"Why now, Bill? I haven't packed; I haven't planned. Where are we going? How are we getting there?"

"Just pack as much as you think will fit in the station wagon; we'll send everything else later," I said.

I did know where we were going. I was all too aware of what returning to Arizona might mean for her, so my plan, already worked out, was to move to San Jose, California, an area she liked, where a sister of hers and a sister of mine both lived, where we had a community of friends. There was a house waiting for us.

The haste and commotion of leaving, of packing, of making sure there would be a crew going to Arizona to accompany my father made it all too easy to overlook the fact that the most dangerous enemy facing the Bonanno Family, and had been all along, was not from our world. The real enemy was omnipresent and invisible at the same time, lurking in alleyways with guns drawn, in courtrooms with writs pointed; the look and shape of the enemy was ever-changing, mystical and magical, as large and broad as the continent, as tiny as a little forgotten credit card.

24

Shortly after we went west—my father to Arizona, Rosalie and I to California—my father received another subpoena to appear before yet another grand jury in New York. Because he had recently had a heart attack, he checked into a hospital, had himself examined by a court-appointed physician, who confirmed that he was too sick to travel and should therefore not be forced to return to New York. So for the time being, the subpoena was put aside.

But while he was in the hospital, he received a death threat. The hospital operator reported the exact time of the call, and that the words used were clear and unmistakable. "We are going to assassinate Mr. Bonanno," the caller said.

As soon as I was informed of this, I left San Jose for Tucson. At my direction, my father was removed from the hospital and taken home, where I arranged to have him guarded around the clock. I did not know if the threat was a crank call—that was always possible with the frequency of our name in the papers—but in my mind I suspected that our war, far from having ended, had followed us cross-country.

My father and mother chafed at having a security detail, making jokes about the unlikelihood of anyone wanting to go after the retired old Angel of Peace. However, I thought that though my father may have been retired, he was not out of the reach of his enemies.

We had a squad of four men, including myself, to guard him. The four of us shared an apartment in town and took six-hour turns standing guard. All through June and July, the sense of danger hung in the air because the death threats had been followed by others, sent by mail. The letters were unusual in that they were written by one or more people who knew things about us that would have been unknown to the general public, including intimate references to Hank Perrone and Joe Notaro. The way the threats were worded suggested that the writers, or writer, were combatants in the Banana War, people with a determined interest in revenge.

Toward the end of July, the air of menace was broken by a bomb blast—directed not at us but at an ally, Pete Licavoli. The bombing injured no one but shook some foundations. Licavoli and my father had known each other for years. Pete came from Detroit and Cleveland and had been in Arizona for a long time, where he had always shown a willingness to defer, in matters of policy, to any decisions made by us. The newspapers were filled with sensationalized accounts of the blast—and the absurd speculation that we might have been behind it.

While we knew we were not involved, we could only hope that Pete understood that, too. The newspapers reported as fact that there had been trouble between different people close to both Licavoli and my father, but just who these people were, neither we nor Pete could say. We talked by phone the next morning about what had happened, concluding that the bombing had come from outside and that whoever was responsible knew something about explosives, because the bombs were powerful enough to destroy a utility shed and four automobiles parked nearby on Licavoli's property.

As a result, we redoubled our security efforts. I brought in additional men and we stood shift not only inside the house but outside, as well, communicating by walkie-talkie. That very next evening, as I was walking around on the patio of my parents' house, I heard my father's German shepherd begin to growl. I quickly grabbed a shotgun and ran to a step-up platform I had constructed at the rear wall of the garden, where I could see the street. Just as I reached the garden wall, I saw an object of some kind come flying over into the yard. The dog bolted toward the front gate, barking loudly. I climbed up onto the platform and saw someone move from the shadows near the house and break into a run. I raised the shotgun and fired. The figure, by now at the end of the block, got away, but I had the feeling that I might have hit him, because he broke stride, seeming to stagger, before getting into a waiting car and driving off. I started to climb down, intending to go out to the front of the house to talk to our men on guard, when I was knocked ten or fifteen feet by the concussive force of a bomb.

My father came running out to the patio. I handed him my shotgun and told him to get back in the house. I didn't realize then that there was a second bomb, as well. It had been tossed on the roof of the garage, and it detonated just as we were going back inside. The blast not only wrecked the garage but blew out the windows of my parents' bedroom, sending glass and debris all over the place. My mother, who was inside at the time, came out screaming, though she was unhurt.

There was no way of telling what more was coming, whether there were gunmen ready to move in, other bombs about to go off. Sirens were now howling in the distance. The men at the front of the house were upset and confused because they had seen nothing. As the sirens grew closer, so did our sense of urgency. Should all of us, a few of us, or only my parents be present to say what had happened? I thought I might have killed or at least wounded someone, so I needed to get out of there as fast as possible. I knew my father would be able to lose the gun and that our men would remain to be with him and my mother. I told my parents I would be back after the cops left; then I took off, moving as unobtrusively as I could till I was out of the area.

I was, believe it or not, now skilled at handling situations such as these. I figured, Let the authorities come and ask questions of my father, who owned the house, rather than of me. That probably would have resulted in my being taken down to the station for further questions. I had learned from Apalachin eleven years earlier that to panic and act instinctively was foolish. When you're in the middle of something, just stay calm and let other people take care of it. I walked rapidly for several blocks, eventually continuing on to the campus of the University of Arizona, my alma mater.

It was still early evening and there were many students strolling around—just the way it had been years ago when I was an undergraduate and thinking about a career in the foreign service or in law. Now I was simply glad to be able to blend in, to breathe more easily and to begin to think more clearly.

We sat around the next afternoon, trying to figure out what to do next. The newspapers were full of stories about the bombing, but there was no mention of a killing or of anyone being wounded. It seemed, however, that reporters and photographers were on the scene even before the police and firemen arrived. There was a photograph of my father in the still-smoking backyard.

The headlines suggested an answer: BONANNO BRINGS N.Y. MOB WAR TO TUCSON. But we were now pretty sure that was not the case. The next evening, another bomb went off—this time at the house of Joe Notaro's cousin, Pete, who had moved to Arizona with us in 1968.

Whatever was going on, whoever was behind this, it was clear that we had a problem, a real one on our hands—and there seemed to be little we could do about it.

The Arizona state legislature, along with the police, soon got into the act. Everyone seemed far more interested in pursuing us than whoever was setting off the bombs. Within weeks, Morris Udall, a member of the House of Representatives, condemned the Bonanno's for bringing mob warfare to the state. What an irony that was. As mentioned earlier, the Udalls, along with the DeConcinis, had for years been grateful recipients of our support, no questions asked, during election campaigns.

A *Tucson Daily Citizen* editorial read:

> Tucson's biggest underworld figure is Joe Bonanno, whose patio was bombed Monday night. Last spring, he brought several bodyguards to Tucson to protect him and his son Bill from a rival faction headed by Paul Sciacca, his former lieutenant.
>
> In so doing he may have moved the Mafia war to Tucson from New York, where several of his followers were gunned down last winter.
>
> There may be no connection between the bombings and fighting within the Mafia. One wonders, though, whether Tucson is not beginning to reap the bitter harvest which may follow having notorious underworld figures as part-time Tucsonians.

While no one could completely rule out the possibility that our own people were involved, that explanation made no sense. As the attacks continued—and they went on for the next fifteen months—there was no pattern to them other than that "known Mafia figures" seemed to be involved.

Obviously, I did not wait for the police to help us—especially as I could not be sure the authorities themselves might not, in one way or another, be involved. I had my own people on the case from the start. We had contacts throughout local and state government, and we tried to run down every lead we could come up with.

We began jotting down the license plates of the cars that were almost always following us around town. A few days into our investigation, we got the plate numbers on two of the cars that had been following us and had them checked out. We came up with a single address for both cars in Phoenix, one hundred miles away. That was strange in itself, but stranger still was the follow-up.

My brother, Joe, then twenty-two and already knowledgeable about our world, was in Phoenix at the time, and I placed a call to him, asking him to check out the address. He called back awhile later and said the street and number listed was a phony. It existed all right, but it was an empty lot. We were back to square one.

A little later, we got a lucky break. One of our men took down the license plate of a car, a snazzy little red sports car, that may or may not have been up to anything. We had the number checked out; it belonged to a young woman with a local address. We followed her around for a while, realized she wasn't a cop or, as far as we could tell, anyone involved with people in our world. She went to a drive-in food place one night, where our people caught up with her and talked to her.

Her name was Sandra Hitchcock. She was obviously frightened and, just as obviously, unaware that her car had been used to follow anyone around town. She had a boyfriend, she said, who wasn't around now, but he used her car from time to time. He was an ex-marine and a stock-car driver. She wasn't sure when she'd see him again, because he said he was out of town, following the racing circuit. She may or may not have been lying, but she provided us with our first lead.

The very next day, as I was walking in the street, one of the cop cars on my tail pulled me over and the officer in the passenger seat beckoned to me. I recognized him immediately—a local detective named Don Lowe. I said hello and offered condolences that he had to be wasting such a nice day following me around. He nodded and told me that the city police chief, Bill Gilkerson, wanted me to go down and talk to him as soon as possible.

I wasn't in a rush to talk to Gilkerson, though I knew him and liked him. He had been in Tucson for years and, before that, had been a lieutenant in an intelligence unit in Nassau County on Long Island, where we came from. We went back a long way together, but I knew he wasn't interested in rehashing old times.

When I finally got around to paying him a visit, he told me that he had information that I was conducting my own investigation into the bombings. I shrugged and said nothing, wanting to learn more. He pleaded with me to let the police handle things and then he asked me if it was possible to share whatever information we had picked up. I told him there was no information to share. Then he said that he knew we had very recently talked with a certain young woman, and that we had been asking all kinds of questions around town.

I told Gilkerson what I honestly felt: that whatever was going on wasn't coming from our world and that he better find out who was responsible before we did. Gilkerson reiterated that he was as baffled as I was but to leave things to him. I promised him nothing, but I did come away with the sense that he was telling me the truth. He—that is, the local police—were not involved in this.

It was almost a year and a half after the bombing of our house when the police finally announced they had made an arrest in the case. In the meantime, there had been a rash of additional bombings and shootings. The man they collared was an ex-marine munitions expert named Paul Stevens—a name unknown to us, but a most interesting character indeed. When he showed up in court for a preliminary hearing, he was recovering from the effects of a shotgun wound to the shoulder, one, he said, he had received in a hunting accident almost a year earlier.

Then there was another arrest. A drifter, William Dunbar, living with his girlfriend in a trailer home in neighboring Pinal County, was hauled in and charged with being an associate of Stevens. Dunbar was a professional stock-car driver, he said. His girlfriend was not Sandra Hitchcock, but when Hitchcock was called to testify, she said that Dunbar was the brother of her boyfriend, that they were both stock-car drivers, and that they had both been working for the FBI.

Under oath, Hitchcock said that she was not sure which agent had recruited the men, but she thought it was someone named Dave. All that her boyfriend and his brother had ever told her, she said, was that the FBI was looking to foment a mob war.

Her testimony created an uproar. There were immediate denials from the FBI—in Arizona and in Washington. Politicians who had been screaming the loudest about the scourge of the Mafia suddenly were in the position of having to back off and quiet down.

But for me, the young woman's testimony went beyond sensation. A little bell went off in my brain as soon as I heard the name Dave. Immediately following the murder of Hank Perrone in Brooklyn, I was visited by two FBI agents in Arizona. I remembered the visit vividly because one of the agents projected a very strong and very unprofessional show of satisfaction at Hank's death. Sandra Hitchcock didn't remember his name, but I did.

It was David Hale.

25

In the weeks following the arrest of Stevens and Dunbar, everyone learned a lot more about David Hale—while learning nothing at all. Hale's name soon came up in the media and in the trials of the two men. For a while, it seemed as though no one was really going to be able to prove anything. When Hale was confronted by the media, he denied any knowledge of the bombings or of knowing Stevens and Dunbar. While claiming ignorance, the FBI office in Washington went one step further by refusing to acknowledge that Hale even worked for them. But too much had happened now for all of this to be conveniently swept under the rug. Between the media and angry local citizens, the story would not die. Finally, Stevens and Dunbar, for whatever reasons, decided to plead guilty and to tell their story in open court. The story sounded plausible, persuasive—and it was as artfully misleading as it could be.

Dunbar, the stock-car driver, worked in an auto-parts shop in town whose manager was someone named Walter Prideaux. Prideaux, or so said the media, had begun working with Hale out of a sense of civic pride. Hale had sponsored a series of seminars on organized crime; Prideaux had attended and volunteered his services to Hale, who then confided to him that he was most interested in organizing a covert campaign to disrupt, confuse, discourage, and ultimately drive Tucson's Mafia population out of town. This sounded fine to Prideaux, something any patriotic, civic-minded citizen would want to get involved with. Wasn't he afraid to be a citizen volunteer against a group known for its proclivity to avenge violence with violence? Not at all. He had God and the FBI on his side.

Prideaux then brought Dunbar into the picture. Dunbar, in turn, re-cruited Stevens, a buddy who he knew had had extensive Marine Corps training in explosives. What followed were the death threats, shootings, and bombings. In all of this, Hale was depicted as a rogue cop, someone who had taken it upon himself to make an end run around the burdens and restrictions of the Constitution for the greater good of eliminating evil.

He was a lunatic, not a civil servant. He had been right there on the scene with Dunbar and Stevens when they bombed Licavoli's ranch and my parents' home. At one point, according to Dunbar, Hale, who knew that Dunbar had skill in the use of a crossbow, tried to talk him into using it to assassinate one of our people—me or Pete Notaro. Dunbar said he had turned Hale down. Hale had a girlfriend, a student at the University of Arizona, who was attracted to him, so the media said, just because he was such a swashbuckling type. Her thesis at school, we were told, was all about crime and criminals. Then one day, she turned up a suicide, leaving behind a note and a will in which, most strangely, she named David Hale as her sole benefactor.

The story read like a bad TV cop show. It was so weird, deranged, illogical, it seemed to have a ring of truth to it. But who was David Hale anyway? Because civil rights and the Constitution had been so badly tram-pled, the media kept digging. Within days of the "official" story breaking in the papers, Hale resigned from the FBI and left town—with no charges brought against him by anyone. It took awhile before reporters caught up with him—in Florida—where he had taken a job with a security company. He was soon subpoenaed to appear at the trial for Dunbar and Stevens, which he did. By then, Dunbar had been pressured into explaining that when Hale recruited him, he had promised to have an old robbery convic-tion removed from his record and that both he and Stevens had been assured that, no matter what happened, they would be under the protection of the FBI.

The involvement of Prideaux was even stranger. The media more or less accepted his story; after all, he was a known and respected figure in town. It took some time—a few years—before the nature of his involvement became clearer.

What was peculiar to us from the start was that not only was he known to us but he had been something of a friend. He once helped my brother, Joe, prepare for his college entrance exams when he was thinking of applying to the University of Arizona. The facade of eager crime fighter just didn't match the man we knew.

Years later, Prideaux ran into my father one day at a local supermarket and apologized to him for all that had happened. We were never sure whether he was sincere, embarrassed, or frightened (or all three), but he said that he been pressured into working for Hale, who had threatened to expose a shady business deal if he did not go along. He later repeated this to a reporter for *Parade* magazine.

In any case, when Hale returned to Arizona under subpoena, guess what? He took the Fifth, refusing to answer any questions. No one made a move to cite him for contempt. He was excused, never to be bothered again, and the two defendants who had pleaded guilty to all those bombings and shootings saw their charges reduced to misdemeanors. Dunbar and Stevens were fined $286 each and released.

It goes without saying that Hale had not been acting on his own in this campaign. The Justice Department placed a lid of silence on what had happened, and for good reason: There was now in place within the federal government a coordinated and carefully elaborated policy, Cointelpro, which permitted agencies like the FBI to break the law at will in pursuing domestic opponents. Originally the program had been designed to go after political enemies, such as antiwar protesters and the Black Panther party, but had now been expanded to include organized crime. Exposing David Hale meant nothing. The campaign against organized crime—and against my Family—continued. The dust had barely settled following the release of Dunbar and Stevens when my father's home was suddenly raided and ransacked by FBI agents and police supposedly looking for evidence that would link my father to a plot to obtain an illegal release from prison of an old associate, Charlie Battaglia, and to kill David Hale. The raid—with properly executed search warrants—took place one morning after my mother had just returned from church. My father was ill with a heart ailment and in bed when the agents barged into the house and tore it apart, turning over furniture, ripping out drawers, throwing clothing around the floor—all in a supposed effort to find some documents that would link my father to this supposed plot.

There was no way, short of gunplay, to stop the raid. It terrorized my parents, confounded us, and presented us with legal problems we could not begin to contemplate. What were they talking about? They found no documents, no evidence of any kind, yet my father was arrested and arraigned on the spot. A judge was brought to his bedside then and there as formal charges were presented.

It seemed obvious that the FBI was trying to get even for the embarrassment they had suffered over Hale, but there was more to it than that. They wanted the Bonannos out of the way. The "plot" they had uncovered was one of their own making and had been as carefully orchestrated as any of the bombings.

According to them, our friend in Leavenworth, Charlie "Bats" Battaglia, had befriended an inmate who was something of a jailhouse lawyer. Charlie Bats told the guy he believed he had been convicted through the use of illegal wiretaps. The inmate agreed to work up a series of writs, petitions, and so forth on Charlie's behalf.

According to this guy, Charlie asked him to smuggle a number of letters out of jail for him, letters to people who would help him prove his case. Some of the letters were supposedly intended for my father, the person Battaglia was pinning his hopes on. In exchange for his efforts, Charlie supposedly wrote that he would see to it that David Hale was eliminated. There was more. The inmate said that he himself was to become a go-between for my father and Charlie when they set up a narcotics distribution empire in Arizona. Copies of all these letters were made by the inmate and handed over to the authorities. The copies of the letters—not the originals—were the only ones the authorities ever had in their possession.

All of this fell apart in court. Al Krieger, who represented us, got the inmate, a man named Reinke, to admit that many of the letters involved had not actually been written by Charlie but had been dictated by Reinke to other inmates working as "legal assistants" for him. Reinke himself acknowledged that he had been pressured by authorities into working for them. It was a miserable show, and my father, Charlie Bats, and another associate of ours were ultimately acquitted.

Meanwhile, I was on a virtual shuttle between New York and the West, responding to additional grand jury subpoenas concerning the ongoing war in the streets, new weapons-possession charges stemming from the Hale business in Arizona, and then, far more seriously, that business of having used a phony credit card.

In November 1969, I went to trial in federal court in New York, charged, along with Pete Notaro, with various counts of conspiracy, mail fraud, and perjury. The government saw that they had an opportunity to nail me—and they took it. They were able to bring their case because they had a witness—Don Torrillo, the owner of that credit card—who was willing to swear in open court that the card had been extorted from him and had then been used illegally.

Though legal form was used in this case, the government's methods were just as flagrant as they had been in the David Hale affair and in the case they had brought against my father. Here, they were on stronger ground, however.

They were able to bring a string of witnesses to the stand who testified that I had used Torrillo's credit card. There was someone from a Mexican restaurant in Tucson who said that I had used the card to pay for a dinner party, which was true; there were other merchants who offered indisputable testimony. Then there was an airlines clerk who said that Pete Notaro had used that same credit card when he picked up a couple of tickets in our names one afternoon—also true. (Actually, Pete would never have been part of this fiasco if it hadn't been for a traffic jam outside the airport that day. I had phoned in the order for the tickets and given the card number and name, but I had sent Pete in to pick the tickets up when I was unable to park the car. I told him—and the court—that I had instructed Pete to use the card and sign Torrillo's name.)

My case depended on a dead man—Hank Perrone. He had gotten the card from Torrillo and told me it was okay to use it. But without him there to verify this, there was no proof, only my word against the government's. Even though defendants in criminal trials normally do not take the stand, I did. I feared nothing by speaking truthfully about the circumstances surrounding my case. I had done nothing wrong and I was confident that I could convince any open-minded juror of that. I was wrong.

My hopes for acquittal rested, ironically, with Don Torrillo, the government's star witness. Torrillo swore that his credit card had been extorted from him, that he had been intimidated into giving it up to Hank Perrone, that he had testified to the authorities and to the grand jury about all of that.

Torrillo looked and sounded perfect as a victim. He was a small, innocuous-looking man, neatly dressed, wearing horn-rimmed glasses, and his manner was that of a clerk or a grade-school science teacher. He said that Perrone had frightened him into giving up his credit card, that he had been with him on that day, had witnessed him beating an old man in an explosion of temper, had noticed that he was wearing a gun—there was just no way he wanted to risk the man's anger when he was asked for his card.

Of course, we knew that Torrillo and Hank went way back, that Torrillo had been a hanger-on in Hank's crew, but that could not be proven. What was provable was that Torrillo had stepped forward at Hank's urging— long before the credit card case—to take title to my house in East Meadow. What was also provable was that Torrillo's testimony to the grand jury— that he had reported to the authorities "within a month of Hank Perrone's death" that his card had been extorted from him—was false.

Before the feds ever got to him, Torrillo had originally reported to the card company that his card had been lost. Al Krieger confronted him with a letter that he had written spelling that out. He had written other letters stating the same thing after the card company began dunning him for the outstanding bills. Then there was an affidavit that he had signed saying that his card had been lost—not stolen or extorted. And, finally, there was Torrillo's testimony to a grand jury four months after Perrone's death to the same effect. Krieger read back Torrillo's own words in court.

"Was your testimony true?" Krieger asked him.

"No," Torrillo replied.

Krieger then led Torrillo through a whole series of documentable lies and distortions of the truth. He got Torrillo to admit he had deliberately falsified his income in statements to the same credit company when he had originally applied for the card, and that he had made up business cards, representing himself as an electrical engineer who held advanced degrees, including a Ph.D. The falsehoods were as clear as the card itself, which Krieger, over the objections of the prosecution, presented as evidence to the court.

Then when it came to the testimony Torrillo had given to the authorities, I was sure we would win. Krieger brought out the fact that just days after Hank was murdered, Torrillo himself had been arrested. Krieger learned that Torrillo had been busted for possession of drugs and that these charges were later—following Torrillo's final grand jury appearances—dismissed. But when Krieger raised this, the prosecution strenuously objected, saying that the charges against Torrillo were totally irrelevant. But in his zeal to make his point, the prosecutor went too far. He not only acknowledged the charges had been trumped up but he inadvertently gave the court a picture of the duress and fear Torrillo must have felt in relation to the government at the time of his arrest and afterward, when he might have been contemplating the consequences of not cooperating.

"About twenty police officers came to Mr. Torrillo's home the day after Mr. Perrone was killed," the prosecutor explained, "and they arrested him on three phony charges, such as possession of heroin on the basis of some white powder he had in his garage, and I am going to ask the court for a ruling directing Mr. Krieger not to ask any questions with respect to that particular arrest because the charges were dismissed. They were trumped-up charges, and the police came in because of all the confusion about Perrone."

Exactly. The feds knew what had happened. Whether or not local cops had acted on their own when they raided Torrillo's home, whether or not the charges brought against him had been "trumped up," the point was that the feds had been able to use the situation in pressuring Torrillo to testify in this case. But when Al Krieger tried to raise this issue, he was cut off by the judge, who maintained, in essence, that any discussion of the charges brought against Torrillo were irrelevant. The court, however, did allow Krieger to ask a narrower question: Did Torrillo himself feel that he had been coerced? It further allowed Krieger to present portions of transcripts made after Torrillo's arrest that seemed pertinent. Against the prosecution's objection, Krieger read into the record excerpts that seemed to indicate clearly that Torrillo had been pressured and that he indeed had been worried about the consequences of not going along with the government.

It did not matter.

The government also quite specifically withheld evidence that it had in its possession that even more dramatically went to Torrillo's possible motives in testifying as he had. Apparently, Torrillo had also been arrested and indicted on a securities racketeering charge six months after Hank Perrone's death. That charge was still pending. We learned of this before sentencing in our case, then had a posttrial hearing on it, where, as far as I am concerned, we were able to demonstrate clearly that Torrillo was a completely unreliable witness and that the government's case against us was therefore bogus.

None of it mattered.

Pete Notaro, who should never have been part of the trial in any way, and I were both convicted. As we stood in the courtroom listening to the judge read out our sentences, we could hear through the windows the sounds of a noisy antiwar demonstration taking place on the streets below. It was bizarre and unsettling. It fit with this larger sense I had of things no longer holding together, of sheer energy and craziness taking the place of order and the reasoned use of power. I had never had put much faith in the legal system because it had always been clear to me that it was weighted to protect the interests of those in power. But the basis for the system, any system, is order, a clearly articulated set of rules and regulations, which even when cynically followed or exploited still produce predictable and reliable results. The rules and regulations in this case, and in the case of what was loose on the streets, no longer seemed to apply. Exploitation in any society is as natural as breathing or at least as natural as one man being stronger, better positioned, or more advantaged than another. But when the legal foundation of the social system itself is no longer reliable, then anything is possible. The sound of those kids in the streets was an echo of the chaos I felt surrounded by in the courtroom.

The government also threw the rule book away when they came after me. Over a sum of little more than two thousand dollars—the amount I had charged to this credit card—the government meant to incarcerate me for as long as they could. In November 1969, I was thirty-seven years old. I received a five-year sentence for mail fraud (each time I signed a slip on the card and it was sent to the company—through the mails—it was mail fraud), perjury (each time I signed the name of Don Torrillo), and conspiracy (I talked to Hank about using the card).

I spent the better part of the next twenty years in and out of prison. The government in that time went after organized crime in a variety of ways, on a variety of fronts. But nowhere did they exert more energy, focus, and determination than in the single-minded effort to remove the Bonanno Family from the scene once and for all.

26

Of course, we were not the only ones the government went after. Around the same time I was convicted, Carlo Gambino was charged with conspiracy to hijack an armored car full of money. Gerardo Catena, the successor to Vito Genovese, who had died in jail, Meyer Lansky, and Joe Colombo were all rounded up in this period, charged, and convicted. There was no question that from the end of the sixties into the early seventies, the government had a made a decision to eliminate the Italian Mafia by any means necessary, much in the manner of Mussolini in the early part of the century. But nowhere was the force of that campaign directed more powerfully than against my Family.

In the years prior to and following the credit card case, fourteen different grand juries were convened whose only purpose was to go after the Bonanno Family. There has hardly been a day since then when either my father, my brother, or I haven't in one way or another been up against the legal system—either under indictment, awaiting trial, standing trial serving time, or waiting out probation and parole.

From the fourteen different Bonanno grand juries, five indictments were handed up against me, resulting in three different convictions, as well as convictions of my father and brother. A roster of all these cases and their proliferating small details wearies the mind, numbs one's sense of what is and is not important. One example will suffice to show just how ludicrous things could get.

Beginning in the mid-seventies, one of many different strike forces convened in the far West decided that my father was the overlord of narcotics trafficking in the United States. They had virtually no evidence to prove this and plenty, going back through my father's life and career, to demonstrate that he was never involved in pushing drugs. The investigation was meant more to defame him than convict him, and the tactics used rather clearly demonstrate that.

The government, when it eventually brought charges against my father—not for drug peddling but for obstruction of justice—did so on the basis of "evidence" they had culled from sifting through his garbage. For years, cans of garbage placed out on the street in front of my father's house were picked up and carted away, replaced by other full cans of garbage lest anyone in the house suspect that someone was running a garbage search on us. What the government turned up after sifting through tons of swill and trash were a few cryptic handwritten notes, torn up, pieced together, which purported to prove my father's involvement in crimes of one sort or another. The notes that were presented in court would have been funny but for the fact of their intended use as evidence. Most of the notes had been written in Sicilian and therefore had to be translated by specialists who were proud of the work they did. One mysterious note they pasted together and translated read: "Call Titone work and pay *scannatore*."

Now the Italian word *scannare* means "to cut" or "to slaughter." Government specialists therefore concluded that my father had written to an underworld assassin named Titone about a murder he had done for him.

But in Sicilian, *scannatore* means "cutting board"; it is a noun, not a verb, and carries no connotation of killing or slaughtering. The ludicrous reality in this instance—which my father was able to prove—was that Titone was a local carpenter who had made a cutting board for my mother. The note was about paying the man for his efforts. My father nevertheless was convicted for obstruction of justice and wound up, in 1981, at the age of seventy-six, serving nine months and twenty days in jail.

Why should the government have so zealously pursued the Bonanno Family in particular? No doubt some of it was payback for the way we had made the FBI look so foolish when my father surrendered in 1966 and then in the David Hale case. It was not Hale per se but the feds themselves who were exposed. I am more of the belief, however, that our Family was targeted not because of what we had done but because of who we were and what we represented.

Looking around the country at that time, all of the old leaders—except my father—were gone. Steve Maggadino was an old-timer but was of no concern to the government because in the scheme of things—as much as his ego might have wished otherwise—he had little authority and even less power.

The Bonanno Family, on the other hand, had not only been powerful in the sense of its political clout over the years but was also very much the bearer of the traditions in our world. My father went back to the beginning of the century not just in chronological age but in his understanding of who we were and what it took to hold a small group together in militant loyalty, absolute devotion to duty. He represented the past, certainly, but he also was a living link to a future that the government wanted redefined. The feds, for very different reasons than the public, were afraid of a Mafia that was well organized, highly efficient, and powerful.

The government had reached a point where it no longer found it expedient to share power with us. The political map had changed. Our power was ebbing from the eastern cities, from the old political machines; it had drifted west and south—as we had—and its roots were no longer blue-collar or even national. And then, far more important, the government in one blazing, irreversible moment came to understand that we were no longer reliable. More than any single act, the assassination of President Kennedy marked a dividing line. On one side of that divide were years of active and fruitful cooperation; on the other side was a plethora of prosecutions, vilifications, and outright acts of sabotage. I had dimly understood this for some time, but when I went to prison, I was brought face-to-face with the conspiracy to murder John F. Kennedy. It was like the sudden twisting of a lens, so that what had been only cloudy and recessed suddenly came sharply into focus.

I received my sentence in the early part of March 1969 but did not begin serving time until January 1971, when all my appeals were finally exhausted. I was transferred first to the Los Angeles County Jail and then out to the nearby Federal Correction Institution at Terminal Island.

Because I had been in jail before, I was more prepared for it this time. Also, Terminal Island, in the constellation of the federal prison system, was a soft place, mostly for white-collar criminals and other nonviolent types.

It was called "a medium-security facility," which meant that while there was a rigid system of head counting and bed checks, there was little visible firepower on display to discourage inmates and remind them where they were. There were plenty of facilities for classes, exercises, self-improvement, and so on. I was looking to cool my heels, do my time, and, if possible, even enjoy myself.

Family visits were encouraged. That was enjoyable—and, as far as I was concerned, instructive for all involved. (While there, I insisted that Rosalie bring the children to visit me so that I could maintain my ongoing relationship with them. The kids played with vending machines; they'd sit with me while I'd tell them stories or ask them about school. I enjoyed keeping my hand in as a dad.)

Terminal Island, to be sure, was a prison, not a country club. The goal was always to keep you in line. There was little courtesy, even less pride of self. I don't know how many times I saw guards knock something over, spill something that belonged to an inmate, and just keep walking. The whole system was designed to promote failure and lack of self-respect. The goal was to hammer you down into a smaller entity than you had been when you entered prison.

But still, I was lucky and did not begin to believe that my time there would prove to be exceptional. I quickly found a job I liked—working as a clerk for the number-three man in the prison administration. In addition to doing all his typing, I researched and wrote reports based on budget figures that I researched and analyzed. I regularly sent these reports off to Washington. My guy wound up depending on me more than I ever did on him.

I was also lucky because other inmates looked up to me. I was elected president of the inmate council within months of my arrival. I was someone others turned to in disputes or when things needed to be done. It gave me a sense of being needed—not in the way I had been needed by others outside. There was no pressure at all to produce here.

One time, prison authorities came to me because they were in a bind over how to handle a new prisoner they had received—G. Gordon Liddy. The warden had made a decision to lock Liddy up—not because he thought he was a bad guy but because he feared that Liddy would not be able to survive in the yard. Liddy, the Watergate burglar, Nixon commando, and former FBI agent was a likely candidate for death in five minutes if he set foot within the general population—at least in the minds of the authorities. But Liddy was creating incredible headaches for the Bureau of Prisons, firing off letters to his lawyers, raising threats of all kinds of lawsuits, actions, press releases, et cetera. Was there anything I could do? the warden wanted to know. "Sure," I told him, "give me a few days."

That was how Liddy and I became friends.

I got the heads of the blacks, the Chicanos, and the Italians together in the yard, told them the authorities were bugging me about G. Gordon Liddy, who they had in lockup, fearing for the guy's safety. Could they do anything? No problem, I was told; Liddy wasn't a rat like John Dean. He was a loyal soldier. I was told he would be perfectly safe. So one day, he emerged in the sunlight and we became friends.

We talked about lots of things. I didn't agree with too much of what he said, but I liked him for the energy of his personality, and because, in absolutely devoting himself to his boss, he reminded me anew of values that were important to me. Liddy also geared me up to thinking much more about the ways in which presidential politics in my time had become a spawning ground for betrayal and ingratitude.

When I talked to Liddy, I kept thinking about Nixon and the secret pleasure I got seeing him up to his eyeballs in Watergate troubles. I didn't say this to Liddy, but I kept thinking how Nixon had turned his back not only on loyal friends—like Liddy—but also on people in our world, people who had helped him in his career. Nixon would never have gotten anywhere without those old allegiances. Through his pal Bebe Rebozo, Nixon did business for years with people in Trafficante's Family, profiting from real estate deals, arranging for casino licensing, covert funding for anti-Castro activities, and so forth. Nixon was a close personal friend of James Crosby of Resorts International. The man and the company had been involved with underworld figures for years. When Nixon ran for President in 1968, Crosby's yacht was there for the asking. Crosby kicked in $100,000 to Nixon's campaign that year. Over the years, Nixon had also had serious business dealings with a man named Arthur Dresser, an associate of Meyer Lansky. At one point, Dresser loaned Nixon large sums of money for real estate investments in Florida, where Bebe Rebozo's Key Biscayne Bank was located. Rebozo's bank was regularly used for casino profit skimming and for money laundering. There were others close to Nixon, people who enabled him to rise through the ranks—such as C. Arnholdt Smith, Lewis Lipton (or Felix Aguirre, as he was known to us), and John Alessio, Californians all connected to the Los Angeles Family, friendly to us.

Liddy wasn't interested (at least as far as I could tell) in any of that. His focus was always on anticommunism and his contribution to it in fighting the enemies of America. But Liddy swung my mind over to thinking about Presidents and their relationships to us.

That was when I ran into Johnny Roselli in the yard at Terminal Island. I remember seeing him as clearly as if it were yesterday. It was an unusually bright, clear day. There were knots of us standing around in the yard. I had just finished typing up a report for the warden on prisoner complaints and I was taking my midmorning break. There was a guy in the yard I was hoping to find, one of the Italians, who was a chess partner of mine. I stepped out of the administration building into the sunlight, looking around for the Italians, when I saw this very familiar figure, fluid and graceful through the shoulders, an almost silken mane of carefully groomed gray hair—as if it had recently been done in a Beverly Hills salon. Though his back was to me and though he was dressed in uncharacteristic prison denims, I knew who he was immediately. I was startled—almost shocked— but I quickly made my way across the yard.

I walked up to the group, and as I did, Roselli turned, saw me, and smiled.

"Hey, *paisan*," he said. "They told me you were in here."

"That's more than anybody told me about you," I replied. We fell on each other like long-lost relatives, embracing and kissing each other on both cheeks.

Roselli was around for only a few weeks before he was transferred to another facility, but what he told me in that time was a revelation, unexpected—even frightening because of the burden of knowledge it placed on me. John was an older man—the same age as my father—and though he was not Sicilian, he was a man of tradition, someone whom I would not have expected to be so free with information better left unspoken.

Inevitably, we reminisced a lot. Johnny was born in 1905 in Esteria, Italy. His real name was Fillipo Sacco. He came to the United States in 1911, got into trouble with the law, and then changed his name to Roselli. He rose through the ranks in Chicago. He was associated with Al Capone, later with Paul Ricca, Tony Accardo, and Sam Giancana. He occupied the kind of position in the Chicago Family that only men of special talent and ability occupy. He was not a captain as such with a fixed crew so much as man who floated from crew to crew, place to place, contributing intelligence, muscle, savvy on behalf of his Family. He was like a minister without a portfolio and as such acquired a special power for himself. He was a leader even though technically he was a follower. He operated—on behalf of Chicago—in many different areas of the country—on the West Coast, for example. He was instrumental in organizing control of unions in the film industry. He became closely associated with studio moguls, union chiefs, and stars. He was a man-about-town; Frank Sinatra and Dean Martin sponsored him for membership in exclusive clubs like the Friar's Club. In his own right, he was as powerful a man as many leaders in our world— and he rightly expected to be acknowledged as such. He may or may not have had a hard time being a number-two man to anyone, particularly to someone like Sam, but he was somebody who never reached a position where his talents and abilities could be used fully, where they were his alone rather than his on loan. He was always a second, however independent he seemed to be. As a number-two man myself, I had special feeling for him—and for the bitterness I found in him.

By then, he had become disenchanted and even angry about his long relationship with Sam Giancana, his boss from Chicago. He believed that Sam had not stood by him in many different situations. He blamed Giancana for his present troubles, convictions for falsifying his birth records and then for conspiracy to cheat the Friar's Club in Los Angeles. And he ultimately blamed him for not being there for him in Dallas.

Roselli had long been rumored to have been involved in the plot against Kennedy. Being linked to Sam made that seem almost logical. And knowing his background—that he was an accomplished marksman, one of the suspected gunmen at the St. Valentine's Day Massacre—made the long-standing rumor that he was involved in Dealey Plaza also seem plausible.

What was totally surprising to me was that Roselli talked about Dallas. He was almost loose-lipped about it. One day in the yard, when I was standing with him and several other Italian inmates, someone made a remark about a Jewish prisoner. It was a bigoted remark, something about Jews and money.

"Jack Ruby was a Jew," Roselli suddenly barked out. "He was far more loyal than his fucking boss." Nobody said anything, and the conversation about the Jewish prisoner continued, but Roselli's linking Ruby openly to Sam shocked me. Not by his connecting Ruby and Chicago, which a lot of people knew, but by that reference to loyalty, which seemed to have only one possible interpretation. Roselli was being careless.

Only it wasn't carelessness. It was indifference. Roselli was also loose-lipped around the handful of Cubans who were doing time. Some of these people had been involved in the Bay of Pigs, were up to their eyeballs in exile politics, and had been engaged in illegal anti-Castro activities for years. They knew that Roselli, on hire to the CIA, had been involved in several attempts on Castro's life. They also seemed to know that Roselli had been a triggerman in the assassination—and they regarded him as a hero because of that. They were effusive, fawning, flattering around him. They did things like openly thanking him for taking out the betrayer of their country's liberation. Roselli should have turned off such talk whenever he heard it, but he didn't. Instead, he'd make little compromising physical gestures of acknowledgment—a nod of the head, a shrug of the shoulders, a quick thumbs-up sign. One time, when someone thanked him for his heroism on behalf of the Cuban people, he replied that that was more thanks than he had gotten from his own government.

One day, John and I were in the yard. We were walking together, just the two of us. I asked him in Italian what the hell was going on with him. He replied, *"Per cosas,"* meaning, "things."

"What do you mean?"

"That fuck always hated your father. You remember the Commission meeting in '56? Joe Bonanno's the chair. Sam gets pissed off about something, stands up to leave the table. Your father orders him, 'Sit down!' That *spingularu* melts right back into his chair—and ever since then there's been bad blood. He don't mind seeing your father go one bit."

"He never made a move against us, John."

"He don't make moves—that's his whole thing. He just lets things take care of themselves. I was supposed to have a car waiting. You think there was a car waiting? There was shit—and I'm coming out of the sewer holding the fucking piece in my hand."

At first, I wasn't sure what Roselli was referring to. I assumed he was probably talking about my father. He was talking about blowing Kennedy's head off.

"Sam and I both knew I was going to be the one to make the hit. I had the best chance. My position is in the storm drain on Elm Street, facing the route of the motorcade. The car'll be ten feet from me. There were four of us including the patsy, but Sam and everyone else knew I was the one who'd have the shot. We had this safe house where all of us got together before—two different times. Sam wants to make sure I understand what to do afterward. I even did a dry run the day before. Three blocks to the Trinity River, car was right there. But then it wasn't, Bill, there was no fucking car. I'm standing there on these iron rungs, I watch the cars make the turn, see the guy's head maybe ten feet away. How could I miss, ya know? I don't miss. I saw his head go up. And I'm thinking all the while I'm going like a rat through that tunnel, I was so close, they saw the flash of the muzzle. I'm never gonna make it. My heart's going like a cannon. And then there's no fucking backup."

The words were not careless; they were reckless. They were coming from the mouth of a man trained in our way of life, but it was as though he were a schoolgirl. But I could no more stop him than stop a freight train.

"I've just killed the fucking President and there's no backup! He says there was a slip-up, that they already took care of the *goomba* who was supposed to be there, but you know what? I know better, because I know Sam. He don't make slips like that. He knew I'd never say anything if I got caught." Roselli then told me that on his own he carried his rifle from the scene of the killing all the way to a farm in upstate New York, where he left it.

I could not tell Johnny what to say or not say—that was strictly his business. There were all kinds of questions I obviously was curious about but did not ask him—about the parade route, for example. Why were the windows in the Texas School Book Depository all opened at the time of the assassination? Why wasn't that storm drain on Elm Street sealed? He couldn't have taken up his position without knowing something about the involvement of the Secret Service, which was responsible for the routine securing of the area, such as the sealing of windows and storm drains. I already had far too much knowledge, and I had no desire for more.

In the veiled manner of discourse in our world, I told John what my father and other old-timers had long ago passed on to me: that the moment you accept a confidence from someone, you bear the burden he is carrying; whether you want it that way or not, you wind up hauling the same load up the side of the mountain. I praised the old-time leaders, who valued discretion among themselves as a way of preserving peace and order among the Families. "The peace they established was effective," I said, "because it allowed them to remain in the background, to fulfill their responsibilities without ever being seen or heard by anyone."

Roselli understood me perfectly, but he just did not care. He shrugged. "It don't matter no more, Bill; all that's over with," he said.

That was the last time we talked about the assassination—or much of anything else. He was transferred from Terminal Island a few weeks later. In 1976, some time after he got out of prison, he stepped out of his house in Florida one evening, saying he was going to buy a pack of cigarettes. He never returned. A week or so later, his dismembered body was found in a sixty-gallon oil drum floating in Biscayne Bay.

The police called his death "an unsolved murder."

It was more like a suicide—the suicide of a man who knew that everything he stood for and believed in was lost.

EPILOGUE

I spent eleven of the next twenty years in jail and was either on parole or probation the rest of the time. One prosecution followed another, one conviction in the wake of the next. Never mind that the government went after me with a stacked deck. I did time in federal facilities at Terminal Island, then McNeil Island, then in Safford, Arizona. I served four years in San Quentin, a guest of the state of California.

The assault on the Bonanno Family continued unabated. My father and brother were also jailed. Federal and state task forces continued gathering evidence and bringing indictments against mafiosi wherever possible. All the while, an unprecedented campaign in the media to vilify us and anyone associated with us continued.

In 1976, for example, there was a headline murder in Arizona, the car bombing of a reporter for the *Arizona Republic*, Don Bolles. He had been an investigative journalist looking into organized crime. It was immediately assumed that he had been done in by the Mafia, led by the Bonannos. A task force of government agents, along with a self-appointed group of angry reporters from around the country, went to work on the case. Ultimately, arrests were made—of people who had no Mafia connections—but that hardly mattered. The heat from the authorities and the stories in the media were intense and unabating.

Another big story that surfaced around the same time came from the *San Jose Mercury*. This supposed exposé suggested that there was a virtual Mafia empire in Arizona and the West and that it was run by us. "Joe Bonanno," this story declared, was "probably the most powerful Mafioso in America, the undisputed Boss west of the Rocky Mountains." And what was the power built on? Drugs, of course. "Today the Bonanno organization moves kilo amounts of heroin through Pueblo, Colo., for shipment to St. Louis." My brother and I were linchpins. "Now that Bonanno's two sons are established in San Jose in Northern California, the old man appears to be making a concerted effort to gain control of rackets in the entire state.

"Federal and local police officials who have plotted all these moves and traced all this action are convinced that Joe Bananas, from his home base in Arizona, is in the midst of bringing it all together under the mantle and protection of the Bonanno Family."

There was no empire; there was no action, least of all around drugs, which my father from day one saw as the source of evil in modern life. The reality was jail, old age, illness, and death. My mother died in this period, and my father's health deteriorated. In the last stages of my mother's illness, she became delirious, fearful that the door to her home would be battered down and "they" would come to take her husband away. But this was all beside the point. The goal was to dismantle the Mafia not only by exposing and jailing its members but by discrediting the philosophy that had allowed us to become a national power. The reality was that our Family was down to fifteen or twenty loyalists who traveled to Arizona from New York and then decided to stay on.

The Mafia, as a national power, was disintegrating as surely as a species of blighted trees. The individual convictions of mobsters were not nearly so important in a personal sense as in a collective one. So it seemed that each headline case had national significance. Politicians and prosecutors fought over themselves in a haste to nail name Mafia figures. And the results showed. By the mid-seventies the Mafia had been thoroughly balkanized.

Jimmy Hoffa "disappeared" in 1975. He had been pardoned years earlier by President Nixon—a gesture, if ever there was one, of the connection to national power we once enjoyed. But Hoffa's death was the direct result of this larger death of national power. When he got out of jail, he wanted to reassert control over all of the Teamster conferences in the country—a power position that was in accord with the world he knew when he was jailed in the sixties.

That world was gone. Others had taken his place in the union. The leadership of the Teamsters, in accordance with the new political realities all of the Families were dealing with, was far more regional than national. When Hoffa insisted that he not only be given back the presidency of the International but that he also have more direct authority in establishing national policy, he was seen not as a threat so much as an annoyance. He did not have allies. Two Families—one in Michigan, one in Ohio—had been telling him to back off, that things were different. And when he persisted, they decided it was no longer convenient to have him around. They elected to eliminate him rather than to continue useless negotiations with him. The Commission, such as it was, was informed by Detroit and Ohio that they wanted to get rid of Hoffa. The Commission was really in no position to agree or disagree; they simply received the news and that was that. Hoffa was abducted and a devastating and exotic poison called curare was shoved down his throat. This poison perfectly feigns a heart attack and it was explained to me that it was untraceable. Afterward, if the body is not quickly attended to, decomposition rapidly follows. Hoffa's unrecognizable remains were left in the car that was used to abduct him. The car, in turn, was put in a compacting machine; Jimmy Hoffa, so the story goes in our world, is part of someone's front fender today.

For prosecutors and politicians looking for an adrenaline shot in their careers, there is nothing like a good Mafia case. Take the career of Rudolph Giuliani, for instance. Giuliani was an obscure federal prosecutor when he decided to go after the Mafia during the 1980s. He made a name for himself with the so-called Commission Case, in which the government sought to prove the existence of an overarching central committee governing all of organized crime. Several people, none particularly known to the public, were indicted on conspiracy charges. The conspiracy charge in itself is a favorite prosecutorial tool in going after the Mafia and other organizations because it allows prosecution on the basis of group behavior as opposed to individual action. If someone has simply met with or had conversations with another person, both may be liable to conspiracy. Proving that the Commission existed, therefore, meant no more than linking several people who used the term in talking to one another—regardless of the nature or context of those conversations. The reality was that the Commission was as dead of the League of Nations at the time Giuliani had his show trial. But he was not interested at all in the reality of what was going on, only in what he could gain for himself politically.

Giuliani's big problem in that case was that he had no big names to offer up. So he got one: my father's. Though he had been in retirement for over fifteen years, had recently been widowed, his health broken, his day-to-day life perfectly visible to anyone interested in monitoring him, my father was summoned by Giuliani as a witness in 1986. Giuliani's goal was to get him on the stand and to have him say, yes, there was and is a Commission.

My father resisted the subpoena, as Giuliani surely suspected he would. In addition, Giuliani knew that my father had a long history of tweaking the authorities with his use of the Fifth Amendment. He was the perfect target.

When my father's lawyers argued in court that he was too sick to travel from Arizona to New York for the trial, Giuliani turned around and asked that a court-appointed medical staff be allowed to examine him. The court agreed to this; doctors were sent to Arizona, where they put my father through a battery of tests. They returned and told the court that he was indeed too sick to travel. That should have ended the matter right there, but it did not. Where another prosecutor might have been embarrassed, Giuliani was emboldened. He was determined precisely because he had no real case other than the one he could build on the back of a someone whose name would make good copy. Giuliani argued that if my father couldn't be moved to New York for the trial, then the court could move to Arizona. Giuliani's motion to change venue temporarily was accepted, the court was moved, and then Giuliani's real intention became clear.

He knew there was no testimony to get. But he had a name in his clutches, that of someone he could not have indicted as a conspirator or as anything else, but one who nevertheless allowed him to do what he wanted. When the conference room at St. Mary's Hospital in Tucson was turned into a temporary courtroom and Giuliani then proceeded to question him, my father, as expected, took the Fifth. Giuliani turned around and asked the judge to cite him for civil contempt, which would allow the government to jail him for the duration of the trial or until he purged himself of contempt. The judge granted the request and my father was then immediately hustled off on a gurney to a waiting ambulance, which took him took to the airport, where he was then taken by medevac to a prison facility in Lexington, Kentucky. There my father stayed for the next seventeen months—until November 1987, when the trial ended with convictions for all who had been indicted.

Though the trial was a farce, Giuliani made headlines by jailing my father. The existence or nonexistence of the Commission was secondary. All the while, Giuliani was aiming not for the Mafia but for political office. After the Commission trial, he, like Tom Dewey, became known as a crime fighter. Before then, he needed a photo ID when he showed up for work.

Why did the government bear down so hard on the Mafia when it had for so many years been in a kind of unofficial partnership with it? Some of that, as I have suggested, had to do with an inevitable change in the political landscape, with the decline of big-city political machines and an even sharper decline in the importance of labor unions. But mostly it had to do with power itself—who was in control, and why. Take the matter of drugs.

My father's strong moral position against drug trafficking not only was considered irrelevant but also, in political terms, dangerous. Drug trafficking by the late 1960s had become an instrument of foreign policy. In the years when drug profits remained relatively small and the number of countries involved was limited, the government unofficially worked with the Mafia, closing its eyes to drugs shipped into the country through, say, Cuba, Haiti, Panama, in exchange for which, the mafiosi helped maintain the power structures in those nations through payoffs, employment, muscle, and intelligence. As soon as trafficking became a really big business—in the early sixties—it became cumbersome for the government to have the mob as a partner—especially when the Kennedy assassination proved it was leaderless, rudderless, and therefore dangerously unpredictable. They did not want to have power in the hands of people they could not trust. By the 1960s, the government had established the capacity, through its vastly expanded clandestine services, to do in-house what they formerly had relied on the Mafia to help them with.

The Vietnam War was very much a war about controlling the new and booming drug trade though it is not usually described in that way. In Southeast Asia, poppy production flourished in places like South Vietnam, Cambodia, Thailand, and Burma. The center of the worldwide drug business had suddenly shifted east.

It was the government, not the mob, that took control of this trade. We became aware in a variety of ways that the government was up to something more than fighting communism in Southeast Asia. One indication came through our ability to interfere with a money-laundering operation the government was running with the government of South Vietnam all through the Kennedy and Johnson years. We had crews working out of Idlewild (later Kennedy) Airport, cargo handlers, people in our unions. We had noticed for some time that large shipments of money were being sent from South Vietnam by government courier to New York, where the shipments were then rerouted to Swiss banks. American Express certificates, freshly minted, were also being sent on to Vietnam. A crew belonging to another Family, which was probably into drug dealing itself, began skimming off money from these shipments. The way it was done was by replacing the money with the AmEx certificates before tabulations were electronically recorded by the government. From the volume and the character of this trade, all of us in New York understood that the government had entered an illegal business of some kind, one that required the hiding and laundering of large amounts of cash, exactly what would be generated by drug dealing.

But we eventually learned that the government was into drugs in a far more direct way. A personal physician of my father's named Al Levin, who began treating him in the 1970s, had been a navy pilot for a couple of years, flying escort missions for CIA units working in Cambodia. Levin (who later documented some of this in sworn testimony before congressional committees) said he flew these operatives into Cambodia and then flew them—and their cargo of drugs—out of the country and then to U.S. air bases in South Vietnam, where the shipments were then loaded on to unmarked civilian aircraft that were then flown to destinations unknown.

South Vietnam obviously profited from this arrangement, but the United States, in exchange, kept the government it wanted in place. It was the United States, not the Mafia, that had its hands at all times on the levers of power, on the dispensing of favors, opportunities, the perks of office and advantage. Because it was all done in-house rather than subcontracted, the risks of political fallout were minimized as political control was tightened. People like Batista, Duvalier, and Noriega were our men as well the government's. But the tin-horn generals of Southeast Asia were all theirs—as are the political leaders today of countries like Colombia, Costa Rica, Panama, the Dominican Republic, Guatemala, Thailand, and Cambodia—countries where, ostensibly, democracies have been established. Russia is the most interesting of all these drug-saturated countries. I marvel at the way the media regularly refers to the way "the Mafia" (meaning organized crime in Russia) is today in cahoots with Colombian and other Latin drug cartels in a giant conspiracy to undermine the moral fabric of American life. Never mind the obvious fact that American political power, money, and even personnel very much dictate who does what in Eastern Europe; the drug business between the old Evil Empire and the Americas could not exist without extensive cooperation between the government and the mob. It is doubly ironic for me, of course, to see and hear Russian criminals—or any other nonmade non-Italians—being routinely referred to as "the Mafia." Crime in Russia has never and will never have anything more to do with us than the cloning of sheep.

It is no credit to our world that the government had to displace the Italian Mafia in controlling aspects of the drug business. We should never have been involved with trafficking in the first place. And if we had not, if we had all the while held to our values, the government would never have had to view us as an enemy or a competitor. It could have made all the deals it wanted to secure whatever foreign-policy objectives were deemed necessary. And we might have gone on, as before, prospering in the shadows.

My father has said many times over that the Kennedy assassination would never have happened if there had been a functioning Commission, able to mediate the complaints of different bosses who were angry at JFK and Bobby. I would expand that to say that the idea of elements in our world attacking government officials remains almost incomprehensible to me and is at the heart of our disintegration as a viable force in American life. Everything we were about was based on cooperation, not confrontation. Our power was based on handshakes and payoffs, not guns and clandestine plots. Who were we to stand up jaw-to-jaw, fist-to-fist with an opponent that had the power to crush us at will?

There was a breakdown of values that led to the killing of JFK. That assassination was not an isolated act at all. Over the last few years, there have been all kinds of sensational tell-all, accounts of government involvement in the murders of everyone from Martin Luther King, Jr., to Marilyn

Monroe to Bobby Kennedy. I am not a conspiracy theorist. For example, I have no information on who killed King or Monroe. I have heard plenty about Marilyn because Bobby Kennedy was widely rumored to have been involved. It seems credible to me that he was having an affair with her and that he was fearful she would wind up exposing him, his brother, and everyone else she ever slept with. In our world, she was known as an unstable and highly neurotic person—and she was often seen with people close to us and also close to those in power, people like Frank Sinatra and Peter Lawford, who was often used as a messenger between the Families and the Kennedy administration. But as for Bobby's being on the scene just prior to Marilyn's being doped up by mobsters who then killed her by inserting a nontraceable poisoned suppository into her anus, I have my doubts.

Far more credible to me is the idea that there was some kind of Mafia involvement in the killing of RFK. That is in accord with the break in the fabric, with the sort of colossal arrogance that led people in our world to believe they could take on the government as though it were just another Family.

The conspiracy buffs have had a harder time with RFK than with the murder of his brother because the shooter was apprehended so quickly and so clearly visible at the scene on TV. Years ago, talk surfaced that there was a second shooter that night in the Ambassador Hotel and that he was a substitute security guard brought in at the last minute. That sounds plausible to me.

When the name of this alleged second shooter, Thane Eugene Cesar, eventually surfaced, I took note in the same way I did when I heard the name Jack Ruby associated with the killing of Oswald. I didn't know Cesar, but I knew a man named John Alessio who for years had been on very friendly terms with the Los Angeles Family. He was not a made member himself, but he was always around. He ran a racetrack in Tijuana, had all kinds of gambling interests that mixed with ours; he used us and we used him. He was a money contributor and man behind the scenes in California Republican politics (he was a big backer of Richard Nixon, for example, and, later, of Ronald Reagan). One of his known strong-arm guys was this Thane Eugene Cesar. Many of us knew this because Alessio talked about him in the context of having to go to court for him to get him off a couple of heavy raps. Cesar did "things" for Alessio—hence, for us.

I spent about six months with Alessio in prison in California. He had been nailed for tax evasion by the Kennedys, and he was very bitter about it. We hung around together, talked a lot. I never raised the subject of Bobby's assassination or of Gene Cesar, but I could not miss the tone of satisfaction in his voice whenever he mentioned the Kennedys.

"I tell you this, Bill, whoever took out those fuckheads knew what they were doing, ya know what I mean?" He reiterated this line, in one form or another, a dozen times in the six months we spent together.

The reason I always thought there was more than idle talk to this was the fact the Ambassador was, like Dealey Plaza, not secured the night of the assassination. The service staff at the hotel was completely controlled by the Los Angeles Family. Waiters, chambermaids, porters, and security people all belonged to unions dominated by Family influence. It is a fact that there was a last-minute replacement in the hotel security team assigned to Kennedy that night. And it is also a fact that this replacement was Thane Eugene Cesar, who just happened to be standing behind Kennedy when the shooting started and just happened to draw his weapon—an H&R .22-caliber nine-shot revolver, the same type of weapon that was taken from Sirhan Sirhan. Even more interesting to me is the fact that several witnesses in that room all said one of Kennedy's security guards had drawn his gun and fired it when the shooting broke out. I repeat: I don't know if Cesar was Kennedy's killer—but I do know he belonged to Alessio in the same way Jack Ruby belonged to Sam Giancana. And I know for sure that however extensive the assault on the government was by people in our world during the 1960s, it violated everything we stood for and was directly responsible for a murderous and fratricidal splintering and falling apart of a once-coherent world.

Our strength always lay in our cohesiveness. If you go into an Italian neighborhood today, you can still see some of the closeness we depended on. People still congregate in social clubs, at street-corner groceries, on front stoops, they still go to church together on Sundays, observe saints' days, share holidays and street festivals, they still joke with cops, and, if need be, they still make sure they get taken care of on Christmas or the third Friday of every month.

The neighborhoods were, and to some extent still are, tiny oases of order. There was little crime, families were close-knit, and day-to-day life was secure. Why? This never depended on the police or on city government but, rather, on a network of relationships that duplicated those of the old country, where people over many centuries had learned to depend on themselves for support rather than on outside forces. Those outside forces—conquerors, landowners, police—could be depended on only to make life better for themselves, and to make deals with us only when they stood to gain by them. In our Mafia tradition, we were the middlemen between the conquerors and the people. But we could do this only because what we did was so clearly rooted in the traditions and values of the communities we came from. Once that was lost, we lost the sense of who we were.

There has been a lot written about violence and intimidation and the way the Mafia moves in and extorts, ruins, and sabotages legitimate businesses, preying on the weak and paying off the mighty. Some muscle-brained groups have obviously and foolishly operated that way. But there is also a lot of propaganda designed to keep from view the fact that the greater part of our success depended on cooperative, mutually beneficial relationships. A gangland slaying exposes the reality that we operate by our own set of rules and justice—but it says nothing more. For each gangland slaying over the years, there have been tens of thousands of the kinds of peaceful everyday social contacts that made our power possible.

We lost the ability to foster those kinds of contacts the moment we lost touch with the values that made us, values that placed friendship and family ahead of money. Our crimes traditionally have been about providing what the government, what the system, could not or would not provide. We got jobs for people, loaned them money when they were without. To be sure, when alcohol was illegal, we made it available, and we provided the means for people to gamble. To paraphrase Walter Lippmann, as much a pillar of the establishment as John Lindsay: The underworld supplies those services that convention may prohibit and the law may declare illegal but that human appetite nevertheless craves.

What went terribly wrong was that all of this got mixed up with wealth and power. There was no wealth in Sicily other than that of the landowners. In this country, there were lots of ways for lots of people to make money. Our people (and many others) happened to make fortunes illegally during Prohibition. The pattern of relationships built up then extended into and well beyond the local police station, to city hall, the state house, both houses of Congress, and even the White House. The payoffs and deals became ends in themselves, the means to ever-increasing amounts of wealth, ever more access to power. And then as fortunes were built, the understanding that money was only a means to power was lost. Money, any way you got it, was what counted. Cocaine addicts feel the same way about crack.

What about the Mafia today? I am tempted to say that the different headline stories are, like those that preceded them, nothing more than propaganda. But I know better. The careers of people like John Gotti and Vinnie "the Chin" Giganti more than anything reflect the sorry internal state of what was once our world, Our Thing.

Consider Gotti for a moment. He was fingered and eventually put away due to the testimony of Sammy "the Bull" Gravano, his closest aide, who went into the witness protection program and then came out of it to tell his story in Peter Maas's best-selling book *Underboss*. Gotti was convicted of being behind the 1983 killing of Paul Castellano, the boss of his own Family. I really am not familiar with the details, though obviously I am suspicious of any case that turns on the word of an informer. I am also suspicious of any story promulgated about John Gotti, the so-called Dapper Don—both because of the media and because of Gotti himself. Recently, for example, there was a big story about Gotti being beaten up in prison, where he is now serving a life sentence. There was even a photograph picked up by the wire services showing Gotti with his face looking a little puffy and his hair messed up. It did seem like someone had worked him over. Only no one had. How do I know? Because Al Krieger, who happens to be a Gotti lawyer and who is still a friend of mine, told me so. Al, who had spoken to his client, told me nothing happened. A rumor got started; a photographer snapped a picture of him—distant and fuzzy enough to create the desired image of a guy who had had his teeth rattled. That was it. Gotti himself said the story was a pure fabrication.

But John Gotti's rise and fall, no matter what kind of imagery is used, represents almost perfectly why the Mafia no longer has any credibility or power today. Gotti is the epitome of everything that has gone wrong in our world.

He was a thoroughly Americanized product, no more than a street tough with ambition who quickly made his way to the top by being rougher and tougher than other street soldiers. He reached leadership only a few years after becoming a made member of his family—not because he had strong backing but because he was audacious. In all likelihood, he did take out his leader, Paul Castellano. He was able to do this because Castellano, though the most prominent leader among New York's Five Families then, was really a man without genuine support, someone ripe for an assassination. To understand anything about Gotti, you first have to know who Paul Castellano was and how he came to power.

Castellano was the designated successor to Carlo Gambino, who died in 1976. Though Gambino's mother was a Castellano, which made Paul's succession seem natural, it wasn't. I don't know this firsthand because I wasn't there, obviously, but the story is that Gambino, on his deathbed, said that he wanted Paul to be the next leader of the Family. I doubt that this story is true because it flies in the face of common sense.

Both Carlo and Castellano had enough awareness of our tradition, had been around long enough, to know that leaders are not appointed, but selected. There is a crucial difference. An appointment is the action of one man; a leader who is selected is elevated by his peers because they recognize in him a certain authority and power that they, by consensus, choose to honor. Yet if Castellano was not made leader by a deathbed appointment, he was also not selected in the sense of his commanding great respect within his Family. Paul was a hardworking, very ordinary guy who had come up as a butcher and a meat packer; he was a laborer but never an administrator. Though he had some knowledge of our tradition, he certainly had no command of it. I don't really know how he got to be leader, but he was a sitting target for someone like Gotti, who had almost no sense of tradition and even less respect for it. What Gotti knew was that Paul did not have the kind of following that would create a backlash were he killed. When Paul was taken out, Gotti became boss because no one else had the will or the means to stand up to him.

I personally do not know John Gotti. I have no idea what he is like at home, how he treats his wife and children. I would accept without question that however rough he was in his profession, he might be equally pleasing and caring among his own. I knew Albert Anastasia well, and Albert had that kind of split in his makeup.

But Gotti is no Albert Anastasia. Albert, as unorthodox as he was, as tough as he was, was also like most leaders at that time—someone who assiduously kept himself out of the limelight. Gotti, as a leader, is someone who has seemed to thrive in public. He has carried himself like a movie star, has made public displays of himself in ways that courted both celebrity and ruin. It is simply inconceivable to me that a real Family leader would ever publically stick his chest out the way Gotti had for so many years with that annual July Fourth party of his, complete with fireworks and throngs of media, at the Ravenswood Social Club in Queens. Gotti may be in jail because there was no loyalty in his organization, but he also set himself up like a duckpin to be knocked over by the first prosecutor who came along.

There is a simple but effective way of comparing Americanized Mafia leaders like John Gotti and those older leaders who operated with a sense of tradition: their tenure as heads of their Families. Gotti lasted for just a few years, as did other Americanized bosses—Lucky Luciano, Vito Genovese, Tommy Lucchese. On the other hand, Joe Profaci led his Family for over thirty years; Vincente Mangano was a boss for almost as long. My father led the Bonanno Family from 1930 until he retired in 1968. Tradition, if it means anything, is about survival. John Gotti, and those others, never had a clue.

I cannot view what is going on in my world now with any sense of satisfaction. The world I grew up in is gone and what is left is in ruins. The Mafia stories continue, however, regardless of the emptiness behind them. Recently I have been following the accounts of the arrest, prosecution, and jailing of Vinnie Gigante, the "crazy" leader of the Genovese Family. For years, Gigante clad only in pajamas, had been wandering up and down Mulberry Street, near his headquarters in Greenwich Village. All of the stories about him and all of the pictures were designed to titillate readers over such questions as whether or not he was crazy, whether he would beat the rap, if there was the heart and brain of a mad genius under the funny hat, the robe, and pajamas. And then the question of questions: Was he or wasn't he the Boss of Bosses?

The spectacle is sickening.

I knew Vinnie Gigante—vaguely—when he was a low-on-the-totem-pole muscle man for Vito Genovese. They called him "Chin" because he was an ex-prizefighter who had taken one too many to the head. His claim to fame was his botched take-out attempt of Frank Costello in 1957. The standard joke in our world then was that Vinnie wasn't the important guy in that job; it was his driver, who took him to Costello's apartment house and then who helped him escape. He was the guy with brains.

What is clear to me is that organized crime in the United States today has little or no bearing on what is left of the Mafia. I look around and read all kinds of stories about drug smuggling, gambling, and big-time political corruption, and none of it involves what is left of the Mafia. Drug trafficking, on a scale never dreamed of by people in our world, is a multibillion-dollar industry run by cartels in Colombia, Southeast Asia, Mexico, and even Africa. (Most recently, the government announced that it had broken up a huge drug-smuggling ring run by Nigerian *women*.) Gambling is flourishing as never before. If Las Vegas and Atlantic City, which still attract Mafia elements, are doing well, state governments with their lotteries and laws against gambling (read competition) are doing even better. Indian reservations, from Arizona to New England, free from federal law, are in the casino business in ways that promise to dwarf enterprises in our world and those of the government, as well.

I can't say what the Mafia is up to these days because I don't know, but I can surmise. Not long ago, there was a well-publicized account of a big drug bust involving New York's "Bonanno crime family." What an irony. The government and the media still use the names of the old Families—Bonanno, Genovese, Lucchese—to get mileage out of the old stereotypes in their reporting, even though all the former leaders and their men are gone.

In its own way, the story perfectly, if ironically, illustrated just how moth-eaten the so-called Mafia has become. The men arrested were little better than school-yard pushers. They apparently were caught red-handed with little bags of white powder on them. Any really powerful organization—an old-time Mafia Family, a present-day cartel—would never have permitted their men to be compromised in such a manner. Petty street crime is always left to petty street criminals, who may or may not be organized from above but who, in any case, are never part of the organization itself.

I am content with the life I have led and have no apologies for it. I fully accept the idea that the traditions I grew up with and which flourished for a time have now gone underground, there to gather and reform in ways that may be impossible to imagine. But I do believe that the best values of my world—loyalty within a group, honor, devotion to one another, responsibility for one's actions (whatever they are), the determination to be independent and free—cannot be extinguished, because they are at the core of human nature itself.

In spite of tremendous odds and sometimes against the power of the state, my family has made it in America. But the success of its individual members is as much in their hearts as in their jobs, their stations in life. Though each of us has been through a lot, Rosalie and I are still together. My brother, Joe, has done his time; he is married and in business for himself. Catherine, my sister, is a widow, very active in her community in California. My father, who is the sole surviving member of the original Commission, is free of the law and, at ninety-four, vigorous beyond his years. He visits my mother's grave a few times a week, places flowers there, talks to her for a time, and returns to his home, where his keenest interests (aside from talking) are reading old classics—Dante and Homer—and watching vintage black-and-white movies on TV that hearken back to the days of his youth.

In his mind and heart, our story does not go back decades, but centuries. If you listen to him talking on a Sunday afternoon when the family is gathered for a traditional dinner, he will seem to drift away, as though his words and the look in his eyes have to do with other times and other places. He tells us he has lived too long, that the modern world with its proliferation of divorces, same-sex marriages, wars, and man-made catastrophes are too much for him, all part of an unbridled marketplace mentality.

But what I draw from him—what I believe each member of our family, in his or her own way, draws from him—is the look and feel of a tradition older and larger than all of us. We still belong to the thirteenth century as much as to the twentieth; we each have the capacity to remember the night of the Sicilian Vespers, to hear in the ringing of ancient church bells the suffering and the promise of an entire people determined to transform the past and present into a better future. That is our history. That remains, as ever, our inextinguishable challenge.

ACKNOWLEDGMENTS

W hen someone sits down to write his autobiography it takes the energy and collective thoughts of many people to help transform the idea into a finished product. Nelson Glueck noted in *The River Jordan* (1946) that, to this very day, there are old men in the tents of Arabia who can recite the history of their ancestors for forty generations, and if in their recital they stray but a jot from the facts, others within hearing will immediately correct them or supply forgotten facts. Sadly, today there are few if any "others within hearing distance" that can correct or supply forgotten details. However, I did find a few within hearing distance to encourage, assist, criticize, and prod me along the journey.

I wish to acknowledge and thank my agent and friend, Mickey Freiberg, of The Artists Agency, who has guided my career and made it into a cottage industry. My sincere thanks and appreciation to Frank Weimann of the Literary Group International, who took the manuscript and made the book possible, and to Bob Wallace, Editor-in-Chief of St. Martin's Press, for his suggestions and refinement of the manuscript.

Additional thanks go to Anne Twomey for developing a brilliant jacket design; to Abigail Rose for a creative photo section; to John J. Murphy and Joe Rinaldi of St. Martin's publicity department.

My gratitude to David Falkner, an accomplished writer in his own right. Even though David was not there at the end it was his original effort and labor that gave this book a beginning.

I wish to thank my wife, Rosalie, for putting up with long sessions of self-doubt on my part about the project, for her encouragement and faith in my ability to get the job done, and for tolerating the overall mess I created in almost all of the rooms in our home.

Finally, I wish to acknowledge and thank my father, Joseph, for being who he is—who, while he may have lost his romantic illusions as he became a man, never lost his ideals, and who by his example and teaching gave me courage, tolerance, strength, and a sense of honor.

—B. B.
December 4, 1998
Tucson, Arizona